I0214625

Book of Gostynin
(Gostynin, Poland)

Translation of *Pinkas Gostynin*

This is a translation of *Pinkas Gostynin*, (Book of Gostynin),
Edited by. J. M. Biderman,
Pubished in Tel Aviv and New York
By the Gostynin Memorial Book Committee in 1960
(440 pages, Yiddish)

Published by JewishGen

**An Affiliate of the Museum of Jewish Heritage - A Living Memorial to the Holocaust
New York**

Gostynin Yizkor Book

Book of Gostynin, Poland
Translation of *Pinkas Gostynin*

Copyright © 2018 by JewishGen, Inc.
All rights reserved.
First Printing: January 2018, Tevet 5778
Second Printing: March 2019, Adar II 5779

Translation Project Coordinator: Jessie Weistrop Klein
Primary Translators: Pamela Russ and Yocheved Klausner
Layout: Lynn Mercer
Cover Design: Rachel Kolokoff Hopper

This book may not be reproduced, in whole or in part, including illustrations in any form (beyond that copying permitted by Sections 107 and 108 of the U.S. Copyright Law and except by reviewers for public press), without written permission from the publisher.

Published by JewishGen, Inc.
An Affiliate of the Museum of Jewish Heritage
A Living Memorial to the Holocaust
36 Battery Place, New York, NY 10280

"JewishGen, Inc. is not responsible for inaccuracies or omissions in the original work and makes no representations regarding the accuracy of this translation. Digital images of the original book's contents can be seen online at the New York Public Library Web site."

The mission of the JewishGen organization is to produce a translation of the original work and we cannot verify the accuracy of statements or alter facts cited.

Printed in the United States of America by Lightning Source, Inc.

Library of Congress Control Number (LCCN): 2017964331

ISBN: 978-1-939561-54-1 (hard cover: 446 pages, alk. paper)

JewishGen and the Yizkor-Books-in-Print Project

This book has been published by the **Yizkor-Books-in-Print Project,** as part of the **Yizkor Book Project** of **JewishGen, Inc**.

JewishGen, Inc. is a non-profit organization founded in 1987 as a resource for Jewish genealogy. Its website [www.jewishgen.org] serves as an international clearinghouse and resource center to assist individuals who are researching the history of their Jewish families and the places where they lived. JewishGen provides databases, facilitates discussion groups, and coordinates projects relating to Jewish genealogy and the history of the Jewish people. In 2003, JewishGen became an affiliate of the **Museum of Jewish Heritage - A Living Memorial to the Holocaust** in New York.

The **JewishGen Yizkor Book Project** was organized to make more widely known the existence of Yizkor (Memorial) Books written by survivors and former residents of various Jewish communities throughout the world. Later, volunteers connected to the different destroyed communities began cooperating to have these books translated from the original language— usually Hebrew or Yiddish—into English, thus enabling a wider audience to have access to the valuable information contained within them. As each chapter of these books was translated, it was posted on the JewishGen website and made available to the general public.

The **Yizkor-Books-in-Print Project** began in 2011 as an initiative to print and publish Yizkor Books that had been fully translated, so that hard copies would be available for purchase by the descendants of these communities and also by scholars, universities, synagogues, libraries, and museums.

These Yizkor books have been produced almost entirely through the volunteer effort of researchers from around the world, assisted by donations from private individuals. The books are printed and sold at near cost, so as to make them as affordable as possible. Our goal is to make this important genre of Jewish literature and history available in English in book form, so that people can have the personal histories of their ancestral towns on their bookshelves for themselves and for their children and grandchildren.

A list of all published translated Yizkor Books in the project with prices and ordering information can be found at:
http://www.jewishgen.org/Yizkor/ybip.html

Lance Ackerfeld, Yizkor Book Project Manager

Joel Alpert, Yizkor-Book-in-Print Project Coordinator

JewishGen
Yizkor Book Project

This book is presented by the
Yizkor Books in Print Project
Project Coordinator: Joel Alpert

Part of the
Yizkor Books Project of JewishGen, Inc.
Project Manager: Lance Ackerfeld

These books have been produced solely through volunteer effort
of individuals from around the world. The books are printed and
sold at near cost, so as to make them as affordable as possible.

Our goal is to make this history and important genre of Jewish
literature available in English in book form so that people can have
the near-personal histories of their ancestral towns on their bookshelves for themselves and for their children and grandchildren.

Any donations to the Yizkor Books Project are appreciated.

Please send donations to:
Yizkor Book Project
JewishGen
36 Battery Place
New York, NY 10280

JewishGen, Inc. is an affiliate of the
Museum of Jewish Heritage
A Living Memorial to the Holocaust

Foreword for the Publication of the Translation

By Jessie Weistrop Klein, Translation Project Coordinator

Daughter of Charlotte Bagno Weistrop and Nathan Weistrop, granddaughter of Julius Bagno and Jessie Druckman Bagno; great-granddaughter of Mendel Bagno and Genendel Grabinska; great-great-granddaughter of Zulim Bagno and Enta Bressler. The Bagno name appears in Gostynin vital records as early as 1826.

Growing up in the New York City suburbs, I was very close with my Grandfather, Julius Bagno. He often spoke about his parents and the ten siblings he left behind in Gostynin, Poland when he came to America in 1910. Prior to World War II my grandfather's siblings emigrated to America or Belgium for better economic opportunities. Three of his siblings, Hinda, Josef, and Zulim and his mother perished in the Holocaust. I had grown up hearing their names spoken in hushed tones but had never seen pictures of them.

Many years later I became interested in family history. In 2009, I took the "Introduction to Jewish Genealogy" course offered by the Jewish Genealogical Society of Greater Boston. In one of the lectures, the speaker referred to Yizkor books and their availability on the New York Public Library website. After class, I went home, found the Gostynin Yizkor book on the library website, and started turning pages. The original book, *Pinkas Gostynin*, was written in Yiddish so I could not read it, but I eventually got to the Remembrance section where I found pictures of Hinda, Josef, and Zulim, my grandfather's siblings. Pictures I had never seen.

I immediately went to the Yizkor Book Project site on JewishGen and saw that the Table of Contents had been translated and found three untranslated chapters written by one of my grandfather's brothers, a sister and her daughter. So began my journey as Project Coordinator for the translation of *Pinkas Gostynin*. I learned a great deal from the former residents of Gostynin. I found their stories and memories extremely interesting and moving, and I hope you will, too.

Acknowledgements

It is with deepest gratitude that I thank Pam Russ, who translated most of the *Pinkas Gostynin (Book of Gostynin)* from Yiddish into English. It was a pleasure working with Pam. Thanks also to Gloria Berkenstat Freund for translating the Table of Contents, Yocheved Klausner for translation of seven chapters and Haim Sidor for translation of the Necrology. Many thanks to JewishGen, Lance Ackerfeld, the Yizkor Book Project Coordinator, and Joel Alpert, Project Coordinator of Yizkor-Books-in-Print, for ensuring that the stories of our ancestral towns will be available for future generations. We are also indebted to the members of the Gostyniner Societies of New York, Chicago and Israel who in 1960 compiled this memoir of Gostynin. It was their effort that has allowed stories of Jewish Gostynin to be preserved.

Special thanks to the National Yiddish Book Center in Amherst, Massachusetts and the New York Public Library for supplying the high resolution images used in this book.

Jessie Weistrop Klein, Translation Project Coordinator

History of Gostynin

Located in central Poland, Gostynin sits on the Skrwa River within the Mazowieckie Province in the Powiat (County) of Gostynin. It is approximately 60 miles northwest of Warsaw. Although there were settlements in the area dating back to the sixth century, the actual town of Gostynin was not founded until the Middle Ages.

A Jewish Community of 157 members was established in 1765. Members were predominantly traders, inn keepers, tailors, furriers and butchers. In the 1800's, there were several Jewish hosiery workshops operating in Gostynin. From 1823 to 1862, the Jewish population lived in a special residential district. The community built a wooden synagogue which was destroyed by fire in 1809. The rebuilt synagogue also burned in 1899. A brick synagogue and study house was then built north of the market square.

In the 19th century, Gostynin was an important center for Hasidism, and the community maintained a traditional religious orientation into the early 20th century with both orthodox and Hasidic groups. In the period preceding and just after World War I, Socialist, Bundist and Zionist organizations were established. Gostynin's Jews also joined trade unions, theatre groups, and choirs.

At the outbreak of World War II, the Jewish population of Gostynin was 2,269 souls. The town was occupied by the German army in September 1939. Persecution of the Jewish population began immediately. In 1940 a ghetto was established and liquidated in 1942. Most of the ghetto inhabitants were sent to the Chemo death camp or other concentration camps.

Today the population of Gostynin is approximately 19,000, but there are no Jews. All evidence of Jewish life and contributions to Gostynin were destroyed in World War II. Both cemeteries were desecrated and the tombstones removed. The few Gostyniner Jews who survived WWII emigrated.

Sources:

www.zchor.org/gosthist.htm ":The Jewish Community of Gostynin, Poland Compiled by Julian H. Preisler of Wilmington, Delaware

sztetl.org.pl/en Virtual Shtetl

Encyclopedia of Jewish Life Before and During the Holocaust.

Encyclopedia Judaica

Cover Design

For this cover of this Yizkor Book, using digital filters, I illustrated a present day photo of the Skrwa River in Gostynin, Poland, to create the illusion of a watercolor painting. My inspiration for the cover comes from the writing of Meyer and Yakov Gostynski (page 4): "Our town of Gostynin was situated in an area of fields, woods, rivers, mountains and valleys, windmills, watermills, brickyards, sugar factories, distilleries, and also peat storehouses..." and from Yosef Keller (page 185): "In everyone's hearts, there glows a painful longing for those times when a lively Jewish life pulsated in our beloved home town."

It is my hope that through this soft rendition of the river and the countryside around Gostynin, this cover will evoke a longing nostalgia for home and a loving memory of Gostynin as it was before the destruction of the people and the community.

Original Photo

Front cover photo of the Skrwa River in Gostynin, Poland used with permission. Photograph by Sebastian Maćkiewicz at the Polish language Wikipedia. Creative photo filters by Rachel Kolokoff Hopper.

Back cover background photo from the hand drawn map of Gostynin in the Yizkor Book.

Back Cover Photo Collage:
Top Left: The Gostynin Cantor Reb Yakov Miller with his choir.
Top right: Door into a starvation cell in Block 11 at Auschwitz, (photograph by Rachel Kolokoff Hopper).
Bottom Left: A group of football players in Gostynin in 1925.
Bottom Right: Rose Shoshana, her sister Chava Bresler (who was killed), her mother Hinda Mozer from Gostynin, her grandmother Chana Jakobowicz, and her brother Philip.

Rachel Hopper
Ft. Collins. CO
r-hopper@comcast.net

Geopolitical Information:

Gostynin, Poland is located at 52°26' N Latitude, 19°29' E Longitude

65 miles WNW of Warsaw, 12 miles SW of Płock.

Alternate names: Gostynin [Polish, Russian], Gostinin [Yiddish], Waldrode [German 1940-45]

Region: Warszawa

The Jewish population was 1,831 in 1900.

	Town	District	Province	Country
Before WWI (c. 1900):	Gostynin	Gostynin	Warszawa	Russian Empire
Between the wars (c. 1930):	Gostynin	Gostynin	Warszawa	Poland
After WWII (c. 1950):	Gostynin			Poland
Today (c. 2000):	Gostynin			Poland

Nearby Jewish Communities:

       Gąbin 11 miles ESE
       Płock 12 miles NE
       Lubień Kujawski 13 miles W
       Żychlin 14 miles SSE
       Kutno 15 miles SSW
       Kowal 15 miles WNW
       Dobrzyń nad Wisłą 16 miles NNW
       Sanniki 18 miles ESE
       Krośniewice 18 miles SW

BALTIC SEA

LITHUANIA

RUSSIA

Vilnius●

POLAND

BELARUS

GERMANY

●Gostynin

●Poznan   Warsaw ●

●Lodz

●Prague

●Krakow

UKRAINE

CZECH REPUBLIC

SLOVAKIA

250 miles

0

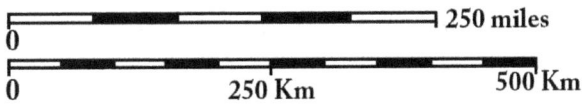

POLAND - Current Borders

0   250 Km   500 Km

Map showing Gostynin in Poland

Notes to the Reader:

We apologize ahead of time for the poor quality of images in the book. Often these images had been scanned from the original Yizkor books which were of poor quality to begin with, being copies of old photographs. Each transfer results in loss of quality. We have done the best we could given the original material and the resources and technology at hand. Even though images often appear of higher quality on computer screens, that does not transfer to high quality images in print. A reader can view the original scans on the web sites listed below.

Within the text the reader will note "{34}" standing ahead of a paragraph. This indicates that the material translated below was on page 34 of the original book. However, when a paragraph was split between two pages in the original book, the marker is placed in this book after the end of the paragraph for ease of reading.

Also please note that all references within the text of the book to page numbers, refer to the page numbers of the original Yizkor Book.

The original book can be seen online at the NY Public Library site:

http://yizkor.nypl.org

then find the book alphabetically

Or at the Yiddish Book Center site:

https://www.yiddishbookcenter.org/collections/yizkor-books/yzk-nybc313774/biderman-i-m-pinkas-gostinin-yizker-bukh

In order to obtain a list of all Shoah victims from Gostynin, the reader should access the Yad Vashem web site listed below; one can also search for specific family names using family name option. These lists are continually updated by Yad Vashem, so it is worthwhile to periodically search these lists.

There is much valuable information available on this web site, including the Pages of Testimony, etc.

http://yvng.yadvashem.org

A list of this book and all books available in the Yizkor-Book-In-Print Project along with prices is available at:

http://www.jewishgen.org/Yizkor/ybip.html

Title Page of Original Yizkor Book

פּנקס גאָסטינין

יזכּור בּוך

רעדאַקטאָר

י. מ. בידערמאַן

אַרויסגעגעבן פֿון

גאָסטינינער יזכּור־בוך קאָמיטעטן

נויאָרק, תּל־אביב   1960 — תּש"ך

Translation of the Title Page of Original Yizkor Book

Book of Gostynin

Memorial Book

Edited by: J. M. Biderman

Published in New York and Tel Aviv, 1960

Table of Contents

Translated by Gloria Berkenstat Freund

In the Years of Destruction   216

There Once Was

Gostyniner Across the World

Remember

Family Notes

Gostynin Yizkor Book

Maps

Legend translated by Pamela Russ

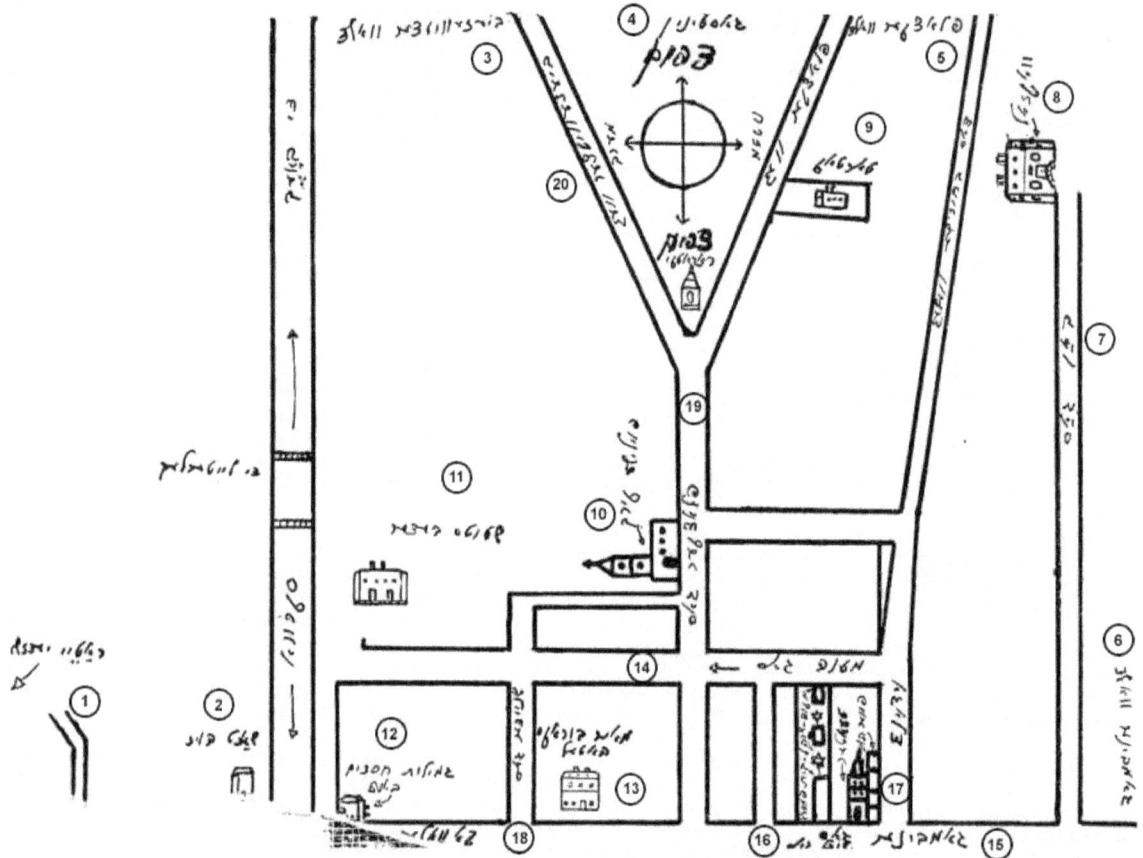

Legend
1 Town hall
2 slaughter house
3 Bierzewice Forest
4 Gostynin (with compass points beneath the city name: north, south, east west)
5 Plock Forest
6 Gombiner Forest
7 Railway Road
8 train station
9 sawmill
10 Polish church
11 city bathhouse
12 Gemillas Chesed Institution
13 hotel
14 mikva street
15 Gombiner Street
16 Mikve, shul, Bais Medrash (House of Learning)
17 theater, next to the fire station
18 tailor street
19 Plock Street
20 Bierzewice Street

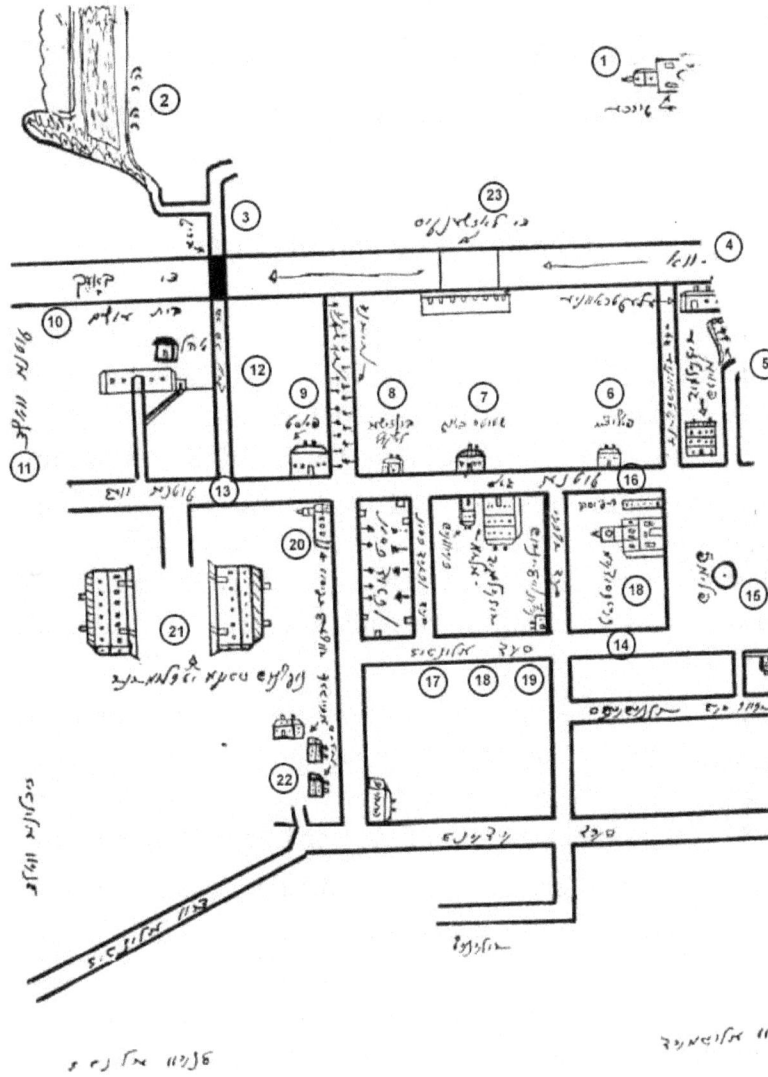

Legend

1	church	12	grave
2	river	13	Kutno Road
3	bridge	14	Kutno Street
4	electricity station	15	fire hydrant
5	women's gymnasium	16	magistrate
6	police	17	local government house
7	city hall	18	men's gymnasium
8	Bundist Center	19	Poalei Tzion Center
9	post office	20	leisure gardens
10	cemetery	21	elementary government schools
11	Kutno Forest	22	Russian workers' center
		23	huts

A Word from the Gostyniner Yizkor Book Committee (Instead of an Introduction)

by Yosef Keller

Translated by Pamela Russ

Now, Gostynin is destroyed and wasted, regardless that the city remained almost untouched by the war operations; the houses, the plazas, the parks, all unharmed in their places – nonetheless, Gostynin, our Gostynin, the beautiful Jewish town, that was proud of its Jewish youth, of its Jewish institutions, no longer exists on the large Jewish world–map. Gostynin experienced the same fate that so gruesomely befell all the large and small cities in Poland. At the time of the last catastrophe, our brothers and sisters who lived there were murdered and destroyed through horrific tortures that demonic Hitlerism contrived.

Of the entire Jewish Gostynin population only those who left to America or settled in Israel in time remained. Only a small number managed to save itself from the destruction. Individual members that were saved from the terrible fires found their refuge in the Land of Israel or in the United States.

In everyone's hearts, there glows a painful longing for those times when a lively Jewish life pulsated in our beloved home town.

The nostalgia for those holy memories of those who died and of the *alter heim* [old homeland] that was destroyed, did not allow for any peace of mind. It beckoned and called. And when finally the end of World War II came, and the great Jewish tragedy became known, the idea to set up an eternal tombstone for our home town Gostynin arose.

At one of the meetings of the "Gostynin Social Club," which was established in New York after the devastation, with the goal of bringing material help and relief to the Gostynin survivors around the world, and especially to those who set up their lives in the Jewish homeland, the idea of publishing a Yizkor Book came about, which would perpetuate our decimated holy community of Gostynin.

[Page 6]

As soon as the "Gostynin Social Club" came in close contact with the union of Gostynin Jews in Israel under the name of the "Irgun of the Emigrés of Gostynin," it seemed that there they had the same idea. After long negotiations, it was decided that the book should be published in partnership with the Gostynin Jews in the New York and in Israel.

Hundreds of Yizkor books were published in the course of the post–war years, in the holy memory of the Jewish communities. Many of these books have great historical value, but they have hugely important sources for the future writers of the Jewish history of Poland. The majority of the material in these books was not written by professional writers. The contributors were all those who had information to relate about the general social life in their settlements, and all kinds of memories that give color to the descriptions of the communities. Separate sections are dedicated to the bloody chapter of the Jewish destruction. Out of all of these books, there pours out love, sentiment, and longing: once there was …

This is exactly how the book about Gostynin was assembled. Those who contributed to this book had the mission for themselves of eternalizing their hometown that possessed a significant Jewish community that dipped itself into the light of the great rabbi who was renowned across the Jewish world, possessed a well–brought up Jewish youth, a great many parties and organizations, a nest of social and benevolent institutions. The majority of article writers had no writing ambitions, so the book does not pretend to be the latest expression of literary art.

[Page 7]

The fact that separate committees in the various global continents – in America and in Israel – took care of the materials, the fact that they had to get the items from people who were scattered and spread out, slowed down the work of the book. Publishing the book was prolonged as well because of these same reasons: It took a long time until both main groups came to a full agreement.

Besides all the other difficulties, the publishers of the book also confronted difficult financial problems. Let the joyful fact be underscored here, that almost all the members of the Gostyniner Social Club contributed to the book fund; significant sums were contributed by the members of the book committee. A completely separate acknowledgment must be given to our compatriot, friend, and close collaborator of the book committee, Herman Krauz (Hirsh Kruczyk), whose contribution to the book fund was substantial, and he served as the foundation for the entire book's undertaking.

Here also should be expressed a heartfelt thanks to all those who in the course of a few years have helped in a practical sense in the follow–through of the Yizkor Book project. Especially to the small group that consisted of Yisokhor Motil, Yosef Keller, Meyer Dovid Tremki, and Yakov Gostinski. The name of our beloved friend, Shmuel Keller, should be especially mentioned here. He worked with us tirelessly, and tragically, in the middle of the work, he left this world. There were innumerable meetings and they worried about each detail of the book, and each detail interested them and concerned them.

If this book, as a whole, will be received with reverence, and will appeal to the broader readership, this will be thanks to the editor of the book, the esteemed writer and educator, Y.M. Biderman. His work was greatly valued by all those who worked along with him.

[Page 8]

The publication of this book is a realization of a long–time dream, of a holy wish to perpetuate the history of Jewish Gostynin, to create a monument for the Gostynin martyrs who died in the years of the terrible rage – 5700–5705 [1940–1945].

Yosef Keller
Secretary of the Book Committee

[Page 9]

Remarks from the Editor

by Y. M. Biderman

Translated by Pamela Russ

The task of an editor of a Yizkor Book is threefold: a) to plan the issue, b) to divide up the themes that individual writers should work on, and finally c) to prepare all the material for printing.

In the case of the *"Pinkus* [Book of Records] of Gostynin," the task of the editor was a lot more straightforward: The material was already written, but for this precise reason the task became more complicated because he [the editor] had to struggle with some moments that could possibly have been avoided if he would have planned this book from the onset. It could be that he may have agreed to include the requisite articles, drafts, and memories written by professional individuals, the complete and full gamut of Jewish life in Gostynin, and all its discoveries – from the very beginning of the Gostynin Jewish settlement until the very tragic end. Maybe in that way, there would not have been unnecessary duplications in the various accounts.

The editor reckons with himself that the contributors to the Yizkor Book are not professional writers and that the members of the book committee have for the first time had something to do with publishing a book. But it should be underscored that the writers of these published works wrote with the best intentions to perpetuate those pieces of Jewish social life in Gostynin of which they were part or about which they had knowledge. In this collective venture, however, they overlooked a series of aspects that should have been taken into careful consideration. The fact that the contributors of the book are spread across the United States, Israel, and a series of European countries did not help them watch out for the required totality of a historical overview.

[Page 10]

Therefore, after the fact, and with this existing situation, after reading the material and preparing it for print, the editor had, to some extent, to fill in the missing parts. He found information about the establishment of the city and knowledge that also shows the beginnings of the Jewish settlement and its development. Not everything was able to be corrected and a series of mistakes remains in the compilation of the *Pinkus* [record book], and a series of stages of public life in Jewish Gostynin have not been covered in this book.

A series of articles were cut, some rewritten because they contained details that others had already extensively described, or other details that were intimately private or familial in nature. Because of the fact that the editor is not a Gostyniner, and he has no connections with this or that Gostynin family, and has no conflict with absolutely anyone in and around Gostynin – he was able to do his work without any partiality. But the editor never changed the central ideas of the writers. Certain manuscripts unfortunately arrived too late, and therefore were not able to be published.

Acknowledgement must be expressed to all the Gostynin compatriots in New York, who demonstrated a sincere respect for the *Pinkus*, and much understanding for this work, and did everything that was in their power to have the book published with the best possible appearance and to its fullest, and so that it can serve as a worthy monument for the decimated Jewish community in Gostynin.

Particular thanks go to our friends Yosef Keller, Yissachar Matil, and Yakov Gostynski, for the huge interest that they demonstrated in the daily work, and for their active participation in all the preparatory tasks of the Gostynin Pinkus. They are also responsible for the final section of the book, the "Yizkor," that they compiled and edited.

Y.M. Biderman

[Page 13]

Pages of History

From the "*Geographical Dictionary of the Kingdom of Poland*" second volume, Warsaw, 1881, Polish

Translated by Pamela Russ

Gostynin is a county in the province of Warsaw near the Skrwa River[1] on the west and Ostenja on the east, lying on the geographical latitude of 52°42'.8 and in the longitude of 37°11'.3, on the highway from Kutno to Plutsk, at a distance of 22 viorst [*one viorst is slightly longer than a kilometer*] from Kutno, 21 viorst from Gombyn, 24 viorst from Koval, 129 viorst from Warsaw; it possesses a brick parish Catholic church, a brick Evangelical church, a beginners school and an English school, a Justice of the Peace from the third district that belonged to the judges association in Wloclawek and which includes the city of Gombyn, the administration of the province, the city hall, the administration of the government forests, and a post–office.

In the year 1827, there were 98 houses in Gostynin and 1523 residents. In 1861 there were 37 brick houses and 138 wooden; 3311 residents, and the total – 1160 Evangelists and 785 Jews.

Now[2] there are 6174 residents in Gostynin (2889 men and 3285 women). The income of the city treasury is 9443 Russian ruble. The city reserve capital – 41985 Russian ruble, the steel capital – 9177 Russian ruble.

Among the factory operations are three tanneries and two small oil mills.

[Page 14]

The local population's business is wool–weaving that developed from the time in 1824 when 105 cloth experts settled here. They were brought over

---

Translator's footnotes

1. In the Yiddish vernacular, Skwra was called Bug.
2. In 1881, when the document was discovered.

from Germany, and a wool press was set up for them, [*as well as facilities for*] shearing, and dyeing.

Gostynin is a real old settlement, and its beginnings are attributed to [being a] defense castle which likely originates from the pre–historic era. This castle as the central point of defense for the entire area, and gave its name to the whole Gostyniner country. This castle was frequently the residence of the Kujawy dukes and others. The castle itself was often the object of conflict: In the year 1286, Konrad from Mazovian forcefully seized it, and captured Woclaw the Czech in the year 1300. Ziemowit, the Mazovian duke, changed the status of the settlement near the castle by giving it municipal rights in the year 1382, receiving the so–called Khelm laws, and gave the city the same rights that Plock had. After the death of the Plocker dukes who did not leave behind any successors, Casimir the Jagielloner integrated Gostynin, in the year 1462, along with the whole country, into the kingdom, thereby establishing the municipal rights and liberties.

In the year 1552, King Sigmund August was the sovereign in Gostynin for the course of a few weeks. Kristof Szydlowiecki, the crown counsellor, rebuilt and reinforced the castle at the beginning of the 16th century, but already in the year 1564, the official examiners determined that in was in a bad condition. They built up the castle once again, when in the year 1611, it was established as a residence for Wasyl Szujski who was imprisoned there along with his family. Here Czar Wasyl died, and his brother Dimiter in the year 1612; also his wife [died there], and their bodies were the first to be buried behind the castle village.

[Page 15]

Gostynin was a city county in the Rawer province [*voivodship*]. Werdum, at the end of the 17th century, found the old castle here surrounded by swamps behind the city. This castle was destroyed during the 18th century; only the four–cornered tower survived thanks to the fact that the remaining walls had been rebuilt into an Evangelical church. In the year 1809, a terrible fire destroyed the entire city...

The government estates of Gostynin, according to the information of the year 1859, existed in the city of Gostynin and the surrounding areas: Bielany, Khoyenka, Nagadow, Ostrovin, Polesie, and Sokhor's sawmill.

The Gostynin county in the Warsaw governorate lies on the left shore of the Vistula River, which is its northeast border, and stretches for 45 viorst in length; the east borders the Sochaczewer and Lowiczer provinces, the south [borders] the Lowiczer and Kutner, and the west [borders] the Wloclaweker provinces.

The Gostyniner county was established, as a result of the last division of the kingdom in the year 1866, into about half of the former Gostynin county, and separated from the Wloclawek county, which today comprises the Duninower municipality...

The main communication artery for grain transportation is the Vistula ... a second rate highway (government) that cuts through the county in the direction of Kutno through Gostynin to Plock. A similar highway runs from the city of Gombyn to the village of Sonyk, and from there it runs in one direction to the city Sochaczew and in the other direction to the city of Lowicz.

The Gostynin county is made up of two cities: Gombyn, and the county-city of Gostynin; of two settlements, formerly towns: Kernoz and Osmolyn, and 676 villages, estates, etc. The county is populated with 78,165 souls (37,336 men, 40,809 women) – Prawoslavs [Russian Orthodox] – 6,139; Catholics – 52,259; Evangelists – 13,646; Jews – 5,279; other religions – 842 ...

[Page 16]

From the *"Jewish Encyclopedia"* with the overall editing of Dr. L. Katzenelson and Baron, D.G. Ginsburg, sixth volume, Peterburg (Russian)

Translated by Pamela Russ

In Polish times,[3] Gostynin was an administration point in the so–called country[4] which was a constituent of the Rawer voivodship [*province*].

According to the numbers of the year 1765, in Gostynin there resided 157 Jews, and 1791 was the total in the whole country.

Now – a county city in the Warsaw province. In the years 1823 until 1862, there existed a Jewish quarter in Gostynin. Only the privileged Jews – who fulfilled certain criteria – were permitted to live outside the designated streets (according to the model of Warsaw).[5]

In the year 1856, there were 2445 Christians and 634 Jews living in Gostynin. In 1897, the population was 6747, of which 1849 were Jews. In the whole Gostynin country there were over 80,000 souls, of which 5709 were Jews.

In each of the settlements in Gostynin with a population of no less than 500 souls, the Jews comprised the largest percentage. In Gombyn, the population was 5137, of which 2539 were Jews; in Kerniezhe the general public was 536, of which 222 were Jews; and in Sonek, there were 1409 souls, of which 216 were Jews.

Translator's footnotes

3. Before the division of Polish kingdom.
4. Gostyniner country.
5. Among others, those Jews had to send their children to public schools, pay a high tax, and [the children had to] be dressed in shorts.

[Page 17]

From the *"Judaistic Encyclopedia"* under the editing of Dr. Yakov Klatzkin and Prof. Dr. Y. Elbogen, seventh volume, original Eshkol, Berlin (German)

Translated by Pamela Russ

A county city in Poland in the Warsaw *voivodship* [province]. In the year 1765, there were 157 Jews living in Gostynin. In 1856 – 634; in 1897 – 1849 Jews (general population 6747); and in the year 1921 – 1831 Jews (general population 6684).

In the year 1823 – 1862 existed in Gostynin, with separate quarters for the Jewish residents. The old synagogue burned down, and in the year 1899 it was rebuilt. The street where the synagogue stood, was formerly the Jewish street. A side street off this very street was called "Death Street" in colloquial speech, because the old cemetery was there.

From the *"Book of Horrors"* with the editing by Binyomin Mintz and Dr. Yisroel Kloizner, first volume, 5705, 1945 (Hebrew)[6]

Translated by Pamela Russ

On Shabbat Shuva[7] the Nazis captured Gostynin. They quickly gave out an order to the Polaks and to the Jews to assemble in the city plaza. After that, they ordered the Jews to move to one side of the plaza and the Polaks to the other side. Later, they ordered the Jews to lie on the ground. Every minute, they [*the Jews*] thought the shooting would bring their end, but suddenly they ordered the Jews to get up on their knees and recite the confession. Everyone had to give up everything they had in their pockets. About five in the evening, the Germans began beating them with their whips. The entire plaza was transformed, in one blink, into a bloody swamp. The screams reached the heavens. After a certain amount of time, they were let go and they were permitted to return to their houses. The following morning, the looting began. The Nazis ransacked all the *seforim* [religious books] from all the Jewish homes, and burned them. Some of the respected Jews in the city were beaten almost to death. There was no end to the mockery [of the Jews]. The Germans forced one Jew to ride on the back of another, to spit in the face of one another, and to beat one another.

[Page 18]

On Yom Kippur, the Nazis assembled all the Gostyniner residents, Jews and Polaks, and herded them into the Christian church. This came as a punishment for the few *"minyanim"* [quorum of men for prayers] that they had discovered that day [Yom Kippur] that is holy for Jews. All of these people were locked into the church for three days without food or drink. They had to take care of their personal needs there, and that's how they desecrated the

---

Translator's footnotes

6.   Protocol of a witness testimony in Tel Aviv, February 17, 1940.

7.   Year 1939, with the onset of World War II.

Christian holiness. After three days, when they were freed, they were forced to clean the floor of the church with their bare hands.

The Germans forced the Rav to collect the horses' feces from the streets of the city and put it into his *shtreimel* [fur–trimmed hat worn by *chassidim*]. They also shaved the Rav's beard and his hair was also put into the *shtreimel*.

They set fire to the synagogue, and they did not permit anyone to put out the fire in the house [synagogue] that burned along with the Torah scrolls. The *Beis Medrash* [Study Hall] was taken over by the Jews themselves who were forced in there by the Nazis who beat them with whips and butts of guns. The *Beis Medrash* was built of wood. The Jews were forced to hand over the wood from the destroyed *Beis Medrash* to the Germans who lived in the city. At great risk, the Jews saved the Torah scrolls and hid them in the ritual baths. The Germans commanded the Jews to break apart the baths and they were terrified that the Germans would discover the Torah scrolls. The Jews were saved by a miracle when they managed to remove the scrolls and the Nazis did not notice.

[Page 19]

From Bulletin of the Historical Institute Number 13–14, Warsaw, 1955, in the detailed work of D. Dombrowska, titled "The Destruction of the Jews in Warsaw" (Polish)

Translated by Pamela Russ

Under the German occupation, Gostynin belonged to Wartheland, to the district of Inowroclaw.

Before September 1, 1939, there were 2269 Jewish souls in Gostynin.

In December 1941, there were 2250 Jews living in Gostynin, of which 1650 were Gostynin residents and 650 were refugees from different cities.

Before April 1942, at the time when there was the evacuation of Jews who were then sent to Chelmno, there were 2000 Jews living in Gostynin.

[Page 23]

The Gostyniner Rebbe

The Good Jew from Gostynin

by Y.M. Biderman

Translated by Pamela Russ

Y.M. Biderman

It is said about the Gostyniner Rebbe, that each time he would return from a trip to Kotzk, he would stop on the small bridge, turn with great earnestness towards the direction of Kotzk, and then tears would flow from his eyes. These were tears of yearning, of great longing for the powerful spirit that beamed out from the fiery sun that shone in Kotzk.

The sun by nature melts things, making softer any blockages, and sometimes burning or desiccating them. The effect of its workings depends firstly on the substance of the object. In the *chassidic* world of his time, Reb Mendele Kotzker affected both types: some he burned and some he softened. The Gostyniner, the Kotzk sun made softer, filled his heart with more mercy, soaked his entire being with heartfelt kindness, superhuman grace, and boundless love.

When the great fire went out in Kotzk because Reb Mendele closed himself off in his room for many years, and from the Rebbe's close surroundings, angry, upset talk circulated that chased away the regular attendants, cooled

down his followers, and caused a great tumult between the closest intimates –
then, the two – Reb Itche Meir from Warsaw, later to be the *Chidushei HaRim*[8]
and Reb Yechiel Meir Gostyniner, later to be called the *Tehillim* Jew [so named
because of his remarkable trait of constantly reciting *Tehillim* (Psalms) with
utmost emotion and fervor] – remained rock solid and loyal in their dedication
to their Rebbe. The genius from Warsaw acknowledged Kotzk as the center of
Torah and scholarship, and the Gostyniner good Jew agreed that in terms of
substance, the ways of Kotzk were dictated from the deepest wells of goodness.

[Page 24]

In his first contact with the Kotzker fiery pillar, he already took some of the
light that came from there.

"Don't worry about us," said Reb Mendele to Reb Yechiel Meyer, "we are not
inventing anything new. We are working hard to bring out from each person
that which is found inside him..."

Moreover, Reb Yechiel Meyer Gostyniner knew that with the Rebbe's
strength, with the force of his glowing spirit that reached the heavens, his own
inner hidden traits, that were covered with heavy layers of flesh–and–blood
notions and drowned under a mountain of human habits and behaviors,
would be elevated and refined to become factors that affect the person who
carries them and affect his fellow man.

One could think that the distance between the strict, sullen Kotzker and
the polite, mild, warm Gostyniner was great. In fact, they were often described
as having opposing characters with distinct traits, differing in their demeanor,
in their behavior, in their speech. But their origins were from one source. They
reciprocally complemented each other. They were in the test of Hillel and
Shammai[9] who expressed thoughts in various categories, and whose spiritual

---

Translator's footnotes

8.   referring to Rabbi Yitzchok Meir Rotenberg–Alter, the first Gerer Rebbe, also called the
Chidushei HaRim, ("New Concepts of Rav Itche Meir") which were the titles of the scholarly
books that he wrote

9.   Hillel and Shammai were two leading sages of the last 1st century BCE and the early 1st
century CE, who founded opposing schools of Jewish thought, known as the House of Hillel and
House of Shammai. The debate between these schools on matters of ritual practice, ethics, and
theology was critical for the shaping of the Oral Law and Judaism as it is today (Wikipedia).

qualities were in contrast to one another. But they sat under one roof of Jewish law, approached one another, and had to depend on one another. Once a rift developed between the two of them – but they were kneaded from one dough and later generations tied them together and brought them closer. Both were the completeness of Jacob's ladder: Reb Mendele was with "his head reaching until the Heavens," he floated in the skies, was removed from earthly matters that are relevant to the world and people; Reb Yechiel Meyer was "with his feet on the ground." He was approached by people, helped them in their pain, and had an ear for their difficulties and woes.

[Page 25]

When the wealthy Gostyniner businessmen asked Reb Yechiel Meyer before Shavuos, as he was preparing himself in his usual manner to travel to Kotzk, why he was travelling to Kotzk, and could they not celebrate the giving of the Torah [which is celebrated by the holiday of Shavuot] in Gostynin just as they do in Kotzk, the Gostyniner good Jew replied to them: "In Gostynin, they translate 'you should not steal' as meaning stealing from another person. But in Kotzk they interpret the phrase 'you should not steal' as meaning you should not steal from yourself. You should not disappoint yourself. Robbing from your mind is also stealing..."

Honesty towards others as well as to oneself was the way of Gostynin.

Both men had their *chassidic* origins in Przysucha. Kotzk was even sharper, more brilliant than Przysucha; Gostynin simplified Przysucha. Przysucha did not accept the concept of reciting Psalms; Psalms can also be recited by the simple people, without intellect. They didn't support the idea of reciting, repeating, or even reciting chapter after chapter of the holy Psalms. Kotzk went even further, saying that he who prayed today because he prayed yesterday, was an evil man because each prayer has to contain newness, and must evoke from it new sparks of holiness. In the opposite manner, regularity merely creates habit.

Gostynin viewed this differently. *Chassidim* tell that once, a sick person came to Reb Yechiel Meyer to ask for relief. The Rebbe gave him his tried and true remedy: reciting a portion of Psalms. The sick man responded:

"But Rebbe, I am a coarse individual, an ignorant man, and I don't understand the meaning of the words...!"

The Rebbe opened the sixth chapter of Psalms that begins with the words: "For the Conductor [God] with melodies..."[10], and then said to him:

"From this chapter you will see it, 'For the Director [God] with melodies King David played on an instrument that had eight strings. There are instruments that have four strings and there are musicians who play on a *katarinka* [portable music box played by cranking], and they play without strings, but turn the handle back and forth and the music comes out of the music box by itself. The least that is required by the musician is to turn the crank. You have to do something. Also, in the prayers to God, you cannot rely on others, you have to pray on your own. Even one who does not understand the meaning of the words is obligated to recite Psalms, and the Creator will send a complete recovery for each word said."

[Page 26]

The Gostyniner Rebbe very often had his eye on the simple Jew. He searched him out to elevate him and give him a taste of Judaism. And in this search for the ordinary person, he himself was the embodiment of simplicity. Not with a simplicity that originates from crudeness or from naiveté, but a simplicity that was built on straightforwardness, refined modesty, and on elevated wisdom that borders on the other side of sharpness and insightfulness. The sharpness tries to peel away the levels and skins and to reach the kernel, to the center, to the essence, to the point, to the simple ordinariness. The Gostyniner simplicity was a step further from this sharpness. As he peels away all the covers and evil spirits, the simplicity reaches the substance, the foundation, to the bare truth.

With this thinking, we have to understand the scene in front of the locked door of the Kotzker Rebbe's room that was besieged by hundreds of *chassidim*. They waited for the moment when the holy Rabbi would reveal himself and they would be greeted by him, and the Rebbe remained alone in his room, in meditation, and did not want to reveal himself to his followers. It was Purim at the time, and the Gostyniner gathered his strength, and banged at the Rebbe's door:

Translator's footnotes

10. King David composed this Psalm when he was sick and in pain. He intended this prayer for every person in sickness or distress, and particularly for Israel when it suffered oppression.

"Rebbe! I am naked and barefoot! I do not have any Torah learnings or any good deeds! We are waiting that the Rebbe should fulfill the *mitzva* [positive commandment] and clothe the naked. Today [because it is Purim], we send gifts of food, and we have to give to everyone who stretches out his hand..."

[Page 27]

How simple and humble were these words about nakedness and bare feet. These words caused every honest soul to tremble with their sharpness and simplicity. They also shook up the dejected Kotzker. He opened the door and took the Gostyniner Rebbe into his room.

"The more we get to the bottom of the treasure of the fear of Heaven, the more we see how much farther away we are from it," he would say. And the same applies to the simplicity for which philosophers strive to find the formulas. The more you search for the simplicity, the more confused and complicated it becomes."

"One can sit and study Torah and its laws for seventy years and hardly move ahead even an iota..."he would say. Of course, studying Torah and praying are great things. But the most important thing for him was the quality of a person's character. He demanded of himself uprightness and compassion. Within himself and his followers he looked not only for constraint and humility, but also for the feeling of unpretentiousness. He would mention the verse in the Torah portion of Vayikra ["...and he called:] "...And Aaron approached the altar..." The commentary Rashi says that Aaron hesitated in humility. Then Moshe asked him, "Why are you hesitating? You were chosen for this." The meaning of this, the Gostyniner said, was that "You were chosen so that you would have the pains of embarrassment..."

The regimen of his daily behavior, tell witnesses, was that the Gostyniner tried to stifle within himself any trace of a negative thought. He took it upon himself to read every day his own personal code to remind himself, to remember, and absolutely never to forget how a person must behave with purity of thought, with honor of character, and with eternal, continuous, permanent self–control. "Do not forsake us in our old age..." – the Gostyniner translated this as — even in old age, may we have the strength to overcome all the bad traits and desires that a person has within him. "Do not throw me into the hands of the Evil Inclination."

[Page 28]

It is a *mitzva* [positive commandment] to live like a Jew. You have to love every Jew. "The Kotzker Rebbe," he would say, "already worked hard on me that love for a fellow Jew should be part of me. But it didn't work," he would sigh, not being satisfied with his levels [of achievement]. "One has to love not only a fellow Jew, but this love has to be on such a level that it should also encompass an enemy."

And the legend that wove itself around the striking personality of this holy Jew, tells of the following:

"Once there was a Jew in Gostynin who became ill. This Jew was known for his antagonism towards the Rebbe. Reb Yechiel Meyer knew about this Jew's hatred towards him, so the Rebbe assembled a quorum of ten Jews, and began to recite Psalms and pray for his recovery. The Rebbe fasted the entire day, and everyone was amazed, and even the Rebbe's mother was astonished.

"Why are you causing such a fuss by fasting because of a person who always persecuted you?"

Reb Yechiel Meyer replied: "You see, Mother, if I have an enemy, probably it was decreed in Heaven that I should have an enemy. Therefore, I am begging the Creator of the Universe that He should send a complete recovery to my enemy because if not this one, then I will have to find another enemy..."

For Reb Yechiel Meyer, love of a fellow Jew was coupled with total faith, and therefore it was completely pure, without biases and preconditions.

The people also say about this fine Gostyniner Jew:

"Reb Yechiel Meyer sent out two important men to collect money among the wealthy Jews, in order to help a needy Jew. The two men returned to the Rebbe and told him about a Jew, a rich man in town, who had closed his hand and in no way would he give any donation. The Rebbe exclaimed: 'You cannot say anything bad about a Jew', as it is written 'You should not hate your brother with your heart.' That means, with your good heart. If your heart is kind, then let it be kind so that you can do good things and not so that you can hate the other person who does not want to do good.

[Page 29]

" 'And you should not be good only in your heart, but be good and pleasing in your words. The good word transposes the bad word and makes the good word even better. Your words have to be guarded, and wherever you can, you must throw in more good words. The word "good," when it is used, brings good, for the good.'" Thus, in this essay about his personal behavior, goodness is the concept and the word that dominates this unusual document.

With love and devotion, he drew close to every Jew. Once, when a Jew, a wealthy man appeared in his courtroom, a clumsy looking man, with broad shoulders and a large belly, Reb Yechiel Meyer called out with such sincerity:

"So much Jew, may there be no evil eye!"

Once, his beadle asked a visitor who had come before daybreak from a journey to Gostynin, whether he had already recited the morning prayers. Reb Yechiel Meyer drew his attention to something:

"A Jew who comes at daybreak after long travels is not asked whether he has already recited the prayers, but is asked if he has already eaten breakfast."

Also, from his religiousness, his fear of God, there shone a boundless love for the Creator and for His creations, to every type of person, to every Jew. They called him – the good Jew from Gostynin. That's how he was known in the Jewish world, and that's how he was popular in the non–Jewish world, who often came for help to the Gostynin *tzaddik* [righteous man]. He was not only a good Jew, a Rebbe, but he was a fine Jew – simply, a Jew, a fine one ...

[Page 30]

***

Small and tossed aside, a town lay on a side road between Kutno and Plock in the kingdom of Poland, an insignificant spot on the map of Jewish settlements in the Polish exile. Unnoticed, the quiet Gostynin would have lived, in the spiritual way of the Polish–Jewish customary manner, had not a local personality, from the daily ordinariness, given the city an unusual aura, a singular aroma and glow with a rare heavenly light.

In the merit of the Rebbe, Gostynin remained part of the history of the wondrous Polish Jew. The Gostynin Jewish community is no longer here. It suffered the same fate as all the other Jewish communities of Poland. It was erased by the terrorizing demon. Its Jews died in the years of the gruesome tragedy.

Gostynin, however, is still alive, because the memories of the good Jew from Gostynin are still alive.

***

And in the hours of pain during the Jewish destruction and waste – go
stand, dear man, on the bridge of generations, as the Gostyniner used to do as
he longed for Kotzk – and drop a tear, a hot, thick tear, for the great lover of
Jews, for the Jewish nation – a tear of longing, a tear of hope, that – – –

May his merit defend us.

[Page 31]

The Gostyniner *Tzaddik* [Righteous Man]

by The Esteemed Rabbi Moshe Aronson (Israel)
Formerly Head of the Jewish Court; Sanik, the Gostynin Circle

Translated by Pamela Russ

Rebbe Yechiel Meyer Lipszycz, the Gostyniner Rebbe, was born in the year 5576 (1815), in Opoczno, Poland, to his father Reb Yakov Czwi, and his mother Soroh, daughter of the Opoczner Rav, Reb Yehuda Leyb Lipszycz. As a child, Reb Yechiel Meyer was already exceptional in his kind–heartedness. He would secretly divide his food and his pocket money among the poor children in *cheder* [religious elementary school].

In his early youth, his parents left him an orphan. First, his mother left this world, and soon thereafter his father, and Yechiel Meyer and his only sister Chaya Szprintze were left as complete orphans.

His uncle, the genius Reb Shmuel Noach Lipszycz, took him in, studied Torah with him, and raised him as his own child.

Years passed, Yechiel Meyer grew up, and became independent. His uncle brought him to Kutno to the large *Yeshiva* [school for religious school for older boys] of the *Gaon* [genius] Rebbe Moshe Yehuda Leyb Zilberberg, the author of the religious text *Zayit Ra'anan* ["fresh olive"]. Each day, Yechiel Meyer grew in his studies and very quickly became known in the Torah world as a prodigy.

One day, Reb Mordechai Wajngart came to the *Zayit Ra'anan* [meaning to Reb Moshe Yehuda Leyb Zilberberg] from Gostynin, having been sent by his wealthy father–in–law Reb Leybish, to ask for a worthy groom for his sister–in–law.

The genius of Kutno selected the best student from his *yeshiva*, Yechiel Meyer, who was also very admired by the rich Gostynin family. The match was made. Reb Leybish promised his future son–in–law lifelong financial support and a large dowry. Yechiel Meyer continued his Torah studies in the Kutno *yeshiva* until his marriage.

[Page 32]

After the wedding, he settled in Gostynin, devoting all his time to Torah, worshipping the Creator, and performing charitable deeds. It is told that after the long day of fasting, on the 17th day of the month of Tammuz, when the entire family sat down to the table to eat something after the day of fasting, Reb Yechiel Meyer disappeared. After a time, he returned, completely soaked from rain, but very cheerful. He had brought a guest with him...

But the good years passed quickly. His father–in–law, Reb Leybish the wealthy man, died suddenly and Reb Yechiel Meyer was forced to seek out a livelihood. He opened a food and tobacco store in Gostynin, where his wife was the primary worker. He only helped her when it was necessary.

Reb Meyer Kowaler, an elderly Kotzker *chassid* who lived in Gostynin at the time, had a great influence on the young Reb Yechiel Meyer, and he convinced him to go see the Kotzker Rebbe.

In Kotzk, Reb Yechiel Meyer became friendly with Reb Wolf Strikewer, and with time, both of them became close to the elderly Kotzker Rebbe. That was still the time when Reb Mendele lived in Tomaszow.

In Kotzk they called him the "religious Yechiel Meyer." As time passed, Reb Yechiel Meyer distanced himself from people, isolated himself from the world, and in secret completely devoted himself to the study of Torah and *chassidus*.

At that time, the Gostyniner Rav, Rebbe Shloime, went to Sieradz; the head rabbinic seat in Gostynin was left empty.

The Kotzker *chassidim* of Gostynin went to see the Rebbe and ask whom they should take on as their new Rav. The Rebbe suggested Reb Yechiel Meyer. Reb Hersh Tomaszower sent along a letter in the name of the Rebbe to Reb Yechiel Meyer, in which he invited him to take on the position of Rav of Gostynin.

At first, Reb Yechiel Meyer declined. But with time, when his livelihood became less and less, he saw it as a sign from Above to address his difficult situation, and he took on the post of Chief Rabbi of Gostynin.

[Page 33]

The moment he became the Gostyniner Rav, he came out of his seclusion, and completely devoted himself to the community. He went from one extreme to the other, and he lowered himself from the isolated levels and lofty, heavenly issues to the basic needs of each Jew in his community. He knew each Gostyniner Jew and tried to help in every possible way according to the person's needs. As the Rav of the city, he had his eye on the entire community in the city. More than once he was involved with appeasing city conflicts, resolving arguments between warring sides, and very often he was also the emissary of his community for the non–Jewish authorities.

The name of Reb Yechiel Meyer Gostyniner became popular very quickly. He was known everywhere as a *Tzaddik* [righteous person] and learned man, a lover of Jews, and a pursuer of peace. His name became famous in many cities outside of Gostynin. Wherever a conflict arose, the people involved would immediately go to Reb Yechiel Meyer, and he, with his good words, would conciliate the sides and restore peace.

"The good Jew from Gostynin," was what he was called, even during his lifetime, not only because he truly was the symbol of goodness, but also because he saw only the good in all people.

"It is easier to be an expert in diamonds than in the simplest Jew," he would say in his goodness. He intentionally gave of himself to the regular businessmen, to the Jews of the nation [committed Jews] and always made efforts for their benefits and well–being. He always made a point to see their grandeur, and to raise up the *pintele Yid* [spark of Jewishness] from the depths of their roots.

Each of his letters ended with the word "tov," "good," a hint that in every contact with the world and with people, goodness must prevail.

He was also called "the Psalms Jew," because for each problem and for any human suffering he had one solution – to recite Psalms. He told one person to recite ten chapters, another one was told to recite the chapters designated for that day of the week, and a third person was told to recite the entire Book of Psalms. And when he himself recited Psalms he tore at the Heavens and nullified bad decrees.

[Page 34]

His teachers were: Rebbe Menachem Mendel Morgenstern, the older Kotzker Rebbe; and after his passing in the year 5619 (1859) he went to the founder of the Gerer court, to the *"Chidushei HaRim"* [named after the title of his Torah works *Chidushei* (new thoughts) *HaRim* (of **R**eb **Y**itzchok **M**eyer)]; and after that to the *Tzaddik*, Reb Avrohm Landau, the Ciechanower Rav. Only after the passing of Rav Landau, in the year 5635 (1875), did Reb Yechiel Meyer consent to become Rebbe. He led his *chassidim* as the Gostyniner Rebbe for thirteen years, and he helped thousands of people with guidance and resources, and with his heartfelt prayers and blessings.

The Rebbe and his family lived in dearth themselves, because the Rebbe did not want to have pleasure from the materials of his *chassidim*, and everything he earned he divided among the needy.

Also, many non–Jews came to the Rebbe for advice and requests because they saw him as a Godly man whose words and blessings were fulfilled.

For forty years, Reb Yechiel Meyer Lipszycz was the Gostyniner Rebbe. On the 28th of the month of Shevat, 5648 (1888), the Gostyniner *Tzaddik* passed away. He left behind two sons: Reb Leybish and Reb Yisroel Moshe, who later was the rabbinic leader in Proskow. He also left behind a daughter, the wife of Reb Aaron Yakov, the son of Reb Dovid Zilberstajn of Gostynin.

The name of the Gostyniner Rebbe shines from holiness among the names of prominent Jews who brought comfort and leadership to the nation of Jews during the times of difficult exile.

[Page 35]

The Rebbe's Word

Translated by Pamela Russ

One can be a passionate person and at the same time a person of stature. There has to be no more explanation here. One can use his stature [intellect] only in the Name of God.

***

There are *Tzaddikim* [righteous men] who have eyes to see and ears to hear, a sense of smell and a sense of touch to recognize whether there is holiness in each thing.

***

There are *chassidim* who praise their Rebbe if he eats nothing. This is in the category of "...they don't see, they don't hear, they don't eat" (describing the idols or false gods who do not hear, see, or eat). This opinion would also include "they don't smell." That means, that they have no scent of the Fear of Heaven. But what? They don't eat. In contrary to that, they don't see with prophecy and don't hear the call of Heaven.

***

I heard in the name of the Gerer Rebbe, may his memory be blessed – the *Chidushei HaRim* – on the verse "that you will merit through your holy work to uproot all the anger from yourself, which means from the depths of your heart." All the people of Israel will heed your words and honor you, as is discussed in a treatise from the sages: "Every person who has the fear of God in him, will have his words heeded."

***

All his years, Reb Yechiel Meyer did not want to become Rebbe. He was a student of the Kotzker Rebbe. After the Kotzker Rebbe's passing, he connected closely to the *Chidushei HaRim* and when the Gerer Rebbe passed on, he became close to Reb Avrohom Ciechanower, to whom he would travel. After the passing of the Ciechanower, under the pressure of his *chassidim*, he consented to become Rebbe. He was sixty years old at that time.

[Page 36]

On the first Shabbath, when he tasted the food at his [ceremonial] "table," he called out to his *chassidim*: "It seems that I am not a Rebbe. I am enjoying the food!"

***

He used to say:

"There is no better remedy book than the Book of Psalms."

Once, he commented to a *chassid*:

The community thinks that I can cure the sick. If this would be the case, I would visit every sick person, go to their home, go to his city, to cure him. But, instead, I recite Psalms. Let him also recite Psalms!

***

Reb Yechiel Meyer would recount:

Once I came to Przasznysz. Reb Hanoch Henech was the Rav there before he became the Alexander Rebbe. When Reb Hanoch Henech found out that I was coming to see him to greet him, he asked that all the candles of the Shabbath candelabrum be lit and he dressed in his Shabbath finery in my honor. He stayed with me all the time and said that a Torah scholar is likened to the Shabbath. A deep love bound us together.

***

When Yechiel Meyer came to the *Chidushei HaRim* in Warsaw, he first went to an inn near the *Beis Medrash* [Study Hall] to put away his packages. At that moment, there was a group of free–spirited young men who were playing cards and at the same time were joking around at the expense of the *Chidushei HaRim*, and were mocking him.

Reb Yechiel Meyer blocked his ears and left the house. He thought that he might have to "tear his garments" [as a sign of mourning], since that is the commandment when one hears a Rebbe humiliated. But then he considered that it would not be becoming to present himself in that manner with torn clothing to the Rebbe. He went to the *Beis Medrash* and searched in the religious books as to what the law would say and he could not determine the answer. He went to the Rebbe and told him what had transpired. The *Chidushei HaRim* replied:

[Page 37]

"Yechiel Meyer, if we would have to tear our garments in mourning for each insult of these types of people, we would have to go around all torn up and tattered."

***

There is a story about a Jew who brought a bottle of aged, expensive wine to Reb Yechiel Meyer. The Rebbe asked him if he had also locked the door with a steel chain, as the wealthy men of that day used to do. When the wealthy man replied that — yes, he had done that, the Rebbe asked him: "And what will you do if Elijah the Prophet will want to enter your home and will find the door locked with a steel lock?"

The Rebbe did not accept the gift.

***

Once, a prominent, wealthy man came to the Gostyniner and wanted to give him a monetary gift. But the Rebbe did not want to accept it. The wealthy man strongly persisted, but the Rebbe remained steadfast. The wealthy man asked the Rebbe: "What is your reason?" The Rebbe replied: "Do you owe anyone money?"

The wealthy man said that he did.

"If so," the Rebbe continued, "then first you must repay your debts, as it is written: ˜First you pay off your debts, then you can give donations..."

***

The Gostyniner Rebbe had a *chassid*, Reb Leyb the estate–owner. Each time that the Rebbe would travel to Czechanow to the Rebbe, Reb Leyb would take him in his carriage.

So, there's a story, that Reb Yechiel and his son Reb Yisroel Moshe and the *chassid* Reb Leyb arrived in Czechanow, and together they went to Reb Avrohom Czechanower to greet him.

[Page 38]

The following day, the Czechanower Rebbe sent his beadle to the inn to invite Reb Yechiel and his son for lunch. Reb Yechiel was very puzzled as to why he had not also invited Reb Leyb to the meal, as was the usual manner. Reb Yechiel Meyer was worried that perhaps Reb Avrohom had simple forgotten. So he went to the Rebbe, and asked why he had not also invited Reb Leyb.

Reb Avrohom replied with great shock: "Was Reb Leyb here last night with me? I did not see him!"

The Gostyniner rushed back to the inn and told Reb Leyb to recite ten chapters of Psalms and to go once again to the Czechanower Rebbe to greet him. Reb Leyb did exactly that. When he arrived, Reb Avrohom looked for him intently and then said: "Now I have seen you. Please join me for lunch."

[Page 39]

A Pamphlet about Behavior
(What the Gostyniner Rebbe Wrote for Himself)

Translated by Pamela Russ

I heard from a holy Jew, who said to me, maybe you were created in order to complete the thought that will take you to the level of the holy ones.

Also, for the love of a fellow Jew – become accustomed to it all your life.

And another holy Jew said to me: "First, adorn yourself. See that your own deeds should be good ones."

I thereby take upon myself a strong and solid vow, with the help of the Creator, blessed be He, and with His great mercy and grace, to chase away from my mind and from my heart all inappropriate thoughts.

Also, the thoughts that the Evil Inclination brings into the mind sometimes, some which he can describe, and some that from the start are recognized to be foolish and empty, and not to infuse them with words of Torah and moral conduct, for the good.

To distance oneself from praise, from all those objects and words that bring to coarseness.

For sure to distance oneself from empty speech.

And from speaking too much, which leads to sin, and distancing oneself from the fear of God and humility, just as a fool who releases every breath from his mouth. And on that subject it is said: "The barrier around wisdom is silence."

And to protect oneself greatly from all sorts of anger and severity.

And if, God forbid, something happens that will stimulate anger and severity, I take upon myself, with the help of the Creator to wait at least a quarter of an hour in order to slowly become calmer and protected from anger and control myself with the help of God.

[Page 40]

And if at some time I will be forced to discipline the people, I take upon myself to recite at least five chapters of Psalms, and to ask for mercy, that I should not stumble with my words.

And to speak with words of love and prayers, as the one who is raising a child speaks to him – with love and with total goodness.

And I am obliged to read these writings every day, for the good.

To keep in mind: May the honor of your friend, that means of your dear soul, be beloved to you with total goodness.

Remember that you are punished for open sins of the past through pain, may it not befall us, through cruel acts that are fitting for this. How good, therefore, is it to suffer for all that is due to a person on this world, and to fulfill his "turning the cheek to the one who slaps," and then be soaked with shame, and with that to celebrate for the good.

Especially, since through that, one suffers and one nullifies his own desires and wishes, and he conducts himself according to the virtues of the Creator Who does good things for everyone and is good to everyone; and he stills his own anger, and contains his temper and is full of mercy – through this, he unites with God, the Almighty, for the good.

And fulfill, "Leave all your worries to God" and He will carry out everything for the good.

And also speak thoughtfully, for the good.

And especially, that in this way the Creator will be able to rest with the people, and enable the person to become......the resting place for His holiness, as it is written "...until I find a place," and also the holiness of the Shabbath should rest upon him, for the good.

[Page 41]

Who is a *chassid?* He who conducts himself piously with his Creator, for the good. A small prophecy, "and you will search," and so on.

A leader must use all his virtues of mercy, as it is written in *Psikto* [commentary], for the good.

The prophet took care of me, etc. That is the well of life and foolishness, all with good.

I heard from the holy Gerer Rebbe, of blessed memory: The children of Noah did not sacrifice any perfect [complete] offerings, but for the children of Israel, just eating the perfect offerings was done with great sacrifice, for the good.

(From the *sefer* [religious book] *"Mei Ha'yam"* [*"Waters of the Sea"*], Lodz, 5648 [1888])Translated from the Hebrew

Bibliography about the Gostyniner Rebbe

Translated by Pamela Russ

Zer Zahav u'Minchas Yehuda [A Golden Wreath and the Offering of Yehuda], printed at the beginning of *Sefer Hamachria* [the Decisive Work], by Reb Yeshaya of Trany.

Siach Sarfei Kodesh [Words of Holy Fire], by Rav Yoetz Kim Kadish.

Mei Hayam [Waters of the Sea], new thoughts on the Torah, published after the death of the Rebbe, by his relative Reb Shimon Menachem Mendel of Gubraczew, together with Reb Nosson Note Hakohen, head of the Jewish court in Kolbiel.

Divrei Shmuel [Words of Samuel], by Reb Noach Shmuel Lipszycz, the Gostyniner Rebbe's uncle.

Admorei Polan [Great Rabbis of Poland], by Eliezer Steinman.

Gute Yidden in Poilen [Good Jews in Poland], by M. Feinkind.

Przysucha un Kotzk [Przysucha and Kotzk], by Menashe Unger.

Migedolei Hachassidus [From the Giants of *Chassidus*], Book 11, *Admor* [esteemed Rav] Reb Yechiel Meyer Lipszycz, may his memory be blessed, by Rav Avrohom Yitzchok Bromberg.

A letter from the esteemed Rav Yitzchok Yehuda Trunk to Sholom Asch in which the last Rav from Kutno tells the famous writer details about the Gostyniner Rebbe, published in the journal *Heimish*, Number 37 and 38–39, 1959.

[Page 45]

Memories

Our Former Gostynin

by Josef Keller

Translated by Pamela Russ

Josef Keller

In a mountain of ashes, destroyed and devastated, lies the city of our childhood years – Gostynin. It's hard to imagine that now Gostynin is a city without Shabbos, without *yomim tovim* (Jewish holidays), that on Friday nights no one is calling everyone to go to synagogue, and that our Jews are no longer rushing to the synagogue on Friday nights to pray. In the same way, it is hard to believe that the lives of our beloved and dearest ones were so horrifically snuffed out.

Yes, for us Gostynin is devoured and dead. The only ones left are we Gostyniner who left to America long before the destruction of Poland. Also, there are those who settled in Israel even before World War II, and several others who miraculously were saved from the plague of extermination that befell our brothers in Poland and are in the Land of Israel along with the other Gostyniner already there, and are part of the organization *"Irgun Yotzei Gostynin Be'Yisrael"* [organization of those from Gostynin in Israel].

We, the surviving Gostyniner, have promised to perpetuate our devastated home, and this very book about Gostynin will be an eternal monument that will leave a memory of our destroyed town and her martyrs for generations to come.

[Page 46]

I remember Gostynin from the early years of this century. A town, clean and neat, surrounded by natural greenery of forests, gardens, green fields and mountains that stretched one higher than the other, such that the tallest mountain was crowned with the name "*har hahar*" which meant "mountain of mountains." Snaking between the mountains were all kinds of roads and footpaths that were hidden by the trees, so much so that these were the most special, beautiful, and discreet strolling places for the youth who did not want to be in the clear view of the older generation.

In the later years, when the political socialist movement tore through our town, the area of the "mountain of mountains" was chosen as the place for secret and illegal meetings.

When there was a Jewish holiday, some of the youth went to the forest in Plock, some to the Kutno forest; others went on the Koval road through the moss to the "mountain of mountains," so that in this way they almost forgot that they lived in a small town.

The town itself was a Jewish one. There were more Jewish than Christian storekeepers because the Jews were primarily occupied in trade. There were grain merchants, lumber merchants, tailor shops and food shops, haberdasheries, and so on.

There were also craftsmen in the town such as tailors, shoemakers, milliners, carpenters, tinsmiths, and a large number of stocking manufacturers.

Among the merchants, there were many who spent a lot of their time in Torah studies; really as they say: "*Tov Torah Im Derech Eretz*" ["Beautiful is the study of Torah along with everyday life"].

This is a general, superficial glimpse of Gostynin. If you want to look more deeply into the Jewish community of Gostynin, then you have to begin with the Rav, Reb Yechiel Meyer, of blessed memory.

Even though this Rav, Reb Yechiel Meyer, lived and was active for some time before my time, I can't say that that time is totally foreign to me, because I heard many stories and many tales about this *Tzadik* [great, pious man]. The truth is that the Gostynin Rebbe's name was known across the entire Poland. His followers were Jews from all corners of Poland, and every one of them who came to see the Rebbe, whether a merchant or a craftsman, a teacher or an ordinary Jew, a rich man or a poor man, all were welcomed, important guests. He received everyone with respect and with heartfelt love. His true greatness lay in his humility. For all problems, he had but one salvation: to recite Psalms as much as possible.

[Page 47]

This awesome story that was told at the time of the Rav's passing characteristically illustrates the holiness with which the Rav was enveloped.

I will retell this exactly as I heard it: When this righteous man died, the town naturally was enveloped in deep sorrow. The Burial Society, for whom doing the purification before burial was one of the most routine things, like (to differentiate) having a drink of whiskey, this time they had no desire to undertake this pre–burial purification simply out of fear of touching such a holy body. But still, the purification had to be done, so the Burial Society held a special meeting and it was decided that the most prominent members of the Burial Society would take care of the task. I don't know exactly who these people were, but I know that one of these was my grandfather Reb Yisroel Itche Keller, definitely an important man in the Burial Society, and someone close to the Rav during his lifetime. The elected Burial Society men went into the room where the purification was to be done, behind closed doors, to do their job undisturbed. But before they had finished, the door to the room suddenly opened and an uninvited member of the Burial Society was there. Wordlessly, but with stern motions, they gestured to the man to leave. When the door closed, they completed their work, and the funeral took place.

A tragic and deep sorrow covered the whole town after the Rebbe's death. But the day after the burial the Burial Society had another purification to do. This was the purification of the man from the Burial Society who had crossed the threshold of the room in which the purification of the pious Rav had been in process.

[Page 48]

This story, as the people in the community told it, is very representational, and illustrates how holy this Rebbe was considered in Gostynin and in other cities in Poland.

These times in which the Gostynin Rav lived I cannot remember, but I will never forget the 21st day of *Shevat* [Hebrew month] which was his *yahrzeit* [anniversary of his death], because on that day Gostynin had a completely different appearance.

One day earlier, in the twilight of the eve of the *yahrzeit*, the study hall was packed with people praying who had come to the town from all corners of Poland. This crowd began to go to the Rav's gravesite right after the evening prayers. The following day, the actual day of the *yahrzeit*, an unending procession went along the Kutno road that led to the cemetery where the Rav's gravesite was situated.

Off the Kutno road, and approaching the cemetery, one could see from afar the *ohel* [structure over the grave] that stood in the foreground of the cemetery. Inside this structure was the grave surrounded by a barbed wire fence through which one could see the actual grave. There was a tall lantern atop a pole that rested on the ground. Inside the lantern was an "eternal light" [a lit candle]. On the day of the *yahrzeit*, this structure at the gravesite was filled to capacity, and outside there were groups of people awaiting their turn to enter.

The gravesite was completely covered with *kvitlech* [pieces of paper upon which people had written personal requests and prayers]. These were all kinds of written requests to the Rebbe. On these pieces of paper, each person, according to his capacity, poured out his heart to the Rebbe asking for his help. And for those who could not write these notes in Hebrew, there was a young man who was the designated "note writer" for the community.

[Page 49]

That's how powerful the day of the Rav's *yahrzeit* appeared in the town. That's why the 21st day of Shevat is so strongly etched in my memory.

After the death of the Gostynin Rav, I don't know exactly how long after, the position of the Gostynin Rav was assumed by the Kinsk [Konskie] genius Reb Yoav Yehoshua. Truthfully, I also remember very little of this Kinsker. But you can't write about Gostynin of those times and not mention him, since it was well known to all that Reb Yoav Yehoshua was one of the greatest scholars with a genius mind. The best students in Poland would come to learn with him. In Gostynin, he was very beloved, particularly by the student of Torah.

But Kinsk could never come to terms with the fact that their community should be without Reb Yoav Yehoshua, so they would often request that he come to them from Gostynin. From the other side, factions began to form and finally the Rav agreed to the requests of the Kinsk community and left Gostynin to return to Kinsk. As I later heard, an argument broke out in Gostynin regarding the fact that this Kinsker had left town.

After the Kinsker left, the seat of the Gostynin Rav was taken over by the Rotsheinzer Rav, Reb Chaim Meshulem Kaufman Hakohen Aterman.

This Rav, Reb Chaim Meshulem Kaufman, I do remember well. This new Rav was a person of magnificent beauty. His appearance and his intelligence were of European style. Other than that he was a great scholar and author of several religious books, he was also very knowledgeable in worldly matters, as were many Polish rabbis of that time. He knew the Russian language that governed at that time, so that he was able to converse easily with the authorities. This was something new at the time in Gostynin, and if something important happened in the community that required an intervention or just something that had to be addressed with a government organization, one would see the elegantly dressed Rav with his beadle at his side going through the marketplace to the then Kommandant, Prince Obolenski.

[Page 50]

The community felt very proud of the fact that the Rav did not have to depend on interceders with the authorities regarding community issues. In fact, the community did become more prestigious in the eyes of the non–Jew population, just as good in the eyes of the government.

Reb Chaim Meshulem Kaufman left Gostynin where he was Rav for thirteen years, to take over the position of Rav in Pultusk. In the year 1924, he went to Warsaw for treatments, but he died that same year.

Since we are remembering the rabbis of Gostynin, we should also mention Reb Shmuel Volf Pinczewski, the *dayan* [judge in Jewish religious court], who answered questions of religious life as well as the Rav, and who was always studying the Torah and its commentaries. I remember him best for his recitation of *selichos* [special prayers before the High Holidays] for the people in the *Beis Medrash* [study hall]. He was also the one who led the morning prayers on Rosh Hashana and Yom Kippur, since evidently, the task of the one who led these High Holiday prayers was an important one. You can see this since the congregation wanted the person who led these prayers to be someone who prayed with significance, and should be worthy to represent the congregation, because after the death of the *Dayan* Reb Shmuel Volf, it was my grandfather, Reb Yisroel Itche who took over this role. My grandfather was really one of the pillars of the Gostynin community, a person whose word was strongly heeded, to whom one turned when there was a disagreement, and one whose arbitration was very reliable. So, he was a most appropriate leader of prayers.

If we are speaking of the people who held religious positions in Gostynin, we undoubtedly have to pause at the cantor/ritual slaughterer of that time, Reb Yakov Miller, of blessed memory, who came to Gostynin from Skidzyel [Skidel], of the Grodno province. This man was beloved in the whole town, without exception. And not for nothing. He was very serious about both his cantorship as well as his ritual slaughtering. This slaughtering was for him an act of holiness, a type of work in which one had to be very strict, and to be a leader of prayers representing the congregation he held as a great responsibility. The prayer *"Hineni He'oni Mimaas..."* ["I come before Thee" recited by the leader of the prayers during the High Holidays], was as if specially written for him.

[Page 51]

The Gostynin Cantor Reb Yakov Miller with his choir. First row from right to left: Eliyahu Meyer Tabachnik, Yechiel Meyer Keller, Marcus Nemach (from Wyszogrod), Yisochor Motil, Yakov Motil
Second row from right to left: Shmuel Keller, Chaim Yehoshua Tabachnik, Cantor Yakov Miller, Chono Zajacz, Pula Danziger

[Page 52]

While the cantor was singing his prayer, the essence of it was clearly expressed because he understood the meaning of the words and knew how to translate them. He was knowledgeable in Hebrew and in Hebrew literature, so the text was not foreign to him. Along with all that, he was a gifted musician.

Music for him was much more than a means of livelihood. Music for him was a holy art and his thirst for this art way surpassed the boundaries of the prayers.

To show how great and how far his achievements in this art went, it will be enough to cite the following fact:

At that time, there was in Gostynin a bandleader from the military band, the very gifted Jewish musician, Gersowycz. When the band leader came into the synagogue and heard the cantor's prayers, he was very moved and quickly became friendly with the cantor. Slowly their friendship strengthened and as a result Reb Yakov Miller, a few times a week, very secretly went to see the bandleader where he studied music and harmony. One has to keep in mind that in those times an act of this sort would be considered by the congregation as a terrible sin, and there were always a thousand eyes directed at the cantor/ritual slaughterer. But this cantor's thirst to learn music systematically was so strong that he risked his livelihood and reputation completely and totally, just so that he could study music.

Naturally, this was a great secret and only the very select, close few knew this secret. But now, this secret of that time can be revealed. Before the holidays one could already hear on Buch Street the cantor's rehearsals with his choirboys until late in the night. His choirboys were not trained singers, and to knock music into these boys' heads – music that was unknown to them, without the help of notes, that none of them understood anyway, was not an easy task. I know that countless times for the cantor, his gall was eaten up [he was very upset] when after practicing for many days the group of choirboys remained coarse, so much so that the cantor angrily told them to shut their holiday prayer books and go to sleep. But because he couldn't proceed without the choirboys, he quickly made amends, reopened the prayer books, and began singing again. The practicing went on for weeks and many times months. But the cantor never tired. His one worry was that while they would be at the podium not one of the singers should lose his memory.

[Page 53]

When it was a few days before the holidays, new problems began. The choirboys came with new problems. One couldn't go to the synagogue because he needed a new pair of boots. Another one needed a proper hat. The third had only a torn pair of pants. What could the cantor do but buy the necessary clothing for the singers. The cantor had to put up with these and all kinds of other problems from the choirboys. But, even so, when the singing at the podium was seamless, the cantor forgave them completely and after the holidays he celebrated a real feast with them.

In the cantor's house there was a warm, pleasant atmosphere. It was a meeting place for the intellectual young generation. They would have social gatherings there along with the cantor's children.

In Warsaw, at that time, there was a *"romanzeitung"* [journal of song] published in which a song with its notes were printed weekly. And as quickly as that journal came from Warsaw, that's how quickly we, the youth, would take this to the cantor and he would teach us the song.

In general, Yakov Miller was very popular and beloved in the city. He had a friendly word for everyone. He had a natural warmth about him that brought people close and attracted people to him. He was one of the major hosts in the city, and even though he didn't have a great income from both his jobs, he nonetheless was very charitable and did it all very discreetly.

[Page 54]

After World War One, when the cantor prepared to leave Gostynin and go to his children to America, there was a general sadness in the city and on the day of his departure the entire city went out onto the Kutno road to accompany him and wish him a heartfelt safe trip.

(It's worth mentioning that in the city of Detroit in America, where Reb Yakov Miller settled, he established ritual slaughter [*shechita*] and cantorialship, and very quickly became famous and beloved.)

Other than this cantor/ritual slaughterer, there were two other ritual slaughterers. One was Leybish the *shochet*, or as they called him Leybush Bobyoker, and that was because he came to Gostynin from Bobyok. Other than being the *shochet*, he was the regular person to lead the prayers [*baal tefilah*] in the study hall [*beis medrash*]. During the High Holidays, his two sons and a son–in–law would help him, as they said in Gostynin. That's when he did the real job of a cantor. The congregants of the *beis medrash* had great pleasure from his prayers because he really was a talented reciter.

The third *shochet*, Binyomin Levi, was a product of Gostynin. Doing the ritual slaughter was appropriate for Binyomin Levi because he came from a very prominent family with generations of rabbis and scholars.

So Gostynin was really equipped with three ritual slaughterers. But whether these three were secure with their livelihoods was always doubtful to me...

It will be appropriate to remember a few of the town's Torah teachers, whose student I was. Because my father Yakov Mendel, may he rest in peace, who in a large fashion had a huge portion of my grandfather in him, that is a piece of Yisroel Itche, with his intelligent view of life, with his logical mind, and whose steps he followed, and for whom he had a great love, hoped that maybe I would also take after my grandfather, he therefore directed me to study. But it ended that I remained only at the foot of the mountain at whose top was my grandfather, Reb Yisroel Itche, may he rest in peace. Nonetheless, I spent some time studying in the *beis medrash*. And in the manner that it was, I studied with some outstanding teachers. I would like to mention them here:

[Page 55]

Dovid Lipsycz: He was a grandson of the Gostynin Rebbe, Reb Yechiel Meyer, of blessed memory, and the son of Reb Leybish Lipsycz. A gentle young man, a prodigy, with a smart head, who learned with desire and enthusiasm.

Nochum Yisroel Shajar: A son–in–law of Mordechai Mendel and Tauba Chaja Danziger. Truly razor sharp, from whose mouth the words fell like pearls, with a harmonious, calm tone.

Avrohom Geizler: A young man, studious, a diligent student, who never tired of learning.

And Chaim Tremski: A young man with a very sharp mind. To study with him was no small feat, because you had to understand him between the lines. I was a student of Chaimel Tremski and at the same time I was a friend of his. Chaim had a sharp head with a mystical undertone, and I understood him well. That's why we were teacher and student and also good friends. That's also why he gave me more time than did the others with whom I studied. In the later years, Chaim Tremski moved over to the neighboring Wloclowek where he was involved in the social life of the city and was one of the directors of the Wloclowker "*Mizrachi*" [religious Zionist movements].

Among these, we should also mention Yitzchok Shtern, who was Yeshayohu Fajnzilber's son–in–law. He was given meals [kest] and was like a scholar who had rabbinic ordination. He had a group of young men around him, with whom he learned.

***

After the Russo–Japanese War, when Russia suffered terrible defeats in the killing fields of the distant East, and in the country they began to feel the bitter chaos of the Russian bear's defeat, and the underground free powers were feeling that it was the right time to release a spark of hope for the revolution that soon burned like a quiet fire, burning and extending to all corners of the country, our Gostynin also could not be saved from this.

[Page 56]

One afternoon there appeared in town a short but wide–boned person with an oversized set of shoulders so that from behind his head hardly showed. With steps and intuition of a hunter he slid through the streets of Gostynin until he made contact with someone from our group, and then brought the others from our circle around him. These others were: Tuvia Jakubowycz, Efraim Motil, Chaim Sender Domb, Zelig Motil (Machles) who is now in Chicago, Yakov Leyb Rosental, and also the author of these lines.

Our first get–together with this unknown person came about in the house of Tuvia Jakubowycz. It's worth spending some time mentioning Tuvia's personality, because Tuvia was an interesting individual. At that time, he already was an independent businessman, with a wife and with his own house. And his livelihood he made from his razor shop [for shaving] that he set up in the house of the black Frieda on Plock Street.

His razor shop was more modern than the others in the city because Tuvia alone was a lot more progressive than a great number of other Gostyniner at that time.

Tuvia Jakubowycz was a little older than the other friends in our group but he was a really interesting and liberal thinking person. Because of that he felt closer to our younger group to which he was really more suited and with which he felt a greater understanding. Even though in that time in Gostynin one could not have a broad worldly education, Tuvia educated himself and read a lot of Hebrew, Yiddish, Polish, and Russian. Other than the Yiddish Peterburg newspaper *"Der Fraind"* [the friend], that was written in partnership with the author of these lines along with Efraim Motil, he also read *"Hatzefira"* [the dawn], in partnership with Yona Boruch Katz, Fishel Tzivia, and the cantor Reb Yakov Miller. They also found by him the Russian newspapers "*Sin Otechestvo*" [son of the fatherland], one of the most radical newspapers of those times. So it's no surprise that we, the younger group, stuck to him. Because of that, Tuvia's house was the most regular and appropriate place for the work of the radicals' upswing. It was natural that the first meeting to be held would be at his place. And so, we did get together at Tuvia's razor shop with the window blinds pulled down so that outside they would not be able to see the not–so–kosher gathering.

[Page 57]

Truthfully, this turned out to be a lecture because we all sat quietly with open ears and listened very carefully to this stranger with the very wide shoulders that looked even wider when he was sitting down. He had such a glib tongue that his words and fine Lithuanian expression came out of his mouth all turned about. He spoke with enthusiasm, so much so that he also relished his own words, as if he had eaten a delicious food.

As we found out later, this man was the Bundist [socialist party] organizer, known by the name of "Avrohom the Hunchback," a member of the Polish district committee.

We listened and swallowed every word. He unravelled for us the Bundist *Torah* [all the philosophies and information], that until that point was absolutely unknown to us, and he tried very hard to infuse into us the fundamentals of the Bundist platform, namely "national cultural autonomy."

It was a long evening, and he, the lecturer, used every minute. And when he was done, the whole concept was not yet clear to us. Nonetheless, just as the Jews at Mount Sinai said "we will do and we will hear," [just before Moses gave the Jews the Ten Commandments], we said the same and *mazel tov*.

[Page 58]

The foundation stone was put down – the foundation for the building to be known by the name of "The Jewish Bund of Poland."

With the establishment of the Bundist committee in Gostynin, it then became evident, that the city was now on the map of Poland, because suddenly delegates from all the parties arrived into the city. First, there came a dandy from Warsaw, with a black mustache, and he looked either Polish or French, maybe even Italian. And even though we didn't know which doctrine he wanted to preach, from his appearance alone we could be educated about the PPS [Polish Socialist Party].

He was not the only guest in the city. There were also delegates from the *Poalei Zionists* [Labor Zionist party], Socialist Territorialists, and even Socialist Revolutionaries, the SRs. Each of them was looking for members to join their party. But the truth was that Gostynin was too small and the Jewish population – particularly the youth – too meagre to digest such a multi–party movement. The end result was that the Bund held 90% of the Gostynin youth of that time. That was because "Avrohom the Hunchback" was the first to preach the Bundist doctrines to a few of the people who had a great influence on the Gostynin youth of that time and who adopted his knowledge.

Soon began the chapter of secret meetings where illegal brochures were distributed with proclamations on white paper with blood–red print, literature that had to be smuggled in under the noses of the police. Suddenly, it became interesting and alive in the town.

The town now had a different face. Suddenly one was able to see with his own eyes that the upper class and even *Chassidic* young men were suddenly friendly with the city's workers, with the tailors, shoemakers, second–hand dealers, and so on. This slightly unsettled the upper class of the city. The mixed marriage of the more privileged with the simple young tailors and shoemakers was for them a bitter medicine that they couldn't swallow so easily. And, as usual, in the homes of those whose names were blackened, there were often fights between the fathers and their sons. The sons really often felt the anger of their prominent but upset fathers.

[Page 59]

The anger of the privileged and the prominent people became more intense when suddenly young men and young women appeared together in the streets, an appearance that until then had hardly ever happened in Gostynin. And these were girls not, God forbid, from the upper class, but from the poor class, and then there were even servant girls. This strongly angered the respected people. But they could do nothing against this. All kinds of reports and rumors came from the larger cities such as Warsaw, Lodz, Lublin, and even from our neighboring cities such as Plock and Gombyn, that this is a type of crowd that wanted to topple governments, so what can ordinary Jews do? So they suffered and were silent.

But there were fanatics who wanted forcefully to hold on to the old–time traditions and in no way would they allow their children to mix with the general rabble. I remember the extremely frequent problems and challenges that my dearest friend Yakov Leyb Rosental had unfortunately to experience because of his father Binyomin Mendel. Binyomin Mendel was a pious Jews, who spread his governance across his entire household as the work of a dictator. He could in no way tolerate that his son Yakov Leyb had left the straight path to become a convert and go around with the "unity" groups along with the young women. Whoever heard of such a thing? … If other young men wish to convert, let them mess up their own heads, but not Binyomin Mendel's son.

I do remember one Shabbos evening, when the group had gone for a pleasure stroll in the gardens near the Russian church, young men and young girls, when out of the clear blue, just as a whirlwind, Binyomin Mendel Rosental came running, looking for Yakov Mendel among the strollers, and then in front of everyone, as they are witness, he gave him a few strong smacks and dragged him out of the garden.

[Page 60]

The group would have liked to give Mendel a lecture on how to slap, but since they wanted to avoid scandals, they remained quiet. But the slap was of absolutely no help to Mendel [like cupping on a dead person] because Yakov Leyb not only continued with his work in Gostynin but later became one of the most important activists of the Bund. His activities were in Wloclavek, a much larger city than Gostynin.

In Wloclawek he was a permanent member of the Bundist committee. From 1921–1929 he was a delegate at the Bundist gatherings. He was also a councilman, a community overseer of Wloclawek, and was very active in the CJSZO (The Central Organization of Yiddish Schools or the *Tzisha*) school affairs.

During the Second World War, when the Nazis established a ghetto in Wloclawek for Jews, Yakov Leyb played an important role. When the community council had to send someone to Warsaw to meet with Joint members to discuss help for the Wloclawek Jews, and if no one of the community representatives was willing to go, Yakov Leyb voluntarily offered to go and went twice to meet with the Joint organization. At the same time, he joined the central committee of the Bund in Warsaw, and brought a lot of information to the Jews in the Wloclawek ghetto.

Yosef Keller and Yakov–Leyb Rosental

[Page 61]

In the Wloclawek ghetto, a kitchen was set up in the cemetery in the room where they would prepare the bodies for burial. From this kitchen hundreds of meals a day were prepared. Yakov Leyb Rosental was the secretary of the kitchen management.

With the last transport of Jews from Wloclawek that were driven out by the Germans and taken to Chelmno, were Yakov Leyb and his son Somke, may their blood be avenged.

For a very short time, it seemed that the echo of the resounding slap of that Shabbos evening in the gardens quietened things down. But that was not so because the "Cossack treatment" – as it was called – of Binyomin Mendel evoked a rage from the committee and there was no doubt that such an ugly deed should not be silenced so that it never would repeat itself. So, in fact, a strict warning was given in the city to the community and to individuals that such intolerable incidents as the garden incident, whose intention was to disrupt the movement, would be punished without mercy in Warsaw's manner. The people knew what the "Warsaw manner" meant: After a punishment like that, you would hesitate to ever slap again...

That was the first time that the Gostyniners heard such clear and sharp words from their own children. And this had the desired effect because after that there was no slapping in the gardens and in no other places either.

Other than with these exceptional incidents, such as Binyomin Mendel's attack on his son, the population as a whole was not opposed to the new movement in the town.

[Page 62]

There were some who were unhappy because the old line of the aristocracy was becoming less noted. But this was a quiet, discreet dissatisfaction because for the time being, this did not cause anyone any material damage ... Gostynin was not an industrial center, the issue of work or capital problems in the broader sense did not exist.

***

There were urban artisans whose products were used by the city and partially by the population in the surrounding areas.

The only trade the Gostynin managed with other cities was the stocking production, and even this on a small scale such that the class struggle, in the true sense of the word, was not applicable.

The terms such as "class struggle" and "exploitation" and "centralization of the capital" were only phrases that one heard on the Bundist exchange that stretched from Plock Street to the Biezewyczer highway.

What did disturb the population was the fear of what could happen to the city if the government would find out what was going on. It was known that "unions" were forbidden; the Jewish children of Gostynin did not want the Kaiser. So the Jews were frightened, went around in fear, but they couldn't help the situation because there was no one to talk to within the "union" crowd.

These fearsome thoughts tormented them and they always thought that their children would be soon arrested and sent to Siberia and the city would be destroyed.

But among these were some who were happy that there was excitement in the city. One of these, it is important to mention him, was Isser Meyer Motil (the father of Regina Margolis, now in Tel Aviv, the secretary of the "*Irgun Yotzei Gostynin be'Yisrael*" (Organization for the Emigris from Gostynin in Israel).

[Page 63]

By nature, Isser was a person who hated to be stifled. That's why – if you can call him that – he was a traitor to the government. He intentionally wanted to do what the government forbade, such as, saccharin was a prohibited item, so Isser Meyer sold it. He also secretly sold bullets for small weapons. It was strongly prohibited to cross the border into another country without a passport but he had his ways that he helped people smuggle across the border. He was the type of person that the tight reins of small town life did not leave him satisfied. He just wanted to spread out his hands to do things that he didn't even know what, and that's why he always did things that others would not even have thought about. He was blessed with natural good humor, such that he could tap any innocent victim on the shoulder and sell him the moon and the stars for payoffs....

Our group was very friendly with him. I remember that after I left Gostynin and had been in New York for a bit of time, a letter arrived from Gostynin with the sad news that Isser Meyer Motil had died. This terrible news really upset me because Isser Meyer was a young, healthy man, and a real friend. But a short while after that another letter arrived from Gostynin in which my friends wrote that the news of Isser Meyer's death was incorrect; he was alive and well. So, what happened? He wanted to hear, while he was still alive, what his friends in America would say about him after this death ....

These were the types of ideas that Isser Meyer Motil had.

It was therefore natural that when the movement began in the city, Isser Meyer would be one of the sympathizers, because it really did bring new life into the city.

And even – as I already mentioned – though in the small towns the movements didn't really create such an upheaval .... they still had a tremendous morale and spiritual influence on the youth in general and on the artisans in particular. First, they began to better understand and appreciate their own worth. The businessmen themselves also began to look at their own workers with different eyes. They knew that behind the workers was the group of "unionists" so you couldn't bother them too much. So, the workers began to be treated better and even received better pay. No one worked late into the night any longer.

[Page 64]

***

There were no large factories in the city at all, only small workshops where there were only two or three apprentices. The only trade that employed more workers in a factory was in the stocking production. By Avrohom Moshe

Holander – who was the largest stocking producer in the city — there were twelve or more workers. There were other stocking producers who employed five or six workers, or even less.

Stocking production was – and I don't know why – considered a more prestigious trade than tailoring or shoemaking, so the workers that were employed in the stocking factory were from a better line of people.

To have an idea about the size of a stocking factory that employed fifteen people, it would be enough to see that the entire factory consisted of one room in a house in which the owner, Avrohom Moshe Holander lived. In summertime, the windows of the factory would be thrown open so that if you just got closer to the intersection of Kovaler and Tandajter streets, you could already hear through these windows all kinds of songs that the stocking makers would be singing while they worked.

As was mentioned, there were no great changes in the city. From time to time, they would smuggle in Bundist brochures. There were all kinds of discussions printed in these brochures, theoretical arguments, and party news and reports from many cities. In an indirect way, these reports stimulated active work.

[Page 65]

The passiveness was sickening, and the committee saw to it that the constant parading at the exchange and rehashing of phrases such as "national cultural autonomy," "exploitation," etc., was becoming monotonous, and they wanted to make it that Gostynin would also be part of the newspaper's party reports.

It did not take long, and the committee adopted a resolution that to infuse some life into the movement and create an upheaval in the city in general, they would have to put out in the name of the workers a demand for higher wages.

And since the greatest number of workers was in the stocking trade, they became the first in the struggle for improved working conditions in Gostynin.

Behind the stables, meetings were held with the stocking producers and as soon as they heard that they would be getting higher wages, they were overjoyed. And when they found out that there was a possibility they would have to quit work and strike if the bosses would not agree to the conditions, they became very enthusiastic. The decision to get better conditions for the stocking makers was approved and the meeting ended on a very optimistic note.

A few days later, the stocking factory owners were informed that the stocking workers under the direction of the Bund had decided to demand higher wages for their work, and if the bosses would not agree to meet their demands, then the workers would stop their work and declare a strike. The bosses ignored the demands and then all the stocking workers quit work and walked out on strike.

[Page 66]

My father, Yakov Mendel Keller, was also a stocking manufacturer, and so naturally his workers didn't come to work either. But when Avrohom Moshe Holander heard that the workers quit because of demands for higher wages he immediately sent out a messenger to find out whether Yakov Mendel's workers had also quit. He wanted to know if the workers in Yakov Mendel's factory quit, ignoring the fact that Yakov Mendel's son was an activist in the "union" groups. When he heard the report, that work was stopped even at Yakov Mendel's factory, he then understood that this was serious business.

Avrohom Moshe Holander was a frequent visitor in the large industrial city of Lodz, and from there he knew that if the Bund put out demands, then it would not be easy to get out of that. Also, he knew that if he would provoke the Gostynin Bund, then maybe he would not be welcomed into the Lodz city gates. So, because of that, he did not delay and immediately agreed to meet the demands of his workers.

With lightning speed, this news spread across the city and the result was that all other smaller factory manufacturers also immediately recalled their workers, agreeing to higher wages. So very soon, the stocking machinery in town once again began to run.

The general workers in the city, and particularly the stocking workers, were stunned by this unexpectedly quick victory. Truthfully, the biggest victory belonged to the movement. This was a great victory to their morale because first of all, the people began to view the party as a strong entity, with which they would have to contend. And the report of the stocking workers' victory, that was described in the Bundist paper "The Worker" of that time, along with the praise of the Gostynin movement, was a great honor for the workers, because that meant that the central organization of the Bund acknowledged the Gostynin movement.

[Page 67]

***

A comical incident that took place at that time is probably interesting to relate here. And this happened because a few comrades ["friends" of the Bundist movement] attended a Gombyner party meeting. This was at the beginning of the summer, when the comrades from our neighboring town of Gombyn, with whom we had regular contact, sent a special invitation to our executive to come to Gombyn to an important party meeting.

Gombyn was one of the exceptional cities in Poland, with extensive party activities that took place there. Even though Gombyn was a smaller city than Gostynin, there were many active party members there with a clear and broad awareness of class and intelligence, and their meetings were very interesting and educational.

But not all members of our executive were able to go over to Gombyn, and Yakov Leyb Rosental and the writer of these lines did not want to let such an opportunity pass, so they went to the meeting.

The Gombyner city synagogue was crowded when the meeting opened at nine o'clock in the evening. Several talented speakers spoke and the meeting went on until the middle of the night.

When the crowd began to disperse, we were then able to talk to some of the Gombyner comrades: Yitzchok Luria, Elya Leizer Tiber, Mailech Tudeles and friend Mindel and Yerachmiel Sofer's son, as they called him at that time in Gombyn. In discussion like that, we went out onto the Gostynin main road, and none of us were thinking about time. Only Mailech Tudeles and Mindel, who were almost always together, returned to the city.

[Page 68]

The evening was mild, the sky deep blue, starry, and the moon with its brightness lit up the wide road, and with the dense trees on either side of the road, the route seemed like a walkway in a rich fruity orchard. All five of us strode in the breadth of the road. Yitzchok Luria, the Bundist theoreticist and gifted speaker, kept us captive with his ongoing speaking. He spoke like that for minutes and hours, and we always walked ahead.

When a little light appeared in the east showing the approach of morning, we looked around and saw that we were already at the Plock forest. Not far from the Plock forest, on the way to Gostynin, was Epshtajn's sawmill. All around were chopped down trees, from which all kinds of boards were made in the sawmill, and we stopped there to examine the sawing machinery.

Near the sawmill, also on the Plock highway, Mordechai Mendel Dancziker and his wife Tauba Chaya had a food store (grocery), and on that very night thieves robbed the store. This awoke Tauba Chaya and she called the police who quickly went out onto the Plock highway to search for the thieves. When the police saw five youths walking around the sawmill area, they were sure that these were the thieves from Mordechai Mendel's store, so they immediately approached them and began to interrogate them. As much as we tried to convince them that we had no connection to the robbery, they were not satisfied. They wanted to know where we had come from so early, at dawn. Although we told them that we had come from a Bundist meeting, and argued with them for some time, it did not help. They arrested us for robbery.

The shops in town were already open when the police marched us with great fanfare though the Plocker Street to the magistrate.

It was not long afterwards that my father found out about this. The people of Gostynin thought that we had been arrested for some political crime. But when my father found out from the magistrate that we had been arrested for robbery, he burst into laughter and they immediately released us into his charge.

[Page 69]

***

It is worthwhile to tell about the establishment of the first public library of Gostynin, the foundation of the Gostynin Jewish cultural life.

The first fruits of the library, still hidden under the surface of the open Jewish socialist life, belong to the last days of October of the fifth year of the current century. Then, in the midst of the fiery freedom movements, in many cities pogroms began to broil, heated up by Russian and Polish hooligans. The Jewish workers, with the help of the revolutionary parties, organized independent security battalions. News about the wave of pogroms threw a fear onto the Jewish population of the cities where there was no protection. Even though we did not expect a pogrom in Gostynin, simply because the Jewish and Christian residents lived together in amicable conditions, nonetheless, we saw this as a golden opportunity to raise monies successfully from the Jewish residents, considering that no one would decline giving monies to such a necessary cause.

We called a special meeting where we elected several committees with the goal to raise funds and not leave out a single home. The committee, of which I was a member, took over Kutner Street, where the city's wealthy man, Aron Bresler, lived. It was an open secret to the entire city that Aron Bresler did not give money to just anyone. But if he thought that there could be a threat to his life, he gave out of fear. I remember that he not only gave a few rubles, but he also gave me his gun for which he had a government permit. Naturally, we left the revolver with him, but took the few rubles.

[Page 70]

As was expected, everyone contributed and a hefty sum was amassed. Meanwhile, news arrived that our security summoned a strong resistance as soon as any unrest would begin, and because of their heroic resistance in all the cities, the flood of pogroms was halted. Now, since the question of self–protection was suddenly taken care of, the finance department and the committee held a conference to decide what to do with the monies collected. That the conference about the money would evoke a hot debate, we all knew as soon as we got together, because we were familiar with the difference of opinions that ruled among those involved. As soon as the debate began, Zelig (Machles) Motil opened with this statement that they should buy guns with the money ... He, Zelig, was convinced overall that the organization needed guns. But the majority, that was opposed to violence, naturally did not agree with him because in Gostynin guns were absolutely not necessary. Elye Jeshan, a party fanatic, without reservation, said that the money should be sent to the district committee of the Bund, from which there already came intimations for the money.

The other members, who were present in majority, argued that since the money was raised from the Gostynin residents, then it should be used in the best possible way for Gostynin. Since there was a shortage and very little cultural resources in the town, it was decided that several Jewish books would be purchased for the money, and that a public library for all the Gostynin residents would be established, and particularly for the Gostynin workers.

This is the history of the public library in Gostynin.

[Page 71]

Without any further discussion, Tuvia's razor shop was to be the home of the library. Since an open library must have a special permit from municipal government, a whole chapter of petitions began, with requests made to the

Warsaw governor, all of course, with Tuvia's name because he was the legal owner of the planned library.

After many and very strained efforts, finally the much coveted permit was acknowledged, and immediately they bought about one hundred books in Warsaw, selected works that were appropriate to the class of readers in Gostynin at that time. That's how, with great fanfare, the first Jewish public library in Gostynin opened in the home of Tuvia Jakubowycz's razor shop.

I was the librarian for some time and on the library's committee until I left Gostynin.

***

The day of my departure from Gostynin came out in the month of May, and even though outside there was actually the fragrance of spring and rebirth, the atmosphere in our home was one of gloomy, cold autumn. My bags were packed, and all of us, the entire household, waited for blond Aron the wagon driver, who took passengers to the Kutno train station.

It's worthwhile to describe the tone of a Jewish house when a member of the household would leave to go across the ocean. One didn't leave for reasons of pride and joy. Immigration was a result of the economic bleakness of the small, and in the long run, old fashioned Jewish towns of Poland. The youth tore themselves away going to unfamiliar faraway places from which there was a glimmer of an existence and success. But really, the fact of leaving home threw serious despair on the children of the house, a real sadness. "Who knows," those who remained thought, "if we willever again see our son or daughter, brother or sister, with our own eyes?"

[Page 72]

I will therefore describe how it looked in our house at the time that I was leaving Gostynin. The picture is representative of hundreds of other houses...

My father, may he rest in peace, a man of strong character, who didn't lose himself even under the worst conditions, was sitting at the table writing something. The silence in the house was so heavy that you could hear the scratches of the pen.

My dear mother, may she rest in peace, who often suffered with headaches, was sitting at the window with her head all bound up, and she followed me everywhere with her cloudy eyes, her trembling lips always whimpering.

Her heartache was tremendous, that I, her Yosef, was leaving to America, a place from which one rarely returned. For my parents, America was a synonym for a far–flung country, and each of them was thinking to themselves, even though they didn't express it, that even the Jewishness there was not in order…

My countless reassurances that I would return did not help. "No, no," my mother said. "No one comes back." My sister Charna, who was always ready to help everyone, and who was a friend and sister to me, sat quietly in a corner of the house, with red, overflowing eyes.

My brother Moshe, an ambitious young man, who was apprenticing to be a merchant and often made business trips – for my father – in the nearby cities, with a youthful tone, commented: "And what is America? You'll see, it won't be too long and I will come to visit you."

For my sister Chava, who by nature was not so cheerful, that morning played right into her mood. With a cloud over her face, she stood next to our mother near the window, and with dismal eyes she looked out onto the street.

[Page 73]

My sister Pesse, who was then working in Warsaw, was not at home. I had made a special trip to Warsaw a week earlier to say my goodbyes to her.

My brother Shmuel, the only one of the family who had left Gostynin to go to America just after the First World War, the only comfort of our family's tragedy on Poland, was already then a compassionate young man, and because I had absolutely promised to come over to America, and he believed me, he stood with very troubled, mixed feelings.

[Page 74]

Yechiel Meyer, Sholom, and Aron, my three youngest brothers, were too young to understand the whole to do. They didn't even begin to understand why going to America was such a terrible tragedy that should cause such a disaster in the home. They went around looking lost and confused about the whole thing.

I had said my goodbyes to my uncles and aunts the night before, and among those were also my father's sister, my aunt Bluma Miriam, and my uncle Hershel. All of us children were very close to Aunt Bluma Miriam because of her warm friendliness. I remember that in my eyes she was the embodiment of compassion, beauty, and love. I never missed even one Shabbos of going to see her, and she always brought the honor of Shabbos to me.

She, Bluma Miriam, as it turned out, did not have enough during our farewells the night before, because as we were in the house the door opened, on the doorstep with her usual Aunt Bluma Miriam smile, there she was. Her arrival brought a little bit of change to the depressed atmosphere. My father immediately put away his writing and a lighter conversation took place with a certain tension in the atmosphere.

Businessmen in Gostynin help promote a theater presentation by raising money for the free kitchen

Seated from right to left: Shimon Yosef Motyl, Mendel Krel, Note Motyl, Yakov Mendel Keller, Yakov Zarchin.

Standing from right to left: Yakov Motyl, Yitzchok Bresler, Efraim Motyl, Moshe Keller, Krigerman, Hershel Motyl, Iser Meyer Motyl, Adam Domb.

But it didn't take long, and the blond Aron arrived with his wagon, thrust open the door, grabbed my packed bags and threw them over his shoulder and said to me in his screechy voice: "Hey, don't delay, it's getting late."

That was the signal that it was time to say goodbye. Such an experience of hysteria and crying I never again had in my entire life. It was more appropriate for a terrible tragedy, Heaven forbid. And at the door, even my father's fixed smile disappeared and there were tears in his eyes that rolled down his pale face.

[Page 75]

My Aunt Bluma Miriam stopped me in the doorway and placed a gold ring – that she had taken off from one of her fingers – onto one of my fingers, and then once again said her goodbyes to me.

I left the house a broken person. There were many people standing outside, who were there to toss a final glance onto a young man who was leaving for America, a land from which one never returned.

I never forgot that day. I also never forgot that promise to my mother – that I would one day return.

But I never returned home. The Hitler murderers destroyed Jewish Gostynin – and my Gostynin no longer exists.

[Page 76]

Jewish Community Life and Jewish Subsistence

by Meir Dovid Tremski

Translated by Pamela Russ

Meir Dovid Tremski

A) The Gostyniner Rav, Reb Yoav Yehoshua

After the passing of the Rebbe, Reb Yechiel Meir, of blessed memory, the city began to think about someone to take over his seat. The city, of course, needed a Torah leader for the town [*morah d'asra*].

As Reb Yekel Alberstajn, the Rebbe's son–in–law, was the scholar and the wealthy man in the city, understandably, everyone listened to him. Reb Yekel Alberstajn was a Sochatczower *chassid*, who displayed the Sochatczower genius, and he occupied the esteemed rabbinic seat in Litermarsk, a small town near Lodz.

The city, with the agreement of the community, decided to bring down the great scholar Reb Yoav Yehoshua as the rabbi of Gostynin. Then again, is it ever possible for all Jews to come to an agreement? So, of course, soon there were factions. The Gerer *chassidim* invested everything to find a Rav from their own court. But no one could compare to those from Litermarsk. To that end, Reb Yisroel Itcze Keller insisted on Alberstajn. Reb Yisroel Itcze also once studied under Reb Avremel Sochatczower.

And so, the city decided to bring in the Litermarksker to Gostynin for a Shabbath and see if he was fitting to take over after the Gostynin *Tzadik* [righteous man], may he be blessed.

[Page 77]

About the issue of engaging a Rav for the city, the businessmen relied on the scholars of the city – they who could study Torah with expertise, and then simply because the Jews looked up to them. Some of these were: the above-mentioned Reb Yekel Alberstajn, Reb Yisroel Itcze Keller, Reb Moshe Aron Lewi, Reb Yeshije Fajnzilber, and others. These were respected individuals, who always found time to study Torah, and to discuss Torah subjects, and even to write innovative responsa to Torah learnings.

And so, it was the candidate Reb Yoav Yehoshua who came to our city. As was done in those years, Reb Yoav Yehoshua came to *shul* on Shabbath afternoon after resting, to deliver a learned address. The address was a combination of great scholarly mastery with intense textual analysis and deep thought. The Gostynin Jews came to *shul* to hear the words of the new Rav. The city's Talmud scholars positioned themselves in the first rows and sharpened their ears so as not to miss one word and later to be able to review [what they had heard] with words of understanding.

The Rav, Reb Yoav Yehoshua, was the opposite of the Gostyniner Rebbe, Reb Yechiel Meir, of blessed memory. And his habits, such as – the Rebbe used to finish the *shemone esrei* [special prayer recited quietly and without interruption until completed] a good bit of time after the congregation. That's what the people were used to. On Rosh Hashana and Yom Kippur, until the Rebbe completed the silent *shemone esrei*, the people meanwhile managed to recite a few chapters of Psalms. The new Rav, however, finished before the people. For the congregants, this was an astounding act: Such a prestigious Jew should complete his prayers, one and two? This, however, was the Sochatczower way, derived from the phrase "Torah precedes prayer." Speed was the characteristic trait of the new Rav, and not only in prayer. He would walk fast and talk fast. They explained that this was a result of his sharpness – of his sharp, genius mind. Gostynin was very proud of Reb Yoav Yehoshua, even though he behaved so differently from the Rebbe.

When the Rav settled in the city, and began to run the city in his new ways, all factions were appeased. Like that, both the *chasidim* and the *misnagdim* [opponents of *chasidim*] grouped themselves around the new Rav.

[Page 78]

In particular, relationships with the Rav improved when he opened a Yeshiva [religious boys' school] in Gostynin. Young boys from far and near came to partake of the Torah fount of the renowned scholar. The city comforted itself with the great loss that it suffered with the Rav's passing. They felt that now a giant of the people of Israel was living among them. No one declined to give a young student a "day"[11] of eating. The students, children of wealthier families, rented places for themselves in local inns. The city became alive with new faces, and knowledge flowed everywhere; light streamed out in the evenings from the *Beis Medrash*, and the young voices that were heard learning, filled each Gostynin Jew with a sense of pride. Very often it happened that when someone was looking for a fitting son–in–law for his daughter, he would come to the Gostynin Yeshiva. The Yeshiva became known far and wide in Poland.

The city Jews regarded the Rav with love, respect, and loyalty. They wanted that Rav Yoav Yehoshua should, to some extent, take the place of the Rebbe, of blessed memory. For example, when someone's family member became sick, he would run to the Rebbe for a blessing [for a speedy recovery]. Gostynin Jews were accustomed to go to Rav Yechiel Meir in such situations, but the Rav pushed everyone aside. With this conduct Reb Yoav Yehoshua resembled Reb Yehoshuale Kutner, such that when anyone would come to him for *Yizkor* [reciting the prayer for the deceased], he would send them off to Reb Yechiel Meir ... for these scholars, the study of Torah far surpassed everything else.

Sadly, Gostynin did not celebrate with this great Rav for very long. Kinsk (Konskie) was jealous of Gostynin and snatched away the great scholar for itself. The Kinsker community was larger than Gostynin and was too strong for Gostynin to win.

The city once again began to worry about finding a new Rav. The Gostynin Yeshiva no longer existed.

Translator's footnote

11. *"Essen teg"* [eating days] is an expression referring to a system where the young students would eat their meals at different homes each day. It was an honor for a family, even the poorest, to host a Torah student.

[Page 79]

B) The Gostynin Controversy of 1894

That year, one shochet [ritual slaughterer] left Gostynin. So, the community businessmen thought that they should acquire a *chazzan* [cantor]– *shochet* that would not cost the city any extra money, and at the same time the *shul* would have its yearly *baal tefila* [leader of prayers].

When the men proposed this idea at a meeting, there was a great outcry, as if they were going to undertake to greatly reform the Gostynin Jewry. Soon there were factions and parties. The *chassidim* called this an argument in the name of God, in which case everything is permitted, even to inform on someone and to spill blood [murder]. They decided not to permit, in any way, such heresy.

Truthfully, in the days of Reb Yechiel Meir, no one would have tried to propose such a suggestion, not in his days, and not even for years after his passing. So, the city stayed in its old ways. The world, however, progressed and even Gostynin Jews moved on in their ways, and the Gostynin businessmen wanted to be like everyone else, particularly when there was an opportunity to do so, and there would be no special cost for this, so then, really, why not?

The Gostyniner had plenty of time, so this controversy actually played right into their hands like a great prize. Between *mincha* and *maariv* [the afternoon and evening prayers] things boiled as if in a boiler. In one corner there was taunting and cursing, and in another corner they let their hands loose. Fortunately, the *gabbai* [beadle] summoned everyone to the *maariv* prayers and the loud opinions were calmed.

The grown boys played not such a small role in this battle. They eagerly listened to each discussion and then often carried what they had heard over to the opposing side.... And the fire burned even more viciously.

The key player in this quarrel was the main speaker Reb Itcze Stupei, a respected personality, a forest merchant, who had his own position at the eastern wall [prominent location for prayers in the *shul*, facing towards Jerusalem], and whose words were heeded by all. His second hand was Reb Moshe Linski, who in those later years went into the feather business, and he "earned a meager dose of impudence" [was very bold], and always jumped to be the first to speak. The third one of the group was Reb Mendel Volf Posner, not a wealthy man, but a Jew with a head on his shoulders. He was the brains of the group, and since his livelihood was done in the streets (he was a peddler), he saw everything and was always useful. This was the trio – the generals. And along with them, there were many prominent businessmen who helped with their strategies. In reserve, there were also others who joined them, who bore old grudges against the *chassidim*. Such as, for example, Reb Aron Brustowski, who was once the *shochet* in the town, and bore a heavy heart against his *chassidic* opponents.

[Page 80]

Also, not all of the *chassidim* opposed a *chazzan–shochet*. Among these, there were others who enjoyed the music and discreetly helped the opponents win the dispute.

From words, the opponents went over to actions. On a certain Shabbath, they brought over the *chazzan* and his fine choir from Plock. There was a double intention with that: one, to increase the *shul*-going Jews' appetite for *chazzanus* [cantorial prayers]; and two, to incite the *chassidim*.

After that, the *shul*-going Jews actually tried enthusiastically to find a good *baal tefila* [leader of prayers] for the *shul*, and meanwhile, the city went upside–down. There was fighting, and not only one person sat under city arrest, and the war went on in full force.

When the *chazzan* from Plock was in Gostynin for that Shabbath, he proposed a fine *chazzan–shochet* that would be appropriate for Gostynin. His candidate was the Inower *chazzan–shochet*, Reb Yakov Miller, whom the community men actually did invite down for a trial on Shabbath.

Reb Yakov Miller came with two choirboys. He conducted the Shabbath prayers and greatly impressed the community. They not only liked his cantorship, but his charming face and friendliness towards the people worked their own way with the people as well.

The following morning, they presented Reb Yakov Miller to the Rav of the city, to see whether Reb Miller was also knowledgeable in the laws of ritual slaughter. He passed the test, even for the position of Rav, one hundred percent. But the *chassidic* side did not give up. Quickly, they circulated a report that a stranger that was Jewish came to Gostynin and stirred up unrest among the Jewish people. The police immediately went to search for the upstart, to make sure he made no trouble. Meanwhile, the "other people" smelled what sort of thing was going on, and so to avoid disgracing God's name, they quickly moved the *chazzan* and his choirboys out of the city. The sharp *chassidim*, who would stop at nothing, were left with great anguish because of this...

[Page 81]

Meanwhile, the cooler *chassidim* looked around and saw what a quarrel like this can lead to, and they decided to discuss the matter seriously. And with everyone's consent, it was decided to employ the Inower *shochet*. Then two businessmen left with a letter in hand to bring over the chazzan–shochet. One of these two was Reb Leybish Tremski – he certainly did not know at the time that he was bringing a wife for his son – Reb Yakov's daughter, Tileh, may she rest in peace, and for him, a future daughter–in–law.

The crowd later calmed down. The *chazzan–shochet* was an honest Jew. Both the sharp and the cool *chassidim* united in their views with their opponents and the above–mentioned. The disdain between them ceased, and Gostynin went back to its daily life. Once again, it became terribly unexciting.

C) Jewish Livelihoods

The geographic location of Gostynin was not very favorable. The city did not have any train or water junctions. The train was established only in the time of Poland's independence. Everything went by horse and wagon. So, there was no great trade or industry going on.

Commerce was generally with the local city and village customers. The farmers from the surrounding villages brought in their products to sell and at the same time they bought everything in the city that they needed for their own business.

[Page 82]

The trade days were Tuesdays and also Fridays. On those days, every homemaker traded for all the products that the farmers had brought. There were fairs several times in the year. At that time there were more buyers and more merchants with all sorts of merchandise that the city merchants did not have. For these fairs, the merchants prepared themselves with more merchandise and hoped for a greater profit. Incidentally, there was also a fair day for the school boys [*cheder* boys], a day off. Like free birds, freed from the *cheder* and the teacher, they wandered around the markets.

It's important to mention the names of the wholesale merchants that brought merchandise for the smaller stores:

Shmuel Klejnbard, a childless *chassid*, who never rushed, not even to do a *mitzvah*. He delivered the flour, so that also became his added name, Reb Shmuel Meller.

A wholesaler of soap was Reb Mendel Eichel, a pious Jew, likely somewhat of a manufacturer because his added name was vinegar–maker. People would also buy from him wine for *Kiddush* [service at the beginning of Shabbath], *Havdalah* [service to end the Shabbath], and for the four cups of wine for Passover.

There were others that supplied the small stores with salt and kerosene, and other products such as tobacco, cigarettes, and sometimes a box of cigars.

Most of the stores were food stores and dry goods stores. These last ones brought their merchandise from Lodz and Warsaw.

Besides these above–mentioned stores, there were Jewish leather merchants, iron stores, lamps and glasses stores, and dye stores, beer taverns (the government handled whiskey, since it was a product that was too dear to leave in Jewish hands).

Many of the stores also traded on the side and were occupied with other businesses because just sitting around waiting for a customer was also something the wife could do. In that way, for example, Yitzchok Srebnegure traded peat, and his wife also ran a stand for dresses for the peasant women. Chaim Domb, the lamp merchant worked with lending out iron beds. Chazan, the leather merchant, was involved in the stocking business. And so on, with many other storekeepers. The average merchant had a businessman status, and while he had no work, he had to do some buy–and–trade. Incidentally, the title "merchant" was honorable, and carried some prestige.

[Page 83]

In the category of larger commerce, there was forest and lumber. Greater capital was required here, as well as skill in the vocation. There were many forests around Gostynin, that belonged to the noblemen and to the government. From time to time, sections of the forest were sold. Mostly, the buyers were from us Jews. This type of merchant went to his store on a Monday morning. He commissioned workers and took care of his earnings. About Friday afternoon, he returned home. When the business grew bigger, this type of merchant would settle in the forest, with his wife and child, until he had nothing left to do there. Other shopkeepers traded grains. They would buy it off the farmers, or directly from the noblemen, the landowneres, all sorts of grains and would sell them to merchants who would load them onto wagons and take them to Germany.

Jewish bus that would take passengers to Kutno and Plock

[Page 84]

In former years, when the farmers would raise sheep around our regions, many Jews had a livelihood from the sale of wool. In the summertime, when they would shear the sheep, the merchants would buy up the wool, give it to be worked into cloth, and then sell it in Lodz or Warsaw.

When there were soldiers in the city, some Jews would deliver products to the military. These were called "*podradczikes*" [contractors]. There was a contractor for flour, another one for meat, a third for heating, and from this they each earned a livelihood.

There were Jews that provided the city Jews with some merchandise from Warsaw: They would add a certain percent for their own labor. This type was called a "*shpiliter*" [expediter]. The expediter would take orders of all kinds and then at the end of the week would bring everything home.

There were also others who made their living from buying eggs, butter, and chickens in the city, and then selling them in the larger cities with a great profit.

There was a larger merchant who established himself in Gostynin manufacturing stockings that were exported beyond Russia, and this gave a livelihood to many young people who learned the trade. The main manufacturers in this business were Reb Mendel Keller, Avrohom Moshe Hollender, and Chaim Goldberg.

There were other Jews who actually earned their living from thin air. Of this type of Jew, there were Moshe Lubiner, Yehuda Mast, and others. This type of Jew completed his prayers at dawn, took his sack under his arm, a stick in his hand, and with faith in the Great Creator, went on his way, ready to buy anything he could get in his hands, a merchant of everything. Even these Jews considered themselves among the businessmen in town.

Others, meanwhile, made their livelihood from leasing certain functions from the city's government – such as lighting the lamps each evening, or collecting the payment from each wagon that rode through the city to come to the market or to the fair.

[Page 85]

Not all the Jews drew their livelihood from trade. There were laborers whose livelihood came from hard work. These were the Jewish bakers of bread and rolls, and the cookies and cake bakers. A separate job was baking matzos for Passover. At that time of year, there were tinsmiths, barbers, butchers, pavers, porters, millers, wagon drivers, carpenters, and tailors that were divided into two types: the jobbing tailor who had ready–made clothes, and the tailor that prepared made–to–measure clothes, such as, for example, Mordechai Warszawski, and a women's tailor like Shmerel.

An exclusively Jewish means of livelihood was orchard work. With the onset of the summer, the orchard keepers rented out orchards from the surrounding villages that were found all around our region. In about the month of May, the orchard keepers packed their wives and children onto a wagon, took some bed linen and some kitchen utensils, and left to go take care of their livelihood. So God helped, and there was an excellent crop of fruit, and so there was lots of profit. If not, God forbid, then the Jew would have worked many months for nothing, and would come back home a broken man.

The pump in the middle of the marketplace

[Page 86]

The fruits sold well in the larger cities. Around the month of Elul [August/September time], the fruit merchants would return to the city. If someone wanted to have an apple during the winter time, then he could get one from one of these merchants.

As in all Jewish communities, Gostynin also had work in religious areas. There were jobs that were purely Jewish, such as the Rav, the *chazzan, shochtim* [ritual slaughterers], *shamashim* [beadles], teachers. They didn't earn a terribly large livelihood with this. When Reb Yoav Yehoshua was the Rav of Gostynin and ran a *yeshiva* [religious school], many young boys came from other parts to learn with him. The wealthier *bochurim* [young students] boarded for money in the homes of the Gostynin Jews, and this gave livelihood to some of the innkeepers.

Gostynin was a typical town in Poland. Probably, in other towns there were also such merchants and the same means of earning a livelihood. That's how the Jews worked, traded, and always hoped for better times...

[Page 87]

The First Sprouts of Jewish Cultural Life

by Rabbi Yona Boruch *Katz Kohan Tzadek* (Israel)

Translated by Pamela Russ

HaRav [The Esteemed Rabbi] Yona Boruch Katz
[*Kohan Tzedek* : righteous Priest]

Reb Simcha Bunim Dancziger was a fiery Jew. From his handsome face, with his broad, beautifully kempt beard and short curly sidelocks, a pair of burning eyes shone. He was a Gerer *chassid*, with a refined tongue, one of the *Chovevei Tzion* [Lovers of Zion][12] that at that time did underground Zionist work. In simple words, Zionist work – work for the Land of Israel, was illegal, because of the persecutions of the Czarist government. Reb Simcha Bunim was over middle age, but filled with the *Chassidic* fire. Better said: with holy, *Chassidic* brilliance. His influence over me was tremendous. He pulled me into the illegal Zionist work, such as the work with the *Keren Kayemet* charity boxes [Jewish National Fund collection "Blue Box"], and so on. Thanks to this work, I maintained a correspondence with Reb Menachem Mendel Ussishkin in Odessa.

---

12. Refers to organizations founded in Eastern Europe in late 1800s that are considered the forerunners of modern Zionism.

Later, with the rise of political Zionism, the cultural work flourished in many cities and towns in Poland. I, a young man just in his thirties, also a Gerer *chassid*, one of the respected people in the *Beis Medrash*, was affected by Zionism and became "tainted" and began to secretly read books of the Enlightenment in the Gostynin women's section of the *shul*. Today, I still remember the books such as *Sefer Habris* ["Book of the Covenant," first printed in 1797, author Rabbi Pinchas Eliyahu of Vilna [Vilna Gaon]. A compendium of astronomy, geography, physics, chemistry, biology, etc., together with a presentation of the kabbalistic (mystical) worldview], *Ben Hamelech Vehanazir* ["The King's Son and the Nazarite," author Rabbi Abraham ben Shmuel Ibn Hasdai, published 1727, an ethical work in prose], *Ben Sira* [a second century BC Jewish scribe, sage, and allegorist from Jerusalem], and *Ahavas Tzion.* ["Lovers of Zion"], and *Ashmat Shomron* ["Guilt of Samaria," author Mapu, 1865, a biblical epic about the hostility between Jerusalem and Samaria in the time of King Ahaz.] – and all kinds of other enlightened books. And I certainly was not the only one who found his way to founts of Hebrew literature, but I was the one and only reader of *Hazfira* [published in Warsaw, mandate was to disseminate knowledge, science, and world news] in Gostynin. Later, I spread the newspaper and got subscribers, not intentionally to receive any payment.

[Page 88]

My home became a meeting house for the forward-thinking young students and youth. At my home, they got together in groups and discussed Zionist and cultural issues. We decided to set up a meeting in the home of Reb Simcha Bunim, of blessed memory. The meeting was attended both by people of the older and younger generations of Zionists. Let's list them (as much as the memory can relate): Reb Shmuel Klajnbord and his brother Dovid, Moshe Zhikhlinski, Mendel Bagno, Mordecai Morycz and his brother Moshe, my brother Dovid Katz, and Mendel Matil. Of the younger generation, there were: the blond Dovid Matil and his brother Moshe, Isser Meyer Matil and his brothers: Aron Mordechai, Efraim, Yakov. Hershel, Shimon Yosef; Chaim Noach Bagno, Yakov Zhikhlinski, Yakov Mendel Keller, Chaim Kuczinski, the blond Leibel Matil, Moshe Dancziger, Hershel Dancziger. There were those who were sympathetic to our work: the cantor Reb Yakov Miller and his son-in-law, Meir Dovid Tremski, Hershel Zilberstajn, Yitzchok Bresler, Yakov Linderman. I felt a real kinship with the people in this crowd, because I was able to show that I had already done some service and practical tasks in this field of work.

This meeting elected a committee – at the head, Reb Simcha Bunim, treasurer – Reb Shmuel Klajnbord, and I was secretary. That's how the Zionist organization was started in Gostynin.

These events evoked a strong opposition among the *Chassidim*. They began to harass us. First, they prevented us from reading the Torah in the *stiebel*, [small synagogue], and some time later they actually chased us out of the *chassidim stiebel*...

Then we decided to invite over a Zionist speaker, who would enliven the work in Gostynin. We invited the *shochet* Reb Sender Tkhursz,[13] who was renowned as a fiery speaker and famous for his sincere love for Zion and Zionism. At that time, we were having difficulty getting the *Beis Medrash* for lectures – the head of the community didn't allow this, so we simply used the *shul*.

[Page 89]

At the first meeting, the *shul* was packed with Jews. Not only were there the organized Zionists, and not only the sympathizers, but also *Chassidim* from all different courts came to hear. Their main concern was that there would be no missionary speeches held...

The speaker stayed with us for a week's time. Every day, he delivered his fiery speeches and attracted souls to Zion.

Then we decided to open a "*cheder metukan*" [the "improved" school, where classes were taught in Hebrew], and that's when the real holy war began from the *Chassidish* faction. They complained that the Zionists were going to convert, God forbid, their children. Disregarding all this, we brought down a teacher from Dobrzyn, Chaim Menachem Lederberg, as a teacher in the *cheder metukan*. As teachers later on, there were Yakov Czekanower, Yakir Warszawski,[14] and others.

The disputes in the city were ablaze. It went so far, that when Reb Simcha Bunim died, the Burial Society refused to take care of the deceased ... did not even want to provide the black death-wagon ... The Zionist activists took care

---

13. Reb Sender Tkhursz belonged to the Mizrachi and all its branches in Wlozlowek. He was a close colleague to the Wlozloweker Rav, the great Zionist HaRav Y.L. Kowalski. Reb Zender Tkhursz, at the end of the 20s, settled in Israel, and was Rav there in Kfar Chitin.

14. Yakir Warszawski later was a teacher in a line of gymnasiums in Poland, and was known as an insightful Hebrew writer.

of the "purification process" of the body, prepared a "bed" and then took the deceased over to the *shul*, where they eulogized him. From the *shul* to the cemetery – quite a distance – the pallbearers were changed.

I want to mention a typical event that happened at that time. We had decided to go with the students of *Cheder Metukan* to *shul* for the holiday of *Simchas Torah* to dance with the Torah scrolls [as is done on that holiday celebration]. There, the crowds carried the Torah scrolls with dance and song. We, the students, and the Zionist flags in hand, went up to the podium and began singing Zionist songs, and when we sang: *Hatikva*, the *dozor*, Moshe Eliyahu Domb, left with a shout. "What does this mean?" he shouted. "In a *shul* one should sing such arbitrary songs? What a disgrace to God!"

[Page 90]

Еврейскій хедеръ   בית ספר עברי
І. Б. КАЦЪ   ידעת
Гостынинъ, Варш. губ.   של י. ב. כ"ץ נאסטינין

דיא 4 יאהר פראקטיקע האבען אונז גינעבען ריא איבערצייגונג,
אז גאסטינין דארף דאבען אזא ארט שולע וואס זאלל גילערענם
ווערען אין אנרויסע מאהם **ידישע למודים**. דארונטער זאלל
אויך מיט נעהן **אלגעמיינע למודים** דארום האבע בעשלאסען
צי פערברייטערן דיא פראנראבע פון אינזער בית ספר הורה ידעת.
ידישע למודים וועם גילערנם ווערען.

גרונדליך עברי. תורה, עם פירוש רשי, נביאים, כתובים גמרא,
העברעאיש, היסטוריה, דקדוק, שרייבען, רעכענען, דיקטאנדע,
שירים, דאיונען, לייענען אין ספר הורה עפ דקדוק, א. ז. וו.

צי אלגעמיינע למודים,

האבע גישלאסען קאנטראקט מיט א רוסישען לערער ער זאלל
קיממען אין שולע לערנען לייט פראנראמע **פין 2**
קלאסען גימנאזיום. איך האבע צי גענימען א נייעם זעהר
גימען ביא הילפער צי ידישע למודים אינטער מיין אויפזיכם,
איך האבע אייך פערברייטערם דיא היגעגישע צישטאנד פון שולע.

מיר קיממען נישם ביט קיינע פוסטע הבטחות, דען אללע וויסען
אז מיר זענען ווייט, פון אזעלכע מיטעלן, אייך איז יעדען גוט
בעוויסט מיין איבערגינעבענהייט אין טרייהייט, צי מיין בית ספר,
וועלכע איז דיא בעסטע גאראנטיע פאר דיא שנעללע פארטשריט
פון מיינע תלמידים, אלזא. בעטען מיר וועהר דיא וואס וויללען אב
געבען זייערע קינדער אין מיין בית ספר, צי קיממען בעצייטענם
אין שולע פערשרייבען זיך, מיר זאללען קאנען איינארדנען דיא
למודים אין יעדע קלאס, הלטידים ווערען אנגינימען אין יעדע
קלאס פון א מעניטמאלן פרייז 1. רוב. ביז 5. רוב.

מיט אכטונג י. ב. **כץ**

A Printed Notice about *"Torah Vodaas"*
["Torah and Knowledge," name of school] School of Torah Vodaas
Y.B. Katz, Gostynin, Province of Warsaw

Translation of the above letter

The four-year experiences have shown us that Gostynin needs to have a type of school where they should learn a large amount of Jewish Studies, along with that General Studies. Therefore, we have decided to extend the program of our school of Torah Vodaas. They will study Jewish Studies.
Fundamental Hebrew, Torah with Rashi commentary, Prophets, Writings, Gemara, Hebrew, Jewish history, grammar, writing, mathematics, dictation, songs, prayers, reading the Torah and grammar, and so on.

For the General Studies, we have sealed a contract with a Russian teacher who will come to the school to teach two classes in the gymnasium. I have hired a new, excellent assistant for Jewish Studies under my supervision. I have also improved the hygiene of the building.

We are not coming with empty promises; you all know we are far from these kinds of things. Also, everyone knows about my loyalty and dedication to my school, which is the best guarantee for the rapid progression for my students. So, we ask that anyone who wants to send their children to my school should come register as soon as possible, so that we can organize the lessons for each class. Students are being accepted into each class at a minimal fee. One ruble, to 5 rubles.

> With consideration,   Y.B. Katz

[Page 91]

A great tumult broke out. But the men, who were of Zionist bent, such as Avrohom Szatan and his brother Yehuda Berish, threw the *dozor* out of the *shul*...

And it was after the death of Reb Simcha Bunim, of blessed memory, that the teacher Yakir Warszawski left Gostynin, and it was decided that I take over the *Cheder Metukan* school and in my free time, I could devote myself entirely to Zionist work. I gave the school the name *Torah Vodaas*. I had postcards printed, of the plans for the school studies. The cards were hung up in all kinds of open places. I also hung up several cards on the inside of the *shul*. But it seems that in Gostynin there were some selfish people who tore the cards down. I decided to wait until Friday late in the evening, and went secretly into the *shul*, hung up the cards, and stuck them down with nails so that they couldn't be taken down on Shabbath... And that's how they remained there over Shabbath.

I ran the school successfully. Today, my students are spread over many different countries. The majority in Israel, are soaked through with pioneering, with the love of Israel, with the love of the land and language. Thank God, I can be very proud of many of them.

When I left Gostynin to take over a *Cheder Metukan* in Kutno, I gave over
the school to my assistant Avrohom Dovid Kuczinski, who was then called the
"small teacher" [*Hamorah Hakatan*].

[Page 92]

Rabbis and *Melamdim*

by Hershel Leib Leizerowitz (Israel)
Translated by Yocheved Klausner

Hershel Leib Leizerowitz

It has been sixty years that I remember you, my town Gostynin. Your name has been shining far beyond your borders, on the merit of your *Thilim Yid* [the Psalms reader], the great *Tzadik*. You have produced a long chain of generations _ scholars, *Tzadikim*, craftsmen and simple Jews, and righteous women. Gostynin was a beautiful Jewish comunity, with a *Bet Midrash* [House of Prayer and Study], a synagogue and a *Shtibl* [a Hasidic house of prayer]. The community managed several institutioms as well: A Home for the Aged, *Linat Tzedek* [charity sleeping accommodation for the needy], a *Gemilut Chasadim* Fund [free-of-interest-loan], *Hachnasat Kala* fund [financial aid for the needy brides] etc. I remember the beautiful Shabat and holiday times. I see before my eyes the Jewish streets, the life of the neighbors, the love and devotion between one another. Everyone took part in the happy and joyful moments of the others, and felt for them in grief. Jewish Gostynin lived together like one family.

Who had shaped the Jewish Gostynin and given it its identity? As everywhere, this was the holy work of the teachers and educators. The following were the Gostynin *melamdim*: R'Sender, R'Leizer and his son Yosef, who inherited the vocation from his father, R'Grunem *melamed* and R'Avraham Fleischman. They were the young children's teachers, who instilled in them the *Mode Ani* [the beginning of the morning prayer] and the *Shema Israel*. When R'Sender the *melamed* died at the age of almost one hundred years, the entire Jewish Gostynin went to his funeral and mourned him. Every person considered himself as one of his pupils.

[Page 93]

In general, the life of the *melamdim* was a difficult life; poverty and need showed in every corner. But they saw their work as a holy mission and they guided their *heder* with love and devotion, bringing up generations of children.

There were also the teachers of *Chumash with Rashi* [the Five Books of Moses with the great commentator Rashi (Rabbi Shlomo Yitzhaki)] and Talmud, for the older children: R'Leibel Tzishik, Avraham Yitzhak Holzman, R'Yechezkel Bagno, R'Levi Melamed, an old man who was a great scholar and died at a very advanced age. All his pupils praised greatly his teaching.

The Gostynin rabbis enriched the Jewish life in town. Not only did they lead their community in the proper Jewish way, but they represented it honorably and were its faithful spokesmen in front of the authorities. They were well-known throughout the country. R'Yechiel Meir Lifshitz z"l became rabbi in Gostynin when he was still a young man. His great scholarship and vast knowledge of Torah, his modesty and his love for every individual brought him to the position of Rabbi and great Tzadik. "The Gostyniner Rabbi" became famous throughout the entire Jewish world. He died on Sabbath eve, 21 Shevat 5648. The position of rabbi was then occupied by the Kinsker rabbi, R'Yoav-Yehoshua, an author of several books and a student of the Sochatchower rabbi R'Avraham, author of the book *Avnei Nezer*. After he left Gostynin, he was followed by the Rav R'Chaim Meshulam Hakohen Unterman, a great scholar, a student of the Ostrowecer rabbi R'Meir Yechiel Halevi, one of the greatest scholars in the rabbinic world. The follower of R'Chaim Meshulam Hakohen was R'David Sillman, a son of the Chmelniker rabbi R'Aharon Sillman and a son-in-law of the Ostrowecer rabbi. He was one of the leaders of the *Mizrahi* party and he supported and strengthened the Zionist movement in town. He died young, on 10 Shevat 5682.

At that time, the question arose who shall take the post of rabbi. Rabbi Yitzhak Meir Bornstein was elected by a large majority. He was a great scholar, a student of the rabbi of Gora [the *Gerer rebbe*], the author of the famous book *Sefat Emet*. He was also a member of the Zionist party *Mizrahi* and he led the community in that spirit. Rabbi Yitzhak Meir was the last rabbi in Gostynin and, together with all the other Jews in Gostynin he perished by the Nazi murderers.

[Page 94]

Simkhah-Bunim Danciger

Moshe Danciger, Israel

Translated by Pamela Russ

Simkhah-Bunim Danciger was born in Wyszogrod in the year 1853. He came from a fanatically religious, *chassidic* home. Nakhum Sokolov, who later became a famous Zionist leader, also lived in Wyszogrod in his younger years. Sokolov left the city of his birth early on, and Simkhah-Bunim Danciger followed him in Wyszogrod in all his wanderings and all the places he went. In the later years, Simkhah-Bunim often confessed that he caught his eagerness to leave the town from his great fellow townsman.

By nature, Simkhah-Bunim was an active man, and at the same time he was an idealist. He participated in the Katowicer convention of the *Khovevei Zion* ["Lovers of Zion"; foundation builders of modern Zionism]. In the year 1885, he went to live in Gostynin. In those years, he was still a Gerer *chassid* [follower of the Gerer *chassidic* dynasty], but along with that, he preached about Zionism in the town. Of course, in the Gerer courts they looked at this very distastefully. The Gerer *chassidim* in Gostynin harassed him for this, humiliated him, and distanced themselves from him.

Simkhah-Bunim's popularity grew, nonetheless, within the *misnagdish* [opposers of *chassidic* ideology] courts and among the general populace. He spread his ideas and found many listeners who wanted to become informed about Zionism and the Land of Israel, and found their support in this Zionism.

Ignoring his illness, from which he suffered greatly – he suffered with asthma – he did not give up his Zionist propaganda and activities. A Zionist group was established at that time that was small in number and not too involved with its growth.

Simkhah-Bunim was 53 when he left this world, in the year 1906.

[Page 95]

Yakir Warszawski

Y. Morbid

Translated by Pamela Russ

Even though he was not born in Gostynin, Yakir Warszawski was considered a Gostyniner. He actually came to our town from Mlawa, his birthplace, near the former border of Germany. But over the years when he lived in Gostynin, he identified with its youth, struggled its struggles, and was its guidepost.

Yakir Warszawski was born on March 14, in the year 1885, into a *chassidic*-business family. He studied in a *cheder*, then in a *shtiebel* [small place of prayer] for *chassidim*, then by himself. While he was studying *Gemara* [Talmud], he also spent time with non-traditional philosophy books, Kabbalah [book of mysticism], and *chassidus*. Under the influence of his fellow townsman Yosef Opatoshu, the great Yiddish writer, he began in his early youth to read Hebrew literature and to study foreign languages. At age 20, he left for Warsaw, and after he was married, he settled in Gostynin where he became a Hebrew teacher.

In Gostynin, Yakir Warszawski already demonstrated great skill as a teacher. His students loved him, and he enveloped them with a lot of love. The mutual relationship was one of faithfulness and high regard. Therefore, from time to time, Yakir Warszawski read the first fruits of his pen to those who were closest to him. Often, in his short stories he would tell about the different characters in the town and he painted homey landscapes.

But the small town became tedious for Warszawski. It was hard for him to earn a living. So he moved back to Mlawa, where he had business as a bookkeeper. Nonetheless, he maintained contact with his friends. Yakir Warszawski's letters went from hand to hand, and the city's intellectuals swallowed them up because of their popularity and because of the direct tone in which they were written. Aside from that, his former students wanted to know what their teacher wrote.

[Page 96]

On the eve of World War I, Warszawski traveled across Germany, Italy, Syria, Israel, and Egypt. He published his travel journal in the Yiddish and Hebrew press at that time, and a newspaper with Yakir Warszawski's articles was read in Gostynin with great interest and enthusiasm.

Returning to Poland, he was hired as a Hebrew teacher in the Jewish gymnasium in Plock, and he frequently visited Gostynin where he spent his younger years. During this time, Gostynin had changed. Many of his close friends had left the city, some to America, and some to other places. But he loved the Gostynin landscape, loved the Gostynin Jews, and in his heart, there was always a small corner for this bright, Jewish town.

A Group of Gostyniner with Yakir Warszawski in Gostynin

Seated from right to left: Yakir Warszawski, Yosef Keller, Tuvia Jakubowycz
Standing from right to left: Iser-Meyer Matil, Yakov Linderman, Efraim Matil

[Page 97]

Between the two world wars, Yakir Warszawski was working in Keren Hayesod [official fundraising organization for Israel], and would travel across the Polish province in the interests of this fund. From 1906, he published literary items and journalistic articles in Yiddish and Hebrew periodicals, also under the pseudonym of Y. Ben-Aharon and Y. Warszai. He published in book form "*Hegeyonot Ve'za'zuim*" ["Reasoning and Shocks"], travel pictures, "*Min Ha'moledet*," ["From the Homeland"], "*Maalot u'Mordot*" ["Rising and Falling"], a series of children's stories in Hebrew.

The beloved and idealistic Yakir Warszawski experienced the fate of the Jews who were locked in the Warsaw ghetto.

The Gostyniner across the entire world will always remember the beautiful character of their Hebrew teacher Yakir Warszawski, may God avenge his blood.

[Page 98]

The Gostyniner *Khazen* (Memories of His Son)

Yoel Miller

Translated by Pamela Russ

Yoel Miller

For just about 30 years, my father, Reb Yakov Miller, was the *khazen-shokhet* [cantor-ritual slaughterer] in Gostynin. His life and impact in this beautiful and Jewish town left an enormous impression there. Until this day, the sweet songs of their *khazen* are still sung by Gostyniner, with a gnawing yearning for their past youth, remembering his name with love.

As other *khazanim* [cantors], my father also aspired, other than to be a leader of prayers, respected and recognized for this, also to bring out Jewish music and heartfelt prayers, and in that way to evoke in his listeners a feeling and taste for characteristically Jewish music. It was difficult for a *khazen* to carry out this mission completely with limited energies and limited means that he had at his disposal. But his [my father's] great desire, however, was always to raise *khazzanus* [cantorial music] to a higher level, so that he alone should be satisfied and that the singers should have enjoyment; and he achieved this. He always sang with a choir. Disregarding how large or how small the choir was, he applied his compositions according to the strengths and capacities of the singers. Once, it happened that he did not have enough singers in town, so he brought choirboys from outside the city. Here the two brothers Lewitt should be mentioned – Aron Hersh and Binyomin, who had beautiful voices and were musically gifted. In the later years, Binyomin Lewitt took on important positions as *khazen* here in America. In his last position, he was the replacement for *khazen* Kwartin in Borough Park, Brooklyn.

[Page 99]

Maintaining a choir according to the requirements of my father was always fraught with great difficulties: from both the financial and musical perspectives. He generally did not use prepared compositions because here he was missing an alto and here a tenor, so he had to get compositions to be appropriate for the skills that he had. The singers changed often, so he had to always prepare new songs, and this was exceptionally difficult. He really had no time for this. He therefore used every opportunity, even outside the house, to sing with his choirboys: in the slaughter-house, or in the forest that was not far from the slaughter-house, waiting for the butcher to prepare the animal to be checked [before the slaughter], he thought up a composition, and once when he was traveling to a village to slaughter [an animal].

He was all music. Everywhere and always, Jewish music poured out of him. The music flowed melodiously, filled with Jewish content, with the Jewish *krekhtz* [sigh, like *kvetch*], and Jewish joy. He submerged himself deeply in the profound content of the prayers, and with a lot of understanding and grace, gave the prayer its fullest interpretation.

My father was not satisfied only with thinking up a melody, he had also to work through the harmonies for the choir. Naturally, it was very difficult to carry this through. How does a young person from Skidel, whose total musical knowledge comprised a few notes that he learned from the Skidler *khazan*, create theoretically sound musical compositions? He gained more musical knowledge by traveling with the then famous *khazen* Meyer Lieder's choir. At that time, they took my father out of the choir and set him up him as a *khazen* in a small city in Poland. But my father was still not satisfied with those few notes that he knew; he was always searching, wanting to get to the bottom of the secrets of musical creations, to learn more of the Torah of music. He used all kinds of methods to acquire this knowledge. He learned a little through a correspondence course which the renowned Czestokhower *khazen* Birnboim ran. But still this did not satisfy him.

[Page 100]

By chance, a Jewish music director [conductor] of the stationed Russian regiment was in Gostynin. This conductor was really a great expert both in worldly and Jewish music. His name was Gersowycz. When he came to *shul* on *Shabbos* and heard my father leading the prayers and singing with the choir, he was captivated. He quickly befriended my father and offered to enhance his musical knowledge. At every opportunity, when both – the *khazen* and the conductor found some free time, they would spend the time together and absorb themselves in theory issues of music.

A new, interesting world opened for my father. Gersowycz taught him harmony, counterpoint, and familiarized him with classical music. Of course, my father used these for his *shul* compositions, and soon you heard a "*Hodu…*" ["Praise to…"] in "*Hallel…*" ["Thanks to…" – prayer recited and sung on special festivals] influenced by the great creations of Hayden; a "*Shoshanas Yakov…*" ["The Rose of Yakov…" – recited on Purim] that smacked of segments of "Troubadour."

It was obvious how great was the influence of the education he received through his *khazen* musical activities. All the hidden treasures opened up to him and a well of Jewish compositions flowed out of him. That period was the most creative time in his life.

That really was why he was so beloved by all. With limited strength, and often with self-sacrifice, he brought out the best of himself. He inspired many young boys who had a good musical ear and nice voices, and they became my father's students. One of them became the famous composer Yisroel Glatsztajn, who was killed by the Hitler murderers. Yisroel Glatsztajn began his musical career as a singer in my fathers' choir and later achieved his recognition as the creator of original melodies to the texts of famous Yiddish poets. He also contributed a lot to Yiddish theater in Warsaw and in Lodz.

[Page 101]

Today, my father's students are spread across many countries – in Israel, in America. And my father had many followers. They absolutely worshipped him. They took my fathers' music everywhere with them. In Gostynin homes in New York you often hear my father's compositions. These Gostynin Jews measure up other *khazzanim* [cantors] and their songs to the *arshin* [measure of length formerly used in Russia; about 28 inches] of the Gostyniner *khazen*, Reb Yakov Miller…

A chapter of the difficulties that my father had with the choir members should also be described here. Among them were also poor children. My father promised them several rubles for singing, saved some from his own small income, and paid them. But it often happened, that a few days before *Yom Tov* [Jewish holidays] the parents of the children came to my father and explained that their little boys could not come to sing because they had nothing to wear; one was missing a suit of clothes, another a pair of shoes; and just as if on purpose, this always happened to the better singers, to the best alto or soprano who was selected to sing a solo. Now my father could not rest, gathered all his resources, and saw to it that everything should be attended to; really, under great strain, but everything was taken care of. The children who had nothing to wear, were dressed up to come and sing. These were small problems. But with bigger children came bigger problems... because the majority of singers could not read notes. So, naturally it was difficult to teach them the compositions. With a lot of energy and patience and hard work, the *khazen* evoked the best from them, and when everything was all done, some of them lost their interest and did not want to sing. Now, once again he had to begin with new singers and once again start to teach a whole new choir. Aside from all these struggles, my father trembled over the singers so that they should not catch cold or become hoarse. He looked behind their eyes, caressed them, invited them to come to his house on Yom Tov morning to have a cup of hot tea and a bite to eat, so that everything should be in order and pass uneventfully. And when it was the time before the High Holidays, the world became lively! Especially the night before *selichos* [special prayers for forgiveness recited during the days preceding Yom Kippur]. In order to be certain that the entire choir would be together and no one would be late, the entire group of singers slept at our home and it was a rollicking time. But when they stood at the *amud* [the head of the congregation] all the problems were gone – it was all worth it, because the choir sang one composition after another and provided pride and joy, both to the *khazen* and to those praying. This Jewish music carried over to the Jewish homes. At the tailors' tables and near the shoemakers' benches, in the warehouses of the stocking manufacturers, you heard the sweet songs. The entire Gostynin sang along with my father, may he rest in peace.

[Page 102]

My father excelled also as a *shokhet* [ritual slaughterer]. He guarded the purity of his holy work with a true fear of God. He was respected and beloved by all classes of the Jewish people. *Chassidim, Misnagdim* [opposers of *chassidim*], God-fearing men, and those who are perfect in their character, all ate from his slaughter [meaning, they trusted his products because of his adherence to the Torah laws of slaughtering and kosher meat]. He was a Torah scholar, and followed the news and evolution of Hebrew literature. A man who was friendly to all people, everyone loved him because he had a kind word for everyone, and he greeted everyone with a broad smile of friendship. With his good advice and smart words, he won over the sentiments of the congregants.

The Gostyniner *khazen* died in Detroit at age 85. On his tombstone, a picture is set in of him wrapped in a *talis* [prayer shawl] as he used to stand at the lectern [in front of the congregation] in the Gostyniner *shul*.

[Page 103]

My Fiddle
(A Song with Notes)

Translated by Pamela Russ

We are herewith printing one of the songs to which the Gostynin *chazzan* [cantor] Yakov Miller, may he rest in peace, wrote this music when he was close to eighty years old.

> I ask of my fiddle: play me a song
> Of love and beauty and good fortune;
> Awaken in my heart at least a little faith,
> Revive my sad gaze.
>
> Oh, play me the song of yearning to live,
> Tones of hope and comfort,
> Choke off the moods that pull at the heart –
> Create a spirit in my body.
>
> Yes, once I took from life,
> Drank wine from the goblets;
> So play, my fiddle, of those joyous times,
> When the glow was still so bright.
>
> And the fiddle replies: Your plea is too large,
> The strings have already been torn, my friend.
> Only moaning and sighing, suffocated wails,
> That's what remained for today.

[Page 104]

Yisroel Glatsztajn

Mikhel Gelbart[15]

Translated by Pamela Russ

Mikhel Gelbart

Thousands and thousands of Jewish children across the entire Jewish world will cry and mourn when they will learn how the Nazi killers murdered their beloved composer, Yisroel Glatsztajn, in such a tragic way. Dear God, why are you silent? Why are You not taking revenge from these murderers who stole so much joy and so many Jewish children? Whoever once experienced a song-lesson in a Jewish public school, or has sat through some children's concert, in whichever city, in whichever country where there are Jews, and have seen the shining faces, the glowing eyes, and the hearts of the young Jewish children filled with joy as they sing Glatsztajn's wondrous

---

15. The writer of this article is the known composer and conductor Michel Gelbart. He sent us the music of Yisroel Glatsztajn to the text of the song of the great Yiddish-Hebrew poet, Yitzchok Katzenelson. Both – the poet and the composer of the melody – died in the years before the destruction [World War II].

children's songs – these people will understand the great loss that Jewish music, Jewish schools, and especially the Jewish child, have suffered.

It was 1908 when I arrived in Zondberg's large theater in Lodz, as choir singer. That same day, Yisroel Glatsztajn also arrived as choir singer. Tall, slim, with a pious pale face, and large, dreamy eyes. I from Ozrokow, and he from Gostynin.

Yisroel Glatsztajn

[Page 105]

He often told me about the Gostyniner *chazzan* [cantor] Reb Yakov Miller with whom he sang in the Gostyniner synagogue and from whom he received his introductory knowledge about music. Yisroel Glatsztajn was a child of Jewish poverty, and was drawn to the world of music. In his home, he already demonstrated a talent for composition. When the newspaper series [booklet] from Warsaw would arrive, he swallowed the notes of each new song and then sang it with a group of accompanying singers. Very often he would try his own abilities, and he would compose his own melody to the text of a song, and the *chazzan* would help him write it down.

Our "salary" was eight rubles a month. Our eyes met, and silently asked: "How can one live from such an income?" Both of us went into the street, strolled around, conversed, got to know each other better, and then found out that each of us came to Lodz with one goal and one purpose: to study music in order to become composers and create Jewish music for the Jewish masses. We decided that it would be easier to starve if we were together. So we looked for, found, and rented a steel bed for both of us in a cheap inn in Balot. We lived on two "portions" [*meals*] with a glass of milk a day. Together, both of us weighed 180 pounds and looked like Reb Zadok's fig after forty days...[16] Going to and from the theater every day, we tried to avoid all the puddles and mud because of our tattered shoes – and thank God there were always enough mud puddles in the knobby small streets. But that's why we learned eagerly, studied and perfected ourselves in music composition.

Every night in our beds, we lay awake for a long time and talked away the hunger with our fantasies about the fortunate time when we would create Jewish music, direct Jewish choirs, and popularize Jewish song.

[Page 106]

After several years of starving and studying, we left Lodz and went out into the world to seek and find our fortune. As I wandered, I came to America and later found out that Glatsztajn was in Lublin where he created superb compositions for young and old. He was particularly outstanding in writing children's songs. In 1920, in Warsaw, his first large collection was published as "Song and Play" – 50 beautiful songs and song-games for children to the text of Moshe Broderson and Y. Katzenelson. These songs were sung in all the Jewish children's schools wherever they were scattered, and children happily sang Glatsztajn's songs. Which Jewish child, who attended a Jewish school, cannot sing Glatsztajn's "*Marsh Lied*" ["Marching Song"]?

> "One and two and three and four,
> That which we are – are we ..."

"Tzipele," ["Little Tzippe"], "Feld Arbet" ["Field Work"], "Felder Grienen, Felder Roishen" ["Fields Are Greening, Fields Are Rushing"], and more and more wonderful songs.

Yisroel Glatsztajn was the first to create a Jewish opera in Yiddish, "Fatima." Later, Glatsztajn settled in Berlin where he created important musical works, which produced great sensations in the Jewish music world.

---

16. Rabbi Zadok lived in the period just prior to the destruction of the Second Temple, 70 CE. He fasted for 40 years before Jerusalem's fall hoping to avert the catastrophe, sustaining himself with sucking the juice from one fig a day, then discarding what was left. In relation to the Yiddish text above, this refers to the gaunt thinness and dried out look (like the fig) of both men described in the Yiddish article above.

Among them were: *"Khurban"* ["Destruction"], *"Shulamit," "Klingen Gleker"* ["Ringing Bells"], *"Wieg Lied"* ["Lullaby"], and *"Tzipele,"* which were published in America.

When Hitler came to power in Germany, and began to torture Jews, Yisroel Glatsztajn fled to Warsaw, from where I received his final letter in which he pleaded: "Have mercy on me and bring me to America." After that, I heard nothing from him, until – I read in the local Jewish press the list of the holy martyrs that the Nazi beasts murdered in Warsaw, among which I saw the name of Yisroel Glatsztajn. Glatsztajn's music will live with us forever.

[Page 107]

"Di Zun Fargeyt In Flamen"
The Sun Sets in Flame

Written by Yitzchak Katzenelson
Music by Yakov Glatstein

Translated by Pamela Russ

The sun sets aflame,
The sun can barely be seen,
So my hope wanes,
So my dream expires.
The night, the night is dark,
The night is mute and black;
So seems my sorrow.
So seems my heart.
World, you world, do not worry,
Soon your day will shine;
Only my sorrow is eternal,
Only my lament is eternal;
The night, the night is dark,
The night is mute and black;
So seems my sorrow.
So seems my heart.

(One can hear selection on the site http://www.milkenarchive.org/ Enter "DI ZUN FARGEYT IN FLAMEN" The Sun Sets, Aflame.)

[Page 108]

Yom Kippur in Gostynin

by Shmuel Keller, New York

Translated by Pamela Russ

Shmuel Keller

For the hallowed memory of my beloved family and of all the Jews from my town Gostynin, who died by the hands of Hitler's beasts in sanctification of the name of God.

It is the eve of Yom Kippur. From all directions, one hears the cries and protests from the birds that are being used for "*kaporah shlogen.*"[17]

Translator's Footnotes

17. The ritual of "kaporah shlogen" is practiced on the day preceding Yom Kippur. A bird is taken into a person's right hand and circled three times over one's head while reciting specific verses related to Yom Kippur. The bird is the atonement or "kaporah" for this person as he prepares body and soul for the upcoming Yom Kippur. The bird is then slaughtered and the meat is given to the poor.

You can smell the heavenly aromas coming from the Jewish bakeries where they are baking the *challos* and artistically braided, tall breads. Women and girls are carrying baked goods through the streets and hurry home with them. Also, the *shochtim* (ritual slaughterers) are exceptionally busy. They are slaughtering hens, roosters, ducks, and geese, and while waiting from one fowl to the other, they hold the special knife in their mouth ...

I clearly remember the face of the cantor, Reb Yakov Miller, who was also a *shochet*. On the day of the eve of Yom Kippur, he would go from place to place slaughtering the chickens, and the *shamash* (beadle) from the *shul* would accompany him. He was the old Reb Hersh Leyb. A fine man, this Hersh Leyb was. But sadly he had one fault – he was deaf. If you wanted to tell him anything, you had to scream into his ears. If he would knock on your shutters for your attention then you would have to go out to him immediately. He did not speak quietly, but shouted, and on the night before Yom Kippur eve, you could hear his voice over the entire city.

[Page 109]

The *mikva* (ritual bath) was busy all night. Jews would go to immerse themselves in the waters to prepare themselves in honor of the upcoming holiday. The wealthier Jews had special baths prepared for them.

The day of Yom Kippur eve, early in the morning, before sun up, the Jews went to say *selichos* (special holiday prayers) in *shul,* and then would stay for the regular services. When they had completed the prayers, they would sit down and recite "*hatoras nedorim*" (a prayer that annuls all vows). Three men were seated and one recited the verses. Many were a little clumsy with their Hebrew reading skills, so they read quietly.

It was also a tradition to visit the cemetery on the day of Yom Kippur eve. The *Chevra Kadisha* (the "Holy Society" – an organization that takes care of funeral and burial needs according to Jewish law) distributed cake and brandy (in order to make a *l'chaim* in memory for the departed soul). As far as I can remember, my grandfather Reb Yisroel Itche Keller, of blessed memory, was the *gabbai* (manager) of the *Chevra Kadisha.* I loved my grandfather dearly and during my childhood years, I spent much time in my grandfather's house. I knew that every year, on the morning of Yom Kippur eve, my grandfather would go out to the cemetery with cake and brandy, so I hurried to be on time.

A funeral in Gostynin

[Page 110]

When I arrived at my grandfather's house, there was already a basket filled with cut up cake sitting on the table. There were also several bottles of brandy on the table, and the two gravediggers – Avrohom Yakov Shaten and Leybish Rudes, were already there.

Avrohom Yakov was a heavy man with a large belly, two ruddy cheeks, and very often his nose was red as well. But he was considered to be an honest man.

Leybish Rudes, generally known as "the tall Leybish," was like a stretched out person with two long legs and a short, black beard. With his two large "sprinters" he would arrive more quickly at the cemetery than those who would go by horse and wagon.

Mendel Fisher went with his own wagon. He was a cold man. No matter what you said to him, even an insulting comment, he was never affected. He would look at you and not even bat an eye.

The two gravediggers carried out the cake and brandy and put it all onto the wagon. Meanwhile, Reb Leybke Wilner arrived, the second manager of the *Chevra Kadisha*. Everyone got into the wagon and was seated, and I sat next to my grandfather. I felt very proud that I was going with him and with all these esteemed Jews.

When we arrived at the cemetery, we already saw many Jews standing near the graves. One person was holding a *Maaneh Loshon* (book of prayers that are said at a gravesite), and another person was holding a *Techina* (book of prayers in Yiddish), and several others were reciting Psalms. The gates to the gravesite of the Gostynin Rebbe were wide open. People were going in and out of there.

Near the fence, many candles were burning. The grave was strewn with *kvitlekh* (handwritten notes) with all types of requests. In the service house of the cemetery, in the so-called "house of purification," there was a long table covered with two tablecloths. On the table were bottles of brandy and nearby, piled high, the cake was set out.

[Page 111]

At the head of the table, were my grandfather and Reb Leybke Wilner, and they were handing out the cake and brandy to everyone and wishing everyone "a good and healthy year" …

I waited for my father to come out to the cemetery. At that time, my father would go only to the Rebbe's gravesite. When my father had finished the prayers, we would go home together.

By the time we arrived home, it was already getting late. We had to hurry. We changed our clothes and went to *Mincha* services. As we were walking, we could see how on all the streets and smaller roads the Jews were on their way, as if in long rows, to the various *shuls*. The *shuls* were filled with candles. Rich and poor people – everyone had lit candles.

At the *Mincha* prayers, you already recited the *Al Chet* (confession of sins) and by now many were crying. In the service house of the *shul* there were many trays with all kinds of notes requesting charitable donations. Every Jew put something into one plate or another.

Going home after *Mincha*, you could see how the Jewish stores were shutting down. The dry goods stores of Reb Avrohom Yitzkhok Lomzer, Yeshaye Wajnzilber, and Avrohom Pinczewski were already locked up. When we came back home, we could feel the holiness of Yom Kippur in every corner. My beloved mother and older sister Charne prepared the table for the final meal before the fast. There were many candles on the table. Washing our hands and reciting the appropriate prayers before eating the *chalah* was also different than it was all year round. We hurried a little through the meal, more than usual. My only job was to get the *mayim akharonim* (water for washing fingers before reciting the "Grace after Meals"). While saying these prayers, all our eyes were on our father. My father's eyes were streaming with tears. When it came to the parts of "*Rachem noh*" (have mercy on us) or "*Ve noh al tatzrikheinu .... Lo leidei matnas bosor vedom*" (please make us not need anything ... make us not dependent on human hands), he said these words with the deepest spiritual and devout pleading. This made a profound impression on us and our eyes also became wet with tears.

[Page 112]

After completing the Grace after Meals, each of us, in order of age, went over to our father to receive his blessings. He placed his hands on one's head, blessed each of us, and his eyes were wet with tears.

My beloved mother was standing next to the candles and was saying the special prayers for candle lighting. My father put on his *kittel* (white robe worn on Yom Kippur) and his *tallis* and overcoat, and we all went over to our grandfather, Reb Yisroel Itche, of blessed memory. When we arrived there, we met aunts and uncles and their children. Everyone had come to the head of the family to receive blessings and good wishes, and to return the blessings as well.

My grandfather was ready to leave and go to *Kol Nidrei* (Yom Kippur eve services). Our grandmother Chaya Soro, a refined, religious woman, a truly modest woman, was standing with the prayer book for Yom Kippur and saying various prayers. We approached her and she gave us each many blessings.

In Gostynin, women did not go to *shul* for *Kol Nidrei*. The same was true for the surrounding towns. All this was because of a tragedy that had occurred in the not-so-distant town of Ledzicz in the women's section of the *shul* during *Kol Nidrei*. A fire had broken out there. One woman let out a scream: "Fire!" All the women tried to run toward the steps that lead to the exit of the *shul*. In the chaos, 30 women were squashed to death. As a result, the rabbis in the entire area issued a decree telling women not to go to *Kol Nidrei*.

As I left the house with my grandfather, I could see how from all streets and smaller roads Jews were streaming forth to *Kol Nidrei*. Everyone's face showed a God-fearing countenance. Everyone who passed my grandfather and father stopped to wish them well. When I turned around and looked toward the west, I saw how the sun was going down between the mountains, leaving bloody-red, fiery stains in the sky. A great fear befell me. I imagined that the heavens were preparing for Judgment Day, that the angels were rushing to do God's bidding and were bringing in the large Book of Deeds, where it is written: "Today it is sealed in the Book of Deeds who will live and who will die." And the prosecutor stands before the Holy Throne and speaks evilly about the Jews, detailing everyone's sins...

[Page 113]

As a result of these childhood memories, a fear overcame me, so I nestled up closer to my grandfather. I loved my grandfather dearly. Whenever I was with my grandfather, I felt protected from all bad things. My grandfather had a great influence on me. All year round he prayed in a small *chasidish shul*, but for the Days of Awe (Rosh Hashana and Yom Kippur) he prayed in the city's *Beis Midrash*. He was the one who began the services. Occasionally, it was the *dayan* (a person knowledgeable in Talmudic law who is consulted for religious questions) Reb Shmuel Volf Pinczewski who did this, but because of his age and frailty my grandfather took over that position.

As we entered the *Beis Midrash,* our eyes were blinded by the glow of hundreds of candles in the hanging light, from chests filled with sand, and from pots. Light was pouring forth from everywhere. Wax candles were burning on the platform from which the Torah was read, and there was hay strewn across the floor.

All the Jews wished each other a good and healthy year. Many Jews who were upset with each other all year, now made up because they knew that Yom Kippur did not forgive the sins of man towards man, but only forgave the sins of man towards God.

Many Jews were already standing with their prayer shawls covering their heads and were reciting *Tefila Zaka*[18]. The *shamash*, Michel Ber, was a tall man with a black beard peppered with some gray. He stood on the raised

---

Translator's Footnotes

18. Introductory prayer said just before the evening services of Yom Kippur, where one expresses forgiveness towards others. Tefila Zaka also proclaims a revalidation of one's faith.

platform waiting for all the Jews to assemble. He knew everyone and so knew who was still missing. This was a man who was in charge of the entire *Beis Medrash* since he came from a wealthy family and was also a scholar unto his own right. He was a strong-minded person and spared no one other than a few wealthier people. He would stand on the platform and shout down, calling to each person by name. If any of the younger people would talk during prayers, he would call them by name so that their fathers would hear. He would chase the younger boys out of the *Beis Medrash* for the slightest antic. But on the eve of Yom Kippur, he was a totally different person. He stood on the platform with his prayer shawl over his head, lifting the shawl that covered his eyes, looked around, then pounded on the table. This was a signal for silence. He approached the eastern wall (place of honor) where Reb Leybish Lifsycz, of blessed memory, was standing. This was the son of the holy Gostynin Rebbe, of blessed memory. Reb Leybish was a tall man with a snow-white beard, a radiating face, one eye smaller than the other, that always gave the impression that he was looking at you.

[Page 114]

With slow steps, Reb Leybish followed the *shamash* Mikhel Ber to the Holy Ark. The *shamash* took out a Torah scroll and put it into Reb Leybish's arms. With great reverence, Reb Leybish turned to the congregation and declared the verse: *"Or zoruah latzadik, u'leyishrei lev simcha"* (trans: Light is sown for the righteous, and for the upright of heart, gladness).

With enormous emotion, each person repeated this verse. With uneven steps, Reb Leybish went down the stairs that led away from the Holy Ark, while still holding the Torah scroll. I remember how my father approached these steps and used his prayer shawl to touch the Torah scroll, then kissed the prayer shawl in the spot that touched the Torah. With the Torah in his arms, Reb Leybish went around the platform and everyone pushed in with their prayer shawls to have a chance to kiss the Torah. The image is unforgettable.

They continued to say *"Or zoruah latzadik"* until Reb Leybish replaced the Torah scrolls into the Holy Ark. He left the doors open until the leader of the services recited the blessing of *"Shehecheyonu"* (in honor of the "new" holiday).

Reb Leybish the *shochet* (ritual slaughterer), the one who led the afternoon services, also led the *Kol nidrei* prayers, but before he began, Reb Leybish

Lifsycz went to stand on one side of him and Reb Avrohom Yitzchok Lomzer, the one who blew the *shofar*, went to stand on the other.

Reb Avrohom Yitzchok Lomzer was a very hairy man. His beard, sidelocks, and mustache completely hid his face. His eyes, overhung with long eyebrows, were almost impossible to see. But if he set his eyes upon you, they looked angry. As far as I remember him, I never saw him with a friendly expression on his face. He was an angry man. Because his nose was always stuffed with tobacco, his speech was not clear and you had to restrain yourself from laughing when he spoke. He always replaced the letter "*mem*" with a "*beis.*" When Reb Leybish said "*al daas hamokom*" ("with the approval of God" is the introductory verse to *Kol nidrei*), he replied: "*al daas abakom*" [with his nose blocked], same was for "*bi'shiva shel maaloh*" ("in the convocation of the court above" is the next phrase of this verse), he said instead "*bi'shiva shel baaloh*" [again with a blocked nose]... But he was a very pious Jew, a scholar, and a God-fearing man.

[Page 115]

Everyone put their prayer shawls over their heads when reciting the "*shmoneh esrei*" (the standing prayer, or the *amidah*). I stood under my father's prayer shawl and felt his tears drip down onto my head. I cried along when I felt my father's tears. I remember the "*yaleh*" and the "*selach no*" and the "*oshamnu*" and the "*ki hinei kachomer*" [all prominent Yom Kippur prayers], the way Reb Leybish the *shochet* said these. And who doesn't remember the heartfelt crying and lamenting of the "*Shema koleinu*" when they reached the phrase of "*al tashlicheinu le'eis zikno*" (do not forsake us in our old age).

After the evening prayers, no one left to go home. Reb Leybish Lifsycz went to the podium to recite the "*Shir hayichud*" (Song of Unity) [a prayer recited responsively after evening services have ended], verse by verse. And even after that, not everyone left for home. Many Jews remained in the *Beis Medrash* all night. Many learned a section of the Talmud, *Mesechta yoma*, and others recited Psalms all night long.

We woke up very early on Yom Kippur morning in order to go to *shul* with our father. I loved to hear my grandfather recite the early prayers, then Reb Moishe Holander who led the morning prayers, and later my father, and also the one who led the afternoon prayers Reb Leybish the *shochet*. I can still clearly hear in my ears as my grandfather sang: "*hokeil be'saatzumois uzecho*" (God, in the omnipotence of Your strength...), and the way Reb Moishe

Holander, with his hoarse voice sang out: *"Hamelech!"* ("King of the Universe!"). I remember how his two sons, Mendel and Yehoshua, assisted him. I even remember the marches that they used to sing.

Somehow they didn't have a feel for music.

I couldn't wait for them to leave the podium. When Avrohom Moishe Holander said the *"Shir hamalos mimamakim korosicho Hashem"* (Song of Ascents, I call to God from the depths...) I cried bitterly. It didn't matter how young I was at the time. He had a strange timbre in his voice and would let out hoarse cries. I could hardly wait until Reb Leybish the *shochet* would go up to do the afternoon prayers.

[Page 116]

I've heard many cantors in my life, but I've never heard anyone recite the *"malchuyos – zichronos – shofros"* (significant sections of the Yom Kippur prayers) as Reb Leybish the *shochet* did.

In the old times, the leader of the prayers did not say *"Hineni he'oni mimaas"* because this prayer had nothing to do with these congregants. This is a prayer exclusively recited by the leader of the prayers. But Reb Leybish the shochet placed his prayer shawl over his head and did recite this prayer, and cried his heart out while doing so.

In my later years, when I sang with the memorable cantor Reb Yakov Miller, of blessed memory, he did the same thing. Reb Leybish the *shochet* also had his two assistants: his son Yitzchok Volf, and his son-in-law. But these two could barely sing. They would always steer him off key. I will never forget how sweetly he prayed. Who doesn't remember what happened when it came to *"Unesana tokef"* (the peak of the Yom Kippur prayer). It was impossible at that point to silence the cries coming from the women's section of the *shul*. No matter how hard Michel Ber pounded on the table hoping to silence the women, nothing helped. It took quite some time before they all became quiet. And only then did Reb Leybish the *shochet* begin his sweet recitation of *"u'veshofar gadol yitoka, vekol demomo dako yishoma"* (trans: "the great shofar will be sounded and a still, thin sound will be heard"), and then took to singing *"kevakoras ro'eh edroi"* (trans: "like a shepherd inspecting the flock"). I've heard many choirs in my lifetime, but nothing even comes close to these prayers as they were recited in the Gostynin *Beis Medrash*.

Now in America, whenever I am standing at the *avoda* (section describing what the Priests and High Priest did in the Temple) part of the Yom Kippur service, as the cantor sings of the Priests ("*Hakohanim*"), and then he comes to the part where he describes how they bowed down and fell to the ground ("*Hoyu Kor'im*), and then only the leader of the prayers and the Rav bow and fall all the way down to the ground, I always remember how when Reb Leybish recited these prayers in the *avoda* describing the Priestly acts ...

[Page 117]

... and even in later years when he sang with the cantor Reb Yakov Miller, of blessed memory, all the Jews, young and old, bowed down until the ground.

Who can forget how the Jews of Gostynin recited the prayer of "*eileh ezkero*" where the story of the death of the Ten Martyrs ("*Aseres Harugei Malchus*") and Rabbi Akiva is told. How many, many tears did our fathers and grandfathers shed during this prayer!

How many tears were absorbed into the Yom Kippur *machzorim* (prayer books). How many tears of our fathers and grandfathers, mothers and grandmothers were buried in these prayers. ...

Between the afternoon and evening prayers, one could already see many pale faces. My father sent me up to the women's section of the *shul* to see how my mother was feeling. Many people were resting, lying on the grass in the *shul*'s courtyard. One individual, whom I still see in front of my eyes, was Mendel Eizenhendler. He was a very dear man, but he was a real clown. All year, he would utter forth all kinds of curses, but he would nonetheless do favors for anyone. He was lying on the grass, and every so often would sniff some sort of drops from a bottle. The drops used to be called "heart strength." Well, here I see a Jew with a silver skullcap on his head and he is bringing the little box of snuff over to my grandfather. This was Reb Yosef Tremski, also an angry man. He was a man that would tell stories. But if someone would annoy him, well God would have to help that person. He was like a gunpowder keg. All in all, though, he was a fine and devout Jew.

I loved all these Jews. And they loved me as well. I learned a lot from them and until today, much of this has remained with me.

My father recited the evening prayers. I remember Epshtajn bought "*maftir Yonah*" (the reading of the Book of Jonah). I don't remember his first name. He was a Lithuanian Jew from the Lomzer region. His business was in forestry and later he built a sawmill where they cut wood. He was expert at reading Hebrew. He would read the Book of Jonah loudly and with the proper cantillations. You could hear every word.

[Page 118]

No one sits idly between the evening services and the closing prayers of Yom Kippur, *Neilah*. People are reciting Psalms. Along the eastern wall, near Reb Leyb Lifsycz there is one Jew who is studying a Hebrew text while wearing two pairs of glasses. This was Reb Fishel Ciwia. He was known as "the black Fishel." They said that in his younger years his beard and his head of hair were a deep black and his face was dark. But when I knew him, he was already snow white, but his eyebrows still contained a few black threads. He was very sharp and full of stories and Torah knowledge. Some said that he even read books with content outside of the religious sphere. They considered him somewhat enlightened. Sometimes, my grandfather would send me to him to get a particular Hebrew text. He had a lot of books. If he would give me a book, he told me not to give it to anyone else but put it directly into my grandfather's hands.

The day does not stand still. The sun moves farther west. The people in the *Beis Medrash* prepare for *Neilah,* the closing prayers for Yom Kippur. These half-faint Jews with their pale faces come back into the *Beis Medrash* from the *shul* courtyard. The air in the *shul* is very heavy with dust that has collected from the hay on the floor, mixed with the smoke from the flickering candles. Rays from the setting sun stream through the windows. It seems as if everything is under a thin mist. A silence hovers in the *Beis Medrash*. The congregation is ready for *Neilah*. The *shamash* bangs on the table, and the prayers of *"U'vo letzion goel..."* (trans: "and a redeemer shall come to Zion...") begin.

The leader of the prayers approaches the podium. Somewhat weak, but with a pure voice, he begins the very familiar melody for *Kaddish* in *Neilah*. Many sing along with him. Everyone says the *shmoneh esrei* of *Neilah* with great devotion. The Holy Ark holding all the Torah scrolls is opened wide. The Ark remains open until *Neilah* is ended.

The sun moves farther. The day is running away. The crowd recites the *"Sholosh esrei middos"* (the "Thirteen Attributes of God"). I can still clearly hear the cries and intonations as they reach the attribute of *rachamim* (mercy) or the leader's prayer of *"yehi rotzon milfonecho shomeah kol bechios"* (trans: "May it be His Will to hear the voice of our cries"). The lamenting, the crying, remains until the end of the prayer services. With the final bits of strength, everyone recites *"Avinu malkeinu"* (Our Father, our King...).

[Page 119]

Only now, after the terrible destruction of the Holocaust, can we understand why the Jews cried so bitterly. When they said: "Our Father our King, act for the sake of those who were murdered for Your Holy Name; Our Father our King, act for the sake of those who went into fire and water for the sanctification of Your Name; Our Father our King, avenge before our eyes the spilled blood of Your servants."[19]

The crying and the devotion of these prayers lasted until sound of the final blast of the *shofar* (*tekiah gedola*) permeated the dusty air and the darkness of the Beis Medrash.

The day of Yom Kippur was very holy in our old home. But the holiness was not just for that one day – every day of our life was filled with a spiritual holiness. Jewish life was complete and had substance, saturated with people's desires and lofty hopes.

This world exists no longer. It was completely cut off. This world will always remain alive deep in our hearts and memories.

Translator's Footnotes

19. From the Hebrew of Avinu Malkeinu in the Yom Kippur prayers: "Avinu malkeinu, kra roah gezar dineinu; Avinu malkeinu, asei le'maan harugim al shem kodshecho; Avinu malkeinu, asei le'maan boei boaish u'vamayim al kidus shemecho; Avinu malkeinu nekom le'eineinu nikmas dom avodecho hashofuch."

[Page 120]

In the Years 1914–1928

by Yisochar Matil

Translated by Pamela Russ

Yisochar Matil

Soon after the outbreak of World War One, the German army invaded the provinces of Poland that were occupied by the Russian military. The Russians retreated back to Warsaw.

At the Russian military's first resistance, the Germans retreated until past Wloclawek.

On the eastern side of Gostynin, a small German unit delayed, and they remained stuck between Gombyn and Gostynin. In order to join up with the regular German army, these Germans, small in number, surrounded Gostynin and shot at it from all sides. The Russians, thinking that this was an attack of the regular German army, hid, and then fled in fear. The civilian population also fled to protect themselves in brick houses and in cellars.

At that time, we lived on Stodolni Street, better known by the Jews of Gostynin as "death street" because all the funerals went through Stodolni Street. Opposite us was a brick apartment house with a large cement cellar. So our whole family – my father, mother, four brothers, and three sisters, and my uncle Ben Zion Keller, who was then in our home – ran across the street to the cellar, to protect ourselves from the bullets. When the shooting stopped, and the Germans passed through Gostynin, everyone came out his hiding place and went to their own homes.

[Page 121]

Our entire family and our uncle Ben Zion also came out of hiding, crossed the road, and went back home. Meanwhile, the Russians, with the help of the anti–Semitic Polaks, took to searching for those guilty of their downfall, whom they could blame for all this. And just as we crossed the road to go home, they immediately came in and accused my father and my uncle Ben Zion of giving signals from a roof to the Germans. In other words, they were accused of being "spies."

We pleaded and cried to them, begging that they leave our father and uncle with us, saying that we were only in the cement cellar to protect ourselves, and that neither our father nor our uncle was a spy. Their reply was that all Jews were spies and they were going to shoot these two Jewish spies. They took my father and uncle with them. We were distraught but could do nothing. A terror seized us all; a dread of the Russian soldiers, and particularly of the Cossacks.

That evening, my two brothers, Moshe and Yakov Leyb, carefully went into the street, with their hats pulled down low over their eyes so as not to be recognized, in order to find out what had happened to our unfortunate father and uncle. They returned with embittered hearts and didn't tell anyone what they had learned. The found out that at 2 AM that night the two Jewish "spies" were to be shot (this is what one Christian told the other). Crying bitterly, we all sat and prayed to God for some sort of salvation.

At 2 AM that night we heard several shots. Moshe and Yakov Leyb cried hysterically. We cried along with them until finally we moved away, exhausted and drained. Early in the morning, my mother and brothers ran to find out what had happened. Their hearts became lighter when they learned that there had been no executions. They also found out that during the night, they had also captured more Jews and Germans, among them the Rav and the German minister.

Iser Meier Matel undertook to go and plea for mercy for the Rav and for the other Jews that were arrested. He went to the Russian colonel who had his quarters in Rzesztowa in the hotel.

[Page 122]

When the Russian colonel heard why the Jew had come, he grabbed his gun and wanted to shoot him on the spot for his *chutzpa*, that a Jew comes to plea on behalf of the Jewish "spies."

Iser Meier just barely escaped with his life. Pale and terrified, he hid in fear. This frightened and upset the Gostynin Jews even more. At midday, the news spread that the pre–war Gostynin authorities had returned. Then, there was a real miracle.

Our uncles, Mote Matel and Yakov Mendel Keller, went immediately to see the prince. They told him that the Rav, my father and uncle, and many other Jews had been thrown into prison and they were accused of being spies.

The prince assured them that he would do everything to free them and he reassured them that no bad would happen to them, if they were lucky and were still alive. Later that same day, the Rav was freed. A day later, my father and uncle. And a few days after that, all the Jews as well as the Germans.

The Gostynin Jews were thrilled with the release of the Rav and with the other Jews.

Our joy was boundless. We were thrilled about the miracle that had delivered our father and uncle alive.

My father and Uncle Ben Zion told us what they experienced in those first hours and on the first night of their arrest. They were guarded heavily and were told that soon, soon they would be shot.

In the room where they were held, they had to kneel the entire time. When more Jews were brought in and some time later the Rav and several Germans along with the minister, they were sure that these were their final minutes. They were sure that the Rav and the minister had been brought to say confession with them. Only later did they find out that the Rav and the minister were also under the same suspicion of guilt. Later in the day, when the Rav was freed, salvation came for them too.

[Page 123]

The slaughter behind Wloclawek went on for a few weeks until the Russians retreated to the western side of Gostynin. At the time, the Gostynin people went through great fear because of the fighting and were terrified that the entire town of Gostynin would be destroyed. The Jews lived in fear of the Russian soldiers. They rarely went out into the streets and, as all the other

Gostynin residents, they slept in their clothes, ready to run for safety in seconds.

After a few weeks, the Russian army retreated to the east, between Gostynin and Gombyn.

Gostynin was also lucky this time. The Russians were running so quickly, that they didn't have enough time to rob the Jews or make any pogroms.

Also, the city did not incur any damage.

The slaughter on the eastern side of Gostynin continued for a few days and the Russian army continued to flee.

In a few months, the Germans occupied all of Poland.

German Occupation

Life under German occupation was very difficult. The city was under guard. German patrols guarded all corners of the city, not permitting any life essentials or other materials to be brought in or taken out. By 10 PM, no one was allowed in the streets. Bread, sugar, and flour ration cards were enforced. There were long lineups in front of the stores. But despite all these difficulties, somehow life began to normalize.

The gymnasiums, schools, and *cheders* opened their doors, and everyone went back to their daily business. Then the Gostynin Jews took to restoring the material and societal damage that the war had left behind, and to set up necessary organizations that the times required.

[Page 124]

The first thing that was established was a community kitchen where meals were distributed to the poor Jewish population in the city and to those who were roving through the city because the war had left them homeless, and also to the many from the big cities who were hungry, since they had left those cities in search of a small piece of bread in the small city provinces.

The entire Jewish youth participated in the work around the kitchen, and the entire Jewish population helped them.

The women cooked and served, and took care of the hygiene. The men took care of the finances of managing the kitchen. With the help of the women they organized all kinds of projects, such as a flower day, raffles for pledges, dance evenings, and often gave theatrical performances.

The Yiddish theater that was once opposed by the *Chassidic* and religious businessmen, who did not permit their children to go and watch the performances, now became very popular. Now they ran to the theater seeing how useful the funds they raised were for the kitchen. The parents no longer prevented the children from going to watch the performances. This led to the fact that at one particular performance, my uncles Nute Matel and Yakov Mendel Keller and a group of other businessmen were the main guests. Nute was the treasurer and Yakov Mendel was the manager. Their wives organized the buffet and were the waitresses.

In 1915, the new group *"Linat Hatzedek"* ["where righteousness dwells," a charity organization that took care of the sick] was founded. The first officials of the group were: Yosef Gonshor, my wife's brother, who died in the Warsaw ghetto along with his wife and two children; Ben Zion Keller, my mother's brother, who died along with his wife and daughter and all the Gostyniners on April 17, 1942, in Chelmno.

Linat Hatzedek had a very large task, because there was a typhus epidemic in the entire Poland. In Gostynin, a large number of Jews became sick with typhus. The Linat Hatzedek raised its funds in the same way that the community kitchen did, and they also sent out men to collect money for weddings and other Jewish celebrations. Also, on Purim, there were masquerading Purim entertainers who went from house to house who raised money for the needs of Linat Hatzedek.

The typhus epidemic subsided after taking many victims, such as: my wife's father Eliezer Gonshor, Yakov Lipe Kaufman, Volf Nosinowycz, Yosef Chaim Hodes, and others. Also, the barber–surgeon Zalman Micholski, who saved many people from the plague, but couldn't help himself and died during the epidemic.

The social energy was used for cultural tasks. A reading room was opened at the Peretz Library, that until then only distributed books for reading, and that now amassed a greater number of books. Other than Yiddish books, the Peretz Library also distributed Polish and Hebrew books. The Peretz Library supported the youth and the progressive well–to–do people.

Assisting greatly were young Jewish students from the surrounding cities and towns – such as Plock, Wloclawek, Kutno, Zychlin, Gombyn, Koval, Radziejow, Lipno, Rypin, Wisograd, and other cities – who studied in the Gostynin gymnasium.

[Page 125]

The "Hatchiya" administration and the drama circle "Habimah" in Gostynin

Seated from right to left: Dovid Katz, Waserman, Tuvia Jakubowicz, Yakov Zarkhyn, Adam Domb, Mordechai Moricz, Yosef Gonshor

First row standing, from right to left: Henokh Kuczinski, Yechiel Zalman Matel, Feige Sarna, Bashe Zaidman, Yakov Leyb Matel, Chaim Sender Zandman, Dvora Zajacs, Hetzke Sarna, and Chana Zajacs

Second row standing, from right to left: Yakov Sarna, Mordecai Reuven Moskol, Yakov Gostinski, Shmuel Keller, Baruch Meier Matel, Chaim Yehoshua Tabacznik, Yisroel Zelig Kuczinski, Yehoshua Noach WilnerThe Linat Hatzedek helped with medicines and money for all those who were in need, and to all those who were sick they sent two members to spend entire nights – sometimes entire days – with them.

In the year 1915, *Hatchiya* was also founded. *Hatchiya* had three units:

– *Herzliya* – a purely Zionist organization

– *Maccabi* – a competition and sport organization

– *Habima* – a drama circle

Herzliya was run by the Zionist group. *Maccabi*, to which the majority of the youth belonged, was managed by a committee that represented all factions. Nonetheless, the uniform hat of the *Maccabi* was colored blue and white, the symbolic colors of Zionism. Every member wore this with pride on every trip and on each sports holiday.

[Page 127]

The *Habima*, under Domb's direction, attracted the most talented youth and prepared to present wonderful performances.

The *Hatchiya*, bought the house on Dlugo near Lustgarten Street, where the first Gostynin cinema was, and before that the Russian teahouse (China). They freshened it up a little, and then moved in with the three units.

Maccabi bought sports equipment and invited Hershel Holczman's grandson, Itche Holczman's son from Kutno, who studied in the Gostynin gymnasium, to be the sports instructor. He set up men's groups and women's groups and taught them to march and to exercise.

With pride, he led the entire sports club, with his men's and women's groups, through the streets of Gostynin, during their excursions. Later, *Maccabi* hired a sports instructor, Finkelstajn from Warsaw, with a monthly salary.

During a trip to Kutno, the entire Jewish population welcomed the Gostynin *Maccabis* and watched how Dovid Katz, the chairman at the time, led the men's and women's teams through the streets of Kutno, and then later watched the practice exercises at the sports festival.

When the Gostynin *Maccabis* later came to Zychlin, there were great festivities in the town.

The *Habima* presented their beautiful performances in town, and also in the neighboring towns – Plock, Kutno, Zychlin – with great success.

In 1915, the director Dzhalowski and his family settled in Gostynin. He came from Lodz. Dzhalowski organized a youth choir and presented beautiful concerts. After a few years, Dzhalowski and his family left Gostynin.

[Page 128]

Men's groups of the competition and sports club "Maccabi" in 1915

First row, sitting, from right to left: Chaim Gerst, Lipe Pluczer, Chaim Bresler, Moshe Yoske Matel, Baruch Meier Matel, Henoch Linderman, Heczke Sarna, Eliezer Flajsman, Chaim Yehoshua Tabacznik, Mordechai Reuven Moskal, Yoske Morycz, Chaim Sender Zandman, the child Yeshiye Zhychlin

Second row, from right to left: Yisroel Shajer, Yisroel Zelig Kuczinski, Henoch Kuczinski, Itzik Bresler, Moshe Morycz, the competition instructor Finkelstajn, Tuvia Jakubowycz, Shmuel Keller, Duvid Levy, Yakov Lefkowycz, Iser Meier Matel, Yakov Zarchin

Third row, from right to left: Avrohom Hershel Matel, unknown, Shmuel Baruch Matel, Yisroel Hersh Zholandz, Yechiel Boczan, Ziskind Goldman, Kahane, Mordechai Morycz, Peretz Keller

Fourth row, from right to left: Fishel Bresler, two unknowns, Swarcbard, unknown, Yankel Nisanowycz, Yosef Kowadlo, unknown

Fifth row, from right to left: Itche Katz, Chaim Zweighaft, Yosef Bagno, Chana Zajacs, Baruch Meier Matel, unknown, Feivish Lichtenstajn, Avrohom Zajacs, Chaim Kruczik

Last row, from right to left: Avrohom Nisanowycz, Kowent, Yitzchok Izak Gerst, Hershel Zweighaft, Yisochar Matel, Shmuel Markowycz, Yakov Sarna, Reuven Lichtenstajn

[Page 129]

The entire income of the theater performances and concerts went to the Peretz Library and the community kitchen.

Adam Domb's performances strongly influenced the love for the theater for all those in Gostynin. And when a Jewish troupe from Lodz or Warsaw came to Gostynin, the theater was always full. Once, Shavuos time, Waksman and his troupe from Lodz came to present three performances in Gostynin. That Shavuos, the Rav gave a sermon in the synagogue during prayers, saying that the Jews of Gostynin were absolutely forbidden from desecrating the holiday by permitting the theater troupe to perform on the holiday. He placed a ban on Waksman and his troupe and placed guards on the streets of Gostynin in order to prevent those who did want to go to the theatre from actually going. Waksman himself performed in the first and second of the three performances for those few who had climbed over the fences on the side streets to get in. The third performance, held on the night when Shavuos ended, when he presented "The Siberian Bells," had a full theater. Waksman went onto the stage, very spirited, greeted the audience, and assured them that he would never forget the Gostynin public. The Gostyniners forgot the ban, but not the theater.

Under the German occupation, the Jewish Community Administration of Gostynin was also established. The municipality directed all the activities in the city involving all the Jewish religious and social activities in the city.

In 1915, the construction of the electric station was completed. And in the middle of the summer the streets of Gostynin were lit up with electric lights. Soon afterwards, the government buildings and many private homes used this light as well. This light was provided from sundown until midnight, and later until 1 AM.

This was life under the yoke of German occupation, but despite all the difficulties because of the Germans, often more was accomplished than under normal circumstances, and times of peace and plenitude.

[Page 130]

In Independent Poland

The establishment of an independent Poland at the end of the First World War filled hearts with a lot of hope, and an optimistic mood enveloped the Polish Jews.

The population organized itself. Unions were set up from every [socio-political] position that existed on the Jewish street: the Bund, leftist and rightist *Poalei*-Zionists [Zionist socialist party]; Zionists in general; communists and their sympathizers, and Agudists [religious opposition to Zionists].

The workers' groups partnered to set up professional unions in the city. In a short time, with the help of the radical voice of the Jewish students and thanks to the ongoing education among the Jewish workers in the city, they were able to organize the professional unions. A needle trade union was established, also transport unions, porter unions, spats [low laced boots] union, and barbers' union.

All these unions had one location where each trade has its representative in the central administration office that managed all the work. In this location of the professional union there were also lectures that were given and readings in Polish and Yiddish. There were also courses in reading and writing.

The lectures and readings were given by the Gostynin young students who were at that time very democratic yet traditional in their disposition.

Aside from this professional work, there were also May First celebrations, and street demonstrations.

Once, before one such street demonstration, we realized at the last minute that although we had prepared everything, we had forgotten a red flag.

It was already late in the evening. We ran to Yehoshua Noach (Wilner), and awoke him and his wife and told them about our dilemma. Yehoshua Noach's face clouded over, and as always, when he had a dilemma, he placed a finger on his upper lip and thought about what to do. We noticed that Yehoshua Noach's face soon lit up. He winked to his wife Faige. Faige quickly grasped what her husband Yehoshua Noach meant and she cried out hysterically: "Not that! It's a new blouse! I haven't even worn it yet!"

[Page 131]

Yehoshua Noach did was not taken aback by her request. He simply said to Faige: "Yes." We still had a few hours to make the flag. A few minutes later, Faige was standing there with a pair of scissors and she cut into the pretty, new blouse, as she began to sew up the red flag. That's how the red flag for the first street demonstration in 1919 in Gostynin was created.

The first time, the police did not interfere with the street demonstrations because in Gostynin they were French units.

As long as the French were in the city, the Polish police behaved in a civil and fine manner during home searches. They were looking for communist literature, and they searched without end. According to them all Jews were communists. When the French left the city, the police became aggressive and rough. They did everything they could to disrupt the street demonstrations, and very often beat the participants. During house searches they behaved terribly and shamefully.

With the rise of the parties, *Hatchiya* and its units dissolved.

The community kitchen was no longer necessary. The only thing that remained was the drama circle under Adam Domb's direction.

In the year 1919, help arrived for the Gostynin Jews from the Gostynin compatriots in America. Later, thanks to American aid, the non–profit fund [*gemilas chesed*] was set up, that helped many Jews with interest free loans.

A break in the activities took place in Jewish Gostynin with the outbreak of the Polish Russian war. The Bolshevik invasion pushed the community life of Gostynin into stagnation. Poland mobilized the military draft. The Jewish youth in general did not want to go into the Polish army, nor did they want to fight against the Russian Red Army. Many of the youth believed that Lenin and Trotsky would bring the ultimate salvation.

[Page 132]

At the height of the war, in the summer of 1920, Yakov Miller, the cantor, who was beloved by all the Jewish residents, left Gostynin and went to America.

At the beginning of 1921, Rav Silman, the Rav of Gostynin, died. When the city calmed down a little, it prepared to take on a new Rav. Then there was a fight between the *Chassidim* and the *Misnagdim* [opponents to the Chassidim]. The *Misnagdim* won. With the help of the Zionists, the Bielsker Rav, HaRav Bernshtajn, became the Rav of Gostynin.

HaRav Bernshtajn was a Zionist sympathizer. He was a charming man. His wife and his two daughters were also charming people and were always very happy to spend time with the people.

In 1921, Poland began taking care of the losses from the war that the Bolshevik invasion left behind. The Jews in Gostynin also resumed their interrupted work, reopening all the cultural, professional, and social organizations that had been closed over the last few years.

The Peretz Library

The Peretz Library was the pride of the town, and everyone, regardless to which party they belonged, was involved in its existence. Everyone did whatever was possible to increase the number of books.

At the opening of the Peretz Library, a general meeting was called. These meetings were called once a year and were charged with the task of electing a new administration and review committee. The administration comprised nine members; the review committee had three.

[Page 133]

The Administration and Review Committee of the Numberg Library in 1933

Seated from right: Lutke Matel, Manja Keller (Zarachyn), Refoel Burak, Shafrin, Ben Zion Morycz

Standing from right: Shmuel Matel, Chana Zajacs, Shalom Keller, Chaim Bresler, Yakov Leyb Pinczewski, Yechiel Meier Keller

[Page 134]

The elections were for budgetary allotments. The administration already had a plan worked out: 65% of the monies went to buy books – 25% for Polish books, 10% for Hebrew books. Still, the cost of Polish books exceeded the number of Yiddish books, because the Yiddish books were much more expensive.

There was peace in the Peretz Library until 1923, when the party conflicts began in town. No doubt, these began to affect the library as well.

Long–standing discussions were of no help. The factions separated, especially since it became clear that Gostynin was too small to have two Jewish libraries.

The *Poalei Zion*, left and right, joined up with the communists and other groups and began a bitter struggle against the *Bundist* group.

The *Bund* pulled out of the Peretz Library, and a few weeks later opened the Medem Library and a reading room in the *Bund* location on Kutno Street, opposite the gardens [*lustgarten*].

After a year, the officials of the Peretz Library saw that it was difficult for them to maintain the library, and impossible to buy new books. So peace negotiations began. The *Bund* conceded to close up the Medem Library and went back to the Peretz Library where the work continued as before. At that time, the library already had a few thousand books, which only increased in number.

When my wife Zisele and I left Gostynin and came to America, I maintained an ongoing correspondence with the comrades and friends of the Peretz Library, and helped them in whatever way possible. In 1933, I received the photographs of the members of the administration and review committee of the Numberg library. The name Peretz Library had to be changed because the Polish government closed down the Peretz Library.

[Page 135]

Reopening of the Professional Movement

The professional unions had one central committee where all the trades were represented. Each trade committee took care that the decisions of the business owners should be implemented and that the workers should be union members.

When there were no professional unions in Gostynin, a worker would labor for endless hours a day. School boys or girls, aside from learning the trade, would do all the dirty work for the boss. When the trades were organized, ...
an eight–hour workday was established and no one had to do any work other

than the work he had learned. When domestic workers organized themselves, a nine–hour day was also instituted and a six–day work week.

The "Bund" and "Tzukunft" ["Future"] in Gostynin (1928)

<u>**Seated from right:**</u> Feivish Lichtenshtajn, Refoel Burak, Shlomo Matel, Chumtche Kaufman, Moshe Morycz, Etke Rok, Yakov Leyb Pinczewski, Yisochar Matel, Lay'tche Makowski, Avrohom Zajacs, Chana Zajacs, Simcha Goldman, Zalman Motelinski, Lipe Pluczer

[Page 136]

That's how the work of the professional union was, where all parties were represented, cooperated peacefully, and everyone understood that the professional movement is not and did not have to be divided into parties.

In 1922, the communists began a struggle to usurp the unions or to destroy them. They came to a union meeting and sat there as if they were not the issue.

Since I was chairman of the union at that time, it was suspicious that everyone without exception suddenly showed up at the meeting. I quickly realized what the communists wanted to do and quickly removed the permit – that was granted by the government – from the table, as well as the rubber stamp with the list of members, and then put it all into my pocket. The communists noticed this and demanded that I put all of it back on the desk. I refused to comply with their demands, so they approached the desk to take the papers with force. But their way was blocked by: Shmuel Wolf Pinczewski, Avrohom Hershel Matel, Shmulik Matel, Shloime Zweighaft, Shimon Reuven Dzenczjol, Eliezer Flajsman, all the *Poalei Zionists*, and some others who did not allow the communists to approach me. When they couldn't get close, they locked the door and did not permit anyone to leave. Out of fear, many of the girls began to cry and scream. There was a great uproar.

The group that protected me, told me to leave through the window. They were sure that as soon as I would leave, everything would be over, because what those communists wanted was permit, the rubber stamp, and the list of members.

I did what they asked, left through the window, and went home. Things calmed down after that.

[Page 137]

They hadn't counted on such a defeat.

We continued with our work with the professional unions. We didn't bar anyone of the communists, but we kept an eye on their activities. And that's how it went until my wife and I left Gostynin.

"The Bund"

The *Bundist* organization was the largest in the city and had a great influence on the Jewish street.

The *Bund* had a building with a reading room on Kutno Street opposite the gardens. The youth group called *Zukunft* [Future], a children's group "*Skif*," and "*Morgenstern*," and a worker's society for physical education.

[Page 138]

The person, thanks to whom the *Bund* was a strong local organization, was Yakov Leyb Pinczewski. He brought a large number of youths to the *Bund*.

Later, before I left to America, there was a *Bundist* alderman, and my brother Shloime Matel and Yakov Leyb Pinczewski and Avrohom Zajacs were *Bundist* councilmen.

The organization continued to win over the youth that was very active. The organization conducted evening courses and education sessions between the *Zukunft* and the *Skif*.

Even though I am here in America, I never broke contact with all these friends in Poland.

The Bund and the Zukunft say farewell to Yisochar Matel

<u>**Seated from right:**</u> Yisochar Matel, Yakov Leyb Pinczewski, Lipe Pluczer, Zalman Aspe, Avrohom Zajacs, Beila Lewi, Refoel Burak

Other Parties

The *Poalei Zion* was situated on Zhikhlyn Street. In the same location there was a club where one could get a drink and some food. The *Poalei Zion* also had its own sports organization.

The director of the *Poalei Zion* was Shmuel Wold Pinczewski.

The Zionists had their organization and did their work for the benefit of the Land of Israel.

Their directors were Yakov Zarchyn, Krysnewski, Tuviah Jakubowycz, Iczik Bresler, Yakov Linderman, Avrohom Dovid Kuczinski, Moshe Morycz, and others.

Other than an organization, the *Agudists* had their own Bais Yakov school where the teacher was Krisa Shtern, the daughter of Shtern.

The communists became very powerful right after Poland's independence, illegal and insignificant in the later years.

All these parties also undertook timely city activities and general political tasks.

[Page 139]

Election in the City

The party quarrels became more embittered every day. And when the first Polish elections for the *Sejm* [Polish parliament] and city council approached, it became lively in town.

On the Jewish street, they put out candidate lists: the *Bund, Poalei Zion, Zionists*, and *Agudists*. There began a fight with election meetings and anger in each individual group. Every organization brought representatives from the organization's central office in Warsaw to their election meetings.

On the day of election to the city council, the whole town was anxious for the results. Late in the evening, when the votes were counted, it was the *Bund* that took first place with three candidates. The elected were: Shloime Matel, Yakov Leyb Pinczewski, and Avrohom Zajacs; the *Poalei Zion* had one candidate: Yehosua Matel; Zionists had one: Moshe Brakman; the Agudists had one: Yakov Lewi.

In general, it was a socialist city council that was elected. Twenty–four councilmen were elected: eleven from the Polish Workers Party (PPS); three from the *Bund*; one *Poalei Zionist*; seven from the Christian citizens; one *Zionist*; one *Agudist*.

The new city council elected a member from the PPS as mayor. From these three aldermen, one was from the PPS and the other from the *Bund*.

The first thing that the new council did was to pass a law that all residents of Gostynin that needed wood to heat their homes should get it for free from the city's forests, which Gostynin had in abundance. Very soon, wagonloads of wood were sent to all the poor residents, on the city's account.

The socialist city council passed other liberal laws, such as the decision to build the first workhouse in the city. This house was built at the edge of Dluga Street, behind the former barracks, where there used to be the elementary government schools.

[Page 140]

In general, there was a good mood among the entire democratic voiced population.

A Train in Gostynin

In the year 1923, the first train line opened in the city. The line was called Plock Lodz. The train went until Radziejow, and a bridge across the Vistula was to take the train to Plock.

In Gostynin, the train station was behind Epstajn – Beker's sawmills, on the eastern side of the "bachelor's path." One had access to it via Gombyner Street that was made longer. And that's how Gostynin became a city with a train station.

At the end of April 1928, my wife and I left Gostynin. We left behind a town filled with social activity, a town filled with lively Jews – a typical Jewish town in Poland.

Once there was a town called Gostynin; Gostynin is no longer. A piece of Jewish life was cut off. In the hearts and thoughts of those compatriots who remained alive, the town and her Jews will remain alive forever.

[Page 141]

The Joint (Distribution Committee) Action

by Shlomo Gostynski

Translated by Pamela Russ

Shlomo Gostynski

The Germans, more and more, removed all sorts of grains and life's necessities from Poland, and that which they left behind for the starving people was carefully controlled by the government. People had no food, and this took its toll on the health of the residents in the cities and in the towns, especially on the poor class of the Jewish sector. Everywhere, epidemics raged. Many died as victims of the typhus epidemic. In the large cities, Warsaw, Lodz, the destruction was not as evident as in the smaller towns, where everyone lived as one family. If one died of typhus, the entire town mourned and cried for the victim.

In a town such as our Gostynin, where the typhus epidemic ripped away tens of victims, the destruction was fearfully huge. The town administration and the magistrate had to extend their aid activities. In a house on Dluga Street, the magistrate set up a hospital specifically for typhus patients; on Pobteczne Street, they changed over Yakov Matil's house into a clinic, especially for the Jewish sick.

There was practically no house without a patient. Everyone lived with the thought that he was a candidate to become sick.

In the town, they began to regard the group "*Linat Hatzedek*" [aid society] differently. Before, they used to look at the organization as company for the youth, whose entire job consisted of dressing up on Purim, and having several gatherings a year for their own honor. But in truth, *Linat Hatzedek* provided great help for the sick. The group would help the poor sick people with money or with medicine. Their greatest assistance was when one of them would come to keep an eye on the sick person throughout the night. That enabled the household, the sick person's family, to rest and then the next day they could continue with their normal daily life. Now when typhus and dysentery were raging, *Linat Hatzedek*, under the directorship of my friend Yosel Gonshor, organized and extended its activities.

[Page 142]

Linat Hatzedek in Gostynin

<u>**Standing from the right:**</u> Feivish Lichtenstajn, Shmuel Keller, Chana Zajacs, Shmuel-Boruch Matil

<u>**Seated from the right:**</u> Yisroel Zelig Kuczinski, Yosef Gonshor, Yitzchok Izak Gerst, Shlome Matil, Henoch Kuczinski,

<u>**Bottom:**</u> Yakov Sarna, Boruch Meyer Matil

Gonshor pulled in the volunteer work of young people, who helped out greatly the hard hit families.

I would like to describe the incident with my friend Shmuel Chaim Hode's. He was not a member of the *Linat Tzedek*, but he nonetheless wanted to help take care of the sick. But he was too young for this work, and no matter how we pleaded with him to take on other work, he remained fixed in his wishes. Tragically, he contracted typhus and he himself died from it.

The relationship between the town and *Linat Tzedek* changed dramatically. The group became completely respected. Everyone gave their deepest thanks to the tireless deeds of my energetic friend Yosel Gonshor. (In the years of the Holocaust, he and his entire family died in the Warsaw ghetto.)

* * *

In the middle of winter 1917, a representative of the American Jewish Joint Distribution Committee came to Gostynin from Warsaw. He had been working there for a while. I don't know if the representative of the Joint had other things to take care of in Gostynin, but I remember well that his main goal was to find out how many Jews there were in town who would need help for the upcoming Passover, in the traditional campaign of *"Maos Chitin"* [donating food for the holidays: matzo, wine, etc.].

At that time, Jewish parties and organizations in Poland were already able to operate legally. Even in towns such as Gostynin, the parties were already all organized, some with more and some with fewer members. The Joint representative began to negotiate with these organized parties, to establish a united committee that should take charge of the assistance campaign. It turns out that in time, the Joint set up an assistance campaign in Gostynin through private individuals, who distributed Joint monies in a wrong and simply dishonest way. The organizational part of this committee was set by the Joint representative through the Local Council [*gemina*]. The synagogue supervisor [*dozor* or *gabbai*], Noteh Matil, permitted a notice to be posted in the synagogue and the *Beis Medrash* saying that the first meeting of the party representatives would be held on Monday, in the hall of the Local Council.

[Page 144]

On Shabbath and Sunday, the town was on wheels [everyone was all excited and busy]. Every party, every court, tried to present their best delegate to this planned committee in order to earn the prestige of the Gostynin Jewish people.

The chairman of the first meeting in the Council was the Joint representative. The Council was represented by Noteh Matil and Hershel Alberstajn; the delegates from the Zionist organization were Avrohom Dovid Kuczinski and Yekel Linderman; the People's Party, although small in number, also sent two representatives: V. Shafran and Dovid Gliksberg; the Orthodox: Yitzchok Shtern and Shmuel Meyer Bruzdowski; from the Poalei Zion: Dovid Levi and the writer of these lines [Shlomo Gostynski]. The Bund did not send any delegate, because at that time the Bund declined to collaborate on any work with the Council. The Joint representative requested that all those present should sign a declaration that each person was bearing the responsibility for the entire job of the committee. Yitzchok Shtern and Hershel Albershtajn declined to put their signature, but they nonetheless remained on the committee because everyone vouched for their honesty. That's how the representatives of the Gostynin Jewish parties and groups constituted the new assistance committee. It was decided with the Warsaw messenger [the Joint representative] that in order that the Joint should know how much flour for matzo Gostynin would need, the committee should send a detailed list to Warsaw of all their needs.

Three days later, the second meeting of the committee took place at the Rav's. At that time, the Zionists withdrew their representative Avrohom Dovid Kuczinski and instead put up the delegate Tuvia Jakubowycz, who was more popular with the Jewish residents. Noteh Matil opened the meeting and suggested that they should elect the Rav as the permanent chairman of the committee. I put forward the candidacy of Tuvia Jakubowycz as the representative of the largest party in Gostynin. But Jakubowycz declined in deference to the Rav. The party representatives brought detailed lists of those who needed assistance. But it turned out that the lists were not exhaustive. Yakov Linderman suggested that on Shabbath in *shul* and in the *Beis Medrash*, they should let it be known that anyone who needs financial aid should sign up in the Council or with one of the committee members. The suggestion was taken on with an amendment by Dovid Levi, that it should be stated in writing, absolutely stressed, that this is not about charity or about handouts, but it is strictly a gift that our brothers in America sent over, and no one has to be embarrassed to come and give his name and receive his share of the gift.

[Page 145]

It's worthwhile to describe a typical incident that occurred at this point, the first of a lineup of later disagreements and difference of opinions in the history of the assistance committee. The representative of the Orthodox, Meyer Bruzdowski, expressed himself in opposition to Yakov Linderman's suggestion, saying that "It's not nice that we should show the Council how to write an announcement, and in general, the youth in the committee have to sit and listen, and not want to be the leaders." The *dozor*, Noteh Matil, interrupted Bruzdowski's speech, and said to him that he does not have to assume the honor of the Council unto himself, and the most important thing was that the assistance activity was not coming from the community and no one will be more worthy than anyone else in front of the committee. Dovid Levy requested that the chairman should underline that all the representatives in the committee, without any age differentiation, have equal rights, and he demanded that Shmuel Meyer Brudzowski pardon himself for his insulting words towards the younger committee members. For the purpose of peace, the chairman tried to diminish the incident; he said that it did not pay do get insulted if someone jumps out with some words. In the end, everyone wants to do a good thing – to distribute the assistance from the Joint honestly. He asked the *dozor* to get the announcement so that they could send the list to Warsaw the following week. And with that, the meeting adjourned.

[Page 146]

Meanwhile, the existence of the committee became known in the city, and of the announcement as well. Many became really excited. Representatives of the committee went from house to house and noted the number of members in each family. It happened that some registered with two or even more committee representatives with the hope that they would get a double share of their promised products. Yidel the watercarrier's wife, *"Potje Minje,"* a Jewish woman, well known in Gostynin, came to the writer of these lines, with lots of complaints about fairness. "How can it be? Where is the wine for the four cups [for the Passover seder]? And meat, fish, and other things?" They told her that all these things were under my responsibility, and in a loud voice, she demanded that I give these things to her. There were also incidents of lending out children in order to receive larger portions of flour. This went on not out of dishonesty, but out of great poverty that existed in the town.

**Founders, managing, and auditing committee of the *Gemilas Chesed* funds
[non-profit, interest free loan organizations] in Gostynin**

Moshe Ziger, Y.M. Krusnewski, Yisroel Meyer Rusak, Efraim Matil, Moshe Matil, Berish
Zhikhlinski, Moshe Morycz, Tuvia Jakubowycz, Ben Zion Keller, Yakov Zhikhlinski, M.B.
Zandman

There was also a great tumult in the parties. Everyone looked to get monies
from the party funds, so they wanted their list of those who needed help for
Passover to be longer than that of the other party's. There were really those
who put their names on the list not because they needed help, but just to do a
favor for a prestigious party man. Factions were set up. Mordechai, Boruch
Matil's, who always felt that the Council was adequate, and that "We don't
need these parties and the youth who want to grab away everything and offer
their opinions on everything," played the leading role in the opposition. His
main opponent was Chaim Leyb Maskal. He proposed the argument that
"We've already seen what has happened in the former years, when the wealthy
businessmen squandered the community's money and the poor had nothing to
eat. They didn't even give them potatoes."

This dispute, as usual in Gostynin, took place in front of Meyer'l Burak's
restaurant where the water carriers would meet. The main spokesman was
Mendel the water carrier. He well represented his colleagues Beryl, Judel, and

Gershon. To this business, would also come Laibe the sand carrier and his son Izak the day-laborer. Mordechai Solmanowycz ran the show. He would deride Mordechai, Boruch's, saying, "It won't help him. The youth will win this time, because they're right." With that, Mordechai Solmanowycz would turn directly to those who were standing around him: "What's wrong? Is Tuvia Jakubowycz not good enough for you? And Yekel Linderman does not have enough respectability for you? He needs his aristocracy. One of ours is not good enough for him."

[Page 148]

Mordechai, Boruch's Matil, did not hold back with an answer. He would talk about the Local Council as if he himself was a *dozor* [overseer of the Jewish community], and he would say: "Without a doubt, the Local Council would give a Mark for each person in the family. What difference would that make to you? But if they don't want the *dozores* [overseers] to have any opinions, then they won't give you any money. And since when were the Zionists concerned for the poor? Just give them Palestine and they'll forgive you for everything right away."

In this type of noisy crowd, there was this small person, who would answer to everyone. Speaking was difficult for him. He would stutter and make long pauses between one word and another. But what he said was always relevant to the issue, thought out, and people would hear him out patiently. He possessed the skill of convincing [winning over] even an opponent who would debate with him. In particular, he felt very much at home when the issues were around the poor, unemployed people. His name was Wajnstajn; he was from Lodz. But he felt like a resident in Gostynin. In these verbal disputes, he would not discuss anything directly with Boruch's Mordechai, but would approach the people around him and ask: "Since when does the Local Council concern itself with the poor people in Gostynin? At the head of the Council are wealthy people, people who own houses and estates, and they have to represent the paupers who need help? Remember how it went in the earlier years. What did the Council do for the poor the entire year? Do the wealthy in Gostynin worry that the poor can't even buy for themselves, unfortunately, that which the Germans give from their ration cards?"

"We must have," Wajnstajn would say with great effort on each word, "our own representatives who should distribute the help honestly and according to the numbers in each family. As it says in the Ethics of Our Fathers [*Pirkei Avos*], "If I am not for myself, then who will be for me?" Those are the sorts of representatives they should have on their lists. Down with the dependence on the honesty of the wealthy! We must put our hands to the task!"

[Page 149]

At these words, Wajnstajn would take out a list from his breast pocket and show that there were already a number of families undersigned, and he would ask that the crowd listening there to him should sign the list and write down the number of people in their families. When Gershon the water carrier said that he had already signed the list of Ber Gonshor and Lipa Pluczer, then Wajnstajn would assure him that this was the same list as the worker's party, and Gershon would already worry that his daughter, who was not yet signed up on any list, should sign up on this list with Wajnstajn.

Understandably, the other parties did not sit idly by. They also worked hard to get large number of signatures on their lists. Krisnewski from the Zionists put in huge efforts. His main argument was that with the Zionists, the most prominent, wealthy men of Gostynin are partnered, and therefore, the poor people should only sign up with them. Apparently, the Zionists made the greatest efforts to have the largest number of names. They didn't do their work with any great noise, but discreetly, from person to person. As it later turned out, it seems that the masses were more loyal to the workers' party. The largest number of families had signed up with them, with the guarantee that the workers' party would take care of their interests better than the other party.

The meeting of the committee that took place on the Wednesday after that Shabbath, was from the onset, a stormy one. The party representatives had to put their cards down, showing the number of families who had signed up with them. On the Council's list, there were 25 families; on the workers' party, Poalei Zion, there were 37 families; on the Zionists' party's list there were 22; of the People's party there were 6; and on the Orthodox, there were only 5. Shmuel Brudzowksi, the representative of the Orthodox, explained that among the religious Jews many were embarrassed to ask for help. In total, the number of people who needed help was about 100 souls, and for a town the size of Gostynin, this was a pretty high percentage. Some of those who had signed up actually did have work, but did not earn enough to live.

[Page 150]

Dovid Levi suggested that the committee set up a commission of three members who should bear the responsibility of distributing the money and the flour. Tuvia Jakubowycz ignored the suggestion and put forth the question of who would distribute the money and flour when it arrived in Warsaw? The majority of the committee members expressed that the entire committee should be involved with the distribution of the help. The *dozor* Noteh Matil remarked that the distribution of money and flour is a time consuming job so that it would be better to designate two people for this task and then they should elect a commission that would supervise the job of those designated. He added that the Council would pay those designated for the task. With a majority of 8 to 3, the *dozor*'s suggestion was accepted. The *dozor* proposed Feivish Unger as one of those designated, and the other Yitzchok Volf Lomski. No one had any opposition to these two, and the suggestions were accepted.

It was a lot more difficult to elect a supervisory commission. Each party wanted to have their person on the commission. Noteh Matil made a fine gesture. He said that the commission should comprise only three, but that every committee member who would wish to work voluntarily with the commission should be committed to the work. Those elected were: Noteh Matil the *dozor*, Tuvia Jakubowycz, and Shloime Gostynski.

The Rav, as the chairman of the committee, remarked that the meeting had done an important job, but the committee members shouldn't think that once the commission of three had been selected, they were exempt from any work. But he proposed that the committee as a whole should undertake to do all possible work.

[Page 151]

Shafran, of the People's party, put the question to the committee that had a special secretary, of whether the secretary's work would be done by the Council's secretary. The *dozor,* Noteh Matil, replied that the Council would accept the decision of the majority, and he thinks that the Council secretary is familiar with the work. And the main thing was that there would be no further expenses. In the end, the committee accepted the suggestion of Tuvia Jakubowycz: The committee should select someone to officially record all decisions of the supervisory commission. As candidates for secretary, proposed were Yekel Linderman of the Zionists, and Dovid Levi of the Workers' party. For voting, the representative of the Orthodox, Shmuel Meyer Brudzowski, explained that he did not see what his group still had to do with this committee, since all the work was controlled by the Zionists. In order to avoid arguments, at the suggestion of the Zionists, H. Shafran, the representative of the smaller parties, was elected as the secretary of the committee.

The representative of the Orthodox, at that same meeting, requested that to the list of those who needed, should be added a designated sum for 20 anonymous families. There are – he explained – many families who don't want to come and ask for help, but they should be given help in the form of *Matan Be'seiser* [discreet donation]. This suggestion evoked a storm. They boiled and stewed and tossed around arguments and the participants were hot.

The youth just sat. The Council had to listen to voices of the parties. The sharp person left the social arena.

The committee distributed the help, without biases, objectively, and honestly.

The first Joint assistance project in Gostynin not only supported the poor, the impoverished, and the victims of the war, but also cemented and impacted the social life in the town.

[Page 152]

Our Youth Leaders

by Gershon Yudkowski (Israel)

Translated by Pamela Russ

Our Gostynin Jewish youth was in large numbers thoroughly infused with the ideals of Zionism and Jewish revival in the Land of Israel. The majority did not see any future for themselves in remaining in their hometowns or in the cities and towns in Poland, where the government's regime always tried to enforce a more difficult life for the Jewish citizens. The Jewish population of Gostynin sympathized with the Zionist youth and gave them all means of expression to their sentiments.

Let us mention the leaders of our youth that planted these holy ideals into their hearts. With the fire of their impassioned souls they lit sparks of idealism and commitment into every single youth who stood in the circle of their influence. They built institutions in the city, built a generation that was prepared to sacrifice themselves for Zionist ideals. Thanks to their activity, a number of Gostyniner saved themselves from the last destruction and, incorporating themselves into the camp of pioneers [*chalutzim*], left their old homes and came to the Land of Israel to build the country and build themselves up as well.

Let us mention the youth–leader Y.M. Krusznewski, of blessed memory. He was the real leader in Gostynin. He was a man who didn't chase honor, but everyone had the greatest respect for him. He was always loyal and vigilant for our movement, and brought help to each person according to his needs. He himself desired to come to Israel – and more than once he explained to the Jews of Gostynin that there is no future in the *galut* [exile]. We are only helping, he would say, to build up foreign countries, that's where we are directing all our energies and potential – and all our possessions will fall into their hands. It is time – he said – to think about our own fate.

[Page 153]

At the time when his other friends were trying to have their children attain some "substantial goal" in life, become certified professionals, he was proud of the fact that his own son was a working man in Israel, a military man and citizen in the country that was to become an independent Jewish land.

Y.M. Krusnewski earlier on, foresaw the destruction of Polish Jewry. He helped every individual immigrate to the Land of Israel.

The youth leaders of all the regions – from the year 1915 to 1920

Seated from right to left: Hershel Moricz, Shloime Matil, Yakov Sarna, Mordechai Reuven Moskol, Feivish Likhtenstajn

Standing from right to left: (unknown name), Zalman Bressler, Yehoshua Domb, Yehoshua Matil, Yechiel Yehoshua Ploczer, Shmuel Keller, Ziskind Goldman, Waserman, Shmuel Boruch Hodes, Simcha Gilman

[Page 154]

... He remained a guide for us, and a pure Zionist activist. May his memory remain pure and holy for us.

* * *

Yakov Linderman was a real Jewish Torah scholar. He possessed a golden heart and a boundless love for every Jew. He always held long and profound speeches and wanted to show that Zionism is a people's movement and an uplifted way of life. He saw the importance of having a Zionist be at the head of all types of Jewish institutions – economic, cultural, as well as socio-political. All the efforts of Polish Jews – including the Gostyniner – must go in this direction to prepare the youth for a new life in the Jewish land. All the years, he dreamed of immigrating to Israel, but it was not fated for him. May his memory remain dear to us.

* * *

Zieger, of blessed memory, had the reputation of a man of extensive knowledge, and his cleverness radiated from him. But he was opposed to using terror tactics in the country. More than once, however, he agreed that only with weapons would they be able to create an independent Land of Israel – and there will come a period of great immigration to the land. May his memory remain eternal.

* * *

Gad Zhikhlinski was a talented and thinking person. He was an opponent of compromise. Only with power – he felt – can one win the struggle and carve out a victory. In the later years, he suffered through a difficult illness. He made efforts to remove the youths' apathy and indifference. The youth must sacrifice itself for the national independence in the Land of Israel – only in that way can there be a victory. He dreamed of remaining active in the underground groups of the land – but it was not fated for him to achieve this goal. He died with all our other martyrs.

[Page 155]

* * *

There should also be mentioned here the person who was in another camp, who did not believe in the Zionist ways, but was deeply infused with love for the Jewish people and their culture:

Yakov Leyb Pinczewski, a man with radiant eyes and sparkling, original ideas. He was raised in the period of revolutions and inhaled the theories of socialism – and he remained loyal to the *Bund*. Sometimes, he became excited with his own unusual way of thinking. He loved Jews just the way they were, with their fate and struggles. He was a spirited follower of folk–culture, of the Yiddish language and Yiddish literature.

Just as the entire *Bund* in Poland, he fiercely defended the "now" [present] and struggled and hoped that Jews would be given their full rights to live, work, and earn a living in Poland. He was the first martyr during the liquidation of the Jews in Gostynin, and was part of the tragic fate of the Jews in Poland.

* * *

Let us remember them all, these idealistic youth leaders, who served as models in their devotion for Jewish ideals and who taught the Jewish youth in Gostynin to live a full, Jewish life.

[Page 156]

The Poalei–Zion Youth in Gostynin

by Shlomo Cwajghaft (Israel)

Translated by Pamela Russ

Shlomo Cwajghaft

Our town of Gostynin totaled 400 Jewish families, about 15% of the general population, and excelled in all areas of cultural, social, and political life. The older generation was still seeped in the traditions of former times, later under the influence of the great Torah leader Rebbe Yechiel Meyer Lifszycz, of blessed memory. This is about the time before World War One. How did Jewish children receive their spiritual education at that time, and who were the educators then – the well–known teachers, generally without pedagogical skills, who because they needed to earn a living, had to teach children. And it was known under what conditions the children would spend their time from morning until late in the evening, in these so–called schools. This *cheder* [school] was the living quarters for the teacher and his family that sometimes totaled from 8–10 souls. And together with the young boys, they generally had all to be in one room. The children were there for 10 hours a day – in the summer without air, and in winter without the necessary light. That's where they received their spiritual education. I would like to mention here several teachers who are definitely known to Gostynin compatriots, such as Leybish Tremski, Leizer Melamed and his son Yosel – the teaching job went by inheritance from father to son – Avrohom Meyer Frajszman, and Leybel Zizhyk.

[Page 157]

It was big news when the well–known teacher and educator Rabbi Yonah Borukh Katz decided to open a modern, Hebrew school under the name "*Torah ve'Daas*" ["Torah and Knowledge"], or as it was called then "*Cheder Metukan*" ["the Improved *Cheder*"]. This school already had a different appearance than a regular "*cheder*." There were two bright rooms; each pupil had his permanent seat, and did not change his seating place without the permission of the teacher. In the corner of each room there was a large blackboard with chalk, as well as a special place for the teacher – a "*katedra*" [like a throne in a cathedral]. They learned how to write and read Hebrew, grammar, *Tanakh* [*Torah, Neviim, Ketuvim*; Torah, Prophets, Writings], and math. The older students also studied Russian and Polish. Other than that, they also studied music and sport. A bell let everyone know the times for the beginning and the end of the learning sessions. Often, we would go for walks outside the city, in the forest (*dibankes* [oak trees]) and in other places and very much enjoyed the beautiful nature and plush pathways with which Gostyninwas exceptional. The pupils organized performances on Chanukah and Purim. On the national and religious holidays, the teacher would explain the background [and purpose] of the holiday, but at the same time he would explain the holiday as nationalist Zionist. In the school, there was also a children's library under the name of "*Perakh*" [blossom]. The children would borrow books from there to read.

[Page 158]

But one fine day, Reb Borukh Katz closed down the school that had already earned itself a fine name. He went over to Kutno, and acquired a teacher's position in the Jewish gymnasium. The appeals from the parents and students did not help at all. Without having any choice, the students had to spread out in many different directions. Some went back to the *cheders*, and some to the general public schools [folk schools], and a large number went over to the government gymnasium. Until then, the Jews avoided the gymnasium, especially those who were forced to study and write on Shabbath. But in an instant, the times changed. Other winds began to blow. The youth began to long for education. Many Jewish students entered into the gymnasium. In the lower classes, 30–40 percent of the students were Jewish.

The Poalei Zion Committee in Gostynin (1932)

<u>**Seated from right to left:**</u> Efraim Matil, Shlomo Cwajghaft, Pesse Izbiczki, Eliezer Flajszman;

<u>**Standing from right to left:**</u> Gershon Matil and Ezra Matil.

The teacher of the Jewish religion in the government gymnasium was Professor Yakov Zarkhyn, who was at the same time director of the Jewish people's school. Professor Zarkhyn himself was not religious, but he was a nationalistic Jew, a committed Zionist. And just like Rabbi Katz, he also raised the children with a Zionist spirit. Along with religion, he also taught Zionism. He infused the holidays with a national, Zionist spirit. And on the national Polish holidays, when the Christian students celebrated their holidays of independence, Professor Zarkhyn would assemble the Jewish students in the synagogue and explain to them – along with the Zionist activists, such as Krusznewski, Linderman, Jakubowycz, and others – the point of the holiday and did not forget to mention and underscore the duties that stand before the Jewish nation, and their efforts for national liberation and their own country.

[Page 159]

Together with the nationalist moment that began to grow within the youth
and the students, also began the first wave of socialist thought. The pupils of
the higher classes, Moshe Klajnbort and Shloime Krancz, who were
ideologically close to socialism, were practically speaking the pioneers in
spreading socialist thought among the Jewish students. They established a
circle [discussion group] to familiarize the youth with the history of the
workers' movement. All this came about in the context of a sports group that
played football. This was in the final years before World War One. With a ball
in hand, we students would stroll twice a week into the forest, to the oak trees,
and with an interest in hearing the lectures of Krancz and Klajnbart.

Our student circle, which completely absorbed the teachings of Zionism
through the teachers Katz and Zarkhyn, at the same time also became familiar
with the idea of socialism – and the circle was in fact the seed of the future
Poalei Tzion movement in Gostynin.

With the formation of the Polish Republic, and at the same time after the
pogrom in Yaffa, when Yosef Khaim Brenner and his friends were murdered, a
group of sympathizers of workers of the Land of Israel, decided to establish a
Poalei Tzion party. The initiators were: Shmuel Wolf Pinczewski, Avrohom
Hersh Matil, Eliezer Flajsman, Efraim Matil, Sender Gerst, and Yehoshua
Matil. I was one of the friends invited to the gathering at the location of the
"Agudah," at the home of Yitzkhok Sarna on Kutner Street. We were the *avant
garde* ones that recruited other friends and prepared the ground–breaking
meeting that already met at its own location at the house of Mendel Bagno on
Olsowe 1.

[Page 160]

Until the establishment of the Poalei Tzion group there was no real party
life in Gostynin. All the social work was concentrated around philanthropic
institutions, around the Y.L. Peretz library, and later to a certain extent,
around the professional unions. Gostynin was exceptional in its beautiful
tradition that in the years of the intense party struggles, also affected the
classes of the Jewish population and preserved the wholesomeness of the
opposing relationships.

The Poalei Tzion did intensive work in all areas. Much was done for Keren
Kayemet, Keren Hayesod Letovat, the fund for the workers of the Land of
Israel. The personalities of the committee for culture and labor were: Shmuel

Wolf Pinczewski, Yehoshua Matil and his wife Ruzhke Rozenberg, Professor Yitzkhok Shor from Kutno, Shloime Neiman. They opened evening courses for the youth who for all kinds of reasons did not attend school.

The Poalei Tzion Committee in Gostynin

Seated from right to left: Kreuczer, Eliezer Flajsman, Shmuel Wolf Pinczewski, Efraim Matil, Dzhencziol

Standing from right to left: Vava Morycz, Kreuczer, Shimon Reuven Dzhencziol, unknown name, Avrohom Mikholski, Shmulek Matil

[Page 161]

In the city council and in the Jewish community, the Poalei Tzion was represented by the comrades Yehoshua Matil and Sender Gers, who energetically defended the interests of the Jewish population.

In the last years, on the eve of the First World War, a unit of *Hechalutz* ["the Pioneers" training Jewish youth who planned to settle in the Land of Israel] was established in Gostynin, with a *Hakhshara* [preparing and education for resettlement] point for two groups of ten comrades. There they received training for collective work and life in the Land of Israel. Several of this *Hakhshara* group, after difficult experiences in the Nazi murder camps and the Russian exile in Siberia – finally found their way to the independent State of Israel.

[Page 162]

"Freedom" and the "Red Scouts"

by Shmuel Wolf Pinczewski

Translated by Pamela Russ

Shmuel Wolf Pinczewski

1923. The youth at that time in Gostynin was governed by the "Bund" and by the assimilated communists that grouped themselves among the youth that was studying in the Polish gymnasium.

Finally a small number of youths, who were soaked through with the ideals of Zionism and democratic socialism, succeeded to break through the anti-Zionist ice that was blocking the road forward. Gradually, we won over new friends to our ideas. We rented a small room and we gathered there in the evenings. We were active in Zionist funds, in the elections to the congress, and in other activities.

At the founding of *"Freiheit"* ["Freedom"] in Poland, all of us affiliated ourselves with the Poalei Tzion (Tz. S.) party. Right then, we set up a unit of the *Freiheit* for younger children. In the course of time, we also established the *"Red Scouts."* When the city council elections approached we had our first opportunity to step forward with our words for the workers' Land of Israel.

[Page 163]

Communist Youth

by Sh. Makowski (Belgium)

Sh. Makowski

Translated by Pamela Russ

The resonance of the October Revolution in Russia carried also to us in the town. Some of the youth that was studying in the Gostynin gymnasium, especially in the student circle, took upon themselves the mission to set up an organizational framework for the leftist–leaning youth. Every Shabbath, groups of youth gathered in the surrounding forests of Gostynin. These groups consisted primarily of the poor, but also attracted some of the wealthier youth.

With this establishment of the professional needle union, a legal opportunity arose for open economic and cultural work – the communist party in Poland was still illegal. Under the direction of the communists, the tailors, who were mainly young apprentices, went on strike. Reports and lectures were organized with political and literary themes, along with discussions. Kettle evenings [evenings of discussion with tea, etc.] went until late in the night. They collected money for the illegal international Red Help Fund that helped the victims of the reactionary Polish regime. Mokowski was the secretary.

The youth that believed in revolution were idealists. They had to bear the Polish government, the police, and no less from the naive, homey, small town mindedness, that could not tolerate the audacity of the Jewish young men and women as they spited authority, be it anti–Semitic and reactionary.

[Page 164]

The independent thoughts nonetheless still embraced a portion of the Gostyniner Jewish youth.

The Committee of the Professional Unions in Gostynin

<u>Seated from right to left:</u> Lieba Mikholski, Yehoshua Apelas, Hersh Kharkowycz

<u>Standing from right to left:</u> Pluczer, Itkowycz, Nisinowycz, Rabinowycz, Khaya Ospe

[Page 165]

The Princess, Gostynin

by Rose Shoshana

Translated by Pamela Russ

Rose Shoshana

In the holy memory of my mother, Hinda Brawarska-Mozer, who was killed by the Hitler murderers.

My mother was a widow for many years, and did not want to marry a second time. She spent her young years, dark and alone, because she didn't want to give us – her little children, a stepfather.

Only when I was a young girl and chose to marry the publisher Lazar Kahan, may his murderers' blood be avenged, did my mother marry a Gostynin resident. And so she became a Gostyniner, and that's how I became tied to Gostynin.

I fell in love with the beautiful, clean town of Gostynin. I remember until today the lovely and powerful impression the town made on me the first time that I came to Gostynin. The cleanliness of the houses and the streets, the beautifully dressed women – completely different from the other provincial towns. Like a queen's daughter, a princess, is how Gostynin looked in my eyes. And as I would come there more often, I was sure that I had not been wrong, and that my first impressions had been right.

Gostynin was a lot more intelligent than other Jewish towns of the same size that time in Poland.

[Page 166]

Maybe this was because there was a gymnasium and officer school in Gostynin. The city was full of students from the surrounding cities, and even from larger cities. Students came to Gostynin to study in the gymnasium because it was easier to get in there than in other larger cities.

Gostynin actually also earned a livelihood from these students. They were given board, food was cooked for them, and the cooks even had a chance to eat these meals as well.

From right: Rose Shoshana, her sister Chava Bresler (who was killed), her mother Hinda Mozer from Gostynin, her grandmother Chana Jakobowicz, and her brother Philip

I see that large gymnasium on Kutner Sreet, a building that would have been proud to stand on any street in the largest city in Poland. Kutner Street could have told many tales, because it stretched for many streets behind the city where it turned into a highway, covered on both sides by dense trees that hid the deepness of the forest in which the youth loved to stroll.

How romantic and beautiful was the Kutner highway on a Shabbos afternoon when the city's youth would go for walks. The Gostynin forest could also have told many tales about all the discussions that took place there, and about lucky and unlucky love. We were young, young with emotion, and yet we were hunched over with the yoke of seriousness. The youth of that time, and that includes those of Gostynin, was filled with obligations and responsibilities; they were not as carefree as today's youth.

[Page 167]

The strolls on the "mountain of mountains," the long, black peat fields, the four-cornered trimmed pieces of peat (heating material with which they used to heat the ovens) that were spread out across the fields to dry, accompany me without end when I remember myself in Gostynin.

Now I see them, the temperamental youth, during discussions about the theater and about other problems.

Now I see them the religious Jews, during heated discussions about politics, as they are spread out in a wide row walking after prayers on Shabbos in the wide open market place.

Now I see her, the large, beautiful, proud *shul* ... and I see them, the proud Jews.

I see before my eyes the amateurs from Gostynin who loved the theater more than life, who sacrificed themselves for art, fanatics about Jewish theater ....

Jewish theater was like air for them, like sustenance, without which one could not exist. They worked tirelessly, rehearsed, studied, and performed in the theater. And they performed well! This was the best amateur troupe from all the surrounding areas, and was there anything they did not perform? Everything was from the better literature, such as: Tchirikov's "Jews," Ansky's "The Dybbuk," Kobrin's "Yankel Boila," Ibsen's "Ghosts," Psibisewski's "Snow," Sholom Asch's "With the Stream," and Yakov Gordon's "God, Man, and the Devil."

And if they only sensed that a professional actor was somewhere in the area, they did everything possible to ensure that this person would come to perform with them, and he ultimately did.

[Page 168]

Actually, once they found out that I was visiting my mother and delegations came right over saying that I had to perform with them. My answer that I was only here for a short time made no difference, and soon they put us all to work.

I see before my eyes Adam Domb, who had a photography studio in Gostynin that served more as a meeting place for the amateurs rather than a place of livelihood.

A customer enters, wants to take pictures, but Domb has no time, he first has to end his discussion with us.

When I performed Pinskin's "Gabri and the Women," with the Gostynin amateur group, Domb played the male lead roles with me. Later, Adam Domb actually became a professional actor. He left the photography studio that gave him a good livelihood and joined WIKT (Warsaw Jewish Acting Theater), and then later the Vilna acting troupe.

And now I see the provocatively beautiful Pela Sarna, and Zandman and Keller and Yakov Leyb Motel and Shloime Gostinski – all, all of them worked for the performance with all their soul, those on stage and those off the stage.

And Yakov Gostinski, what didn't he do for the benefit of the theater! And all the others whose names I cannot remember who always supported the goal of improving the Jewish theater in Gostynin and in the surrounding areas wherever they went.

Now I see the theater, the firemen's coach house on Gombyner Street not far from the *shul*, a guardhouse, very primitive, but the beloved Jews would flow there in masses to the Yiddish performances.

When I came for a second time to visit Gostynin, and at that time there was also the famous singer and performer Yakov Kelter, well, would the stubborn Gostynin amateurs miss an opportunity like that? They got both of us, and to deny them, these beloved Gostyniners, was impossible ... so we performed in several one-act plays (understandably without honorarium). Again, they were exceptional both in their acting and in their commitment and love for this project.

And now I see before me the beloved Chana Bagno, Shmuel Keller, and others in Mark Ornstein's "The Eternal Song," and in Peretz's "After the Burial" that we performed at that time.

And this youth was not only busy with activities of the theater, but they were also busy with other cultural activities and projects.

I remember well the warmth of the Gostynin Jews also towards the Polish speakers. The Jews respectfully attended the speeches that were brought from Warsaw and Lodz. My husband as well, the deceased publisher Lazar Kahan, was among those who came to Gostynin with a presentation. How hungry they were for worldly knowledge, they swallowed ideas of Strindberg and his views about which my husband spoke.

Only memories remain ....

[Page 170]

Gostyniner Jews

by Yitzhak Zandman (Israel)

Translated by Pamela Russ

Sometimes one thinks that there was no yesterday at all. You never had any parents, no brothers or sisters, no wife and children, no friends and acquaintances – you think that you were born from a stone...

Here I am going back and stepping on Gostynin ground. I am taken over by a chill, by a shudder. No one is left. The murderers eliminated everyone. And a longing takes over you for what once was. You see the people, the shops, the houses, the homes, and you want to eternalize each voice, each nuance. The cheerful laughter of children greet me, a father's worry as he admonishes his children with love, the tender whispers of a loving couple; I would eternalize the groaning of an invalid, the cries of the unfortunates, the rhythmic melody of those studying a page of *gemara* or a chapter of *Tanach*.

* * *

It's the year 1946, after my return to Gostynin. No one – I meet no one. And my ear catches no Jewish sound, does not pick up any familiar voice.

There is the train station – the appearance is the same as it was. The railroad street did not change either. But on Gombyner Street I immediately see the gruesome changes. There is no trace of Jewish life in Gostynin. The *Beis Medrash*, the small *shul*, erased – there is no *shul*, the Rav's house, the municipal office, the ritual baths.

I go around, deep in my thoughts and mourn over the gruesome destruction. Here was our *Beis Medrash*.

[Page 171]

The Beis Medrash

A large wooden building with big windows looked out onto Gombyner Street. Inside, long tables were set out with even longer benches, and opposite that, there was a bookcase on the wall filled with religious books (*seforim*). The podium stood at the eastern wall – and several steps up directed you to the Holy Ark. Right in the middle of the Beis Medrash you could see the table used for the people [who had been called up to the reading of the Torah]. On both sides there were steps for those people going up and for those going down. At that table, they honored many congregants who had been called up to the Torah reading. In that same place, the Rav delivered his Rosh Hashona sermons just before the blowing of the *shofar* and then on Shabbos *Tshuva* [the Shabbos between Rosh Hashona and Yom Kippur]. From that same table, other rabbinic speakers that were passing through penetrated the hearts of the Beis Medrash Jews with their sharp words as they called the congregants to repentance. From that same place, there were also speeches about the rebirth of Zionism. Also from there were the protests against the world for the Jewish problems and pains, as well as eulogies for scholarly, true sages of Torah.

The uncrowned (?) manager of the Beis Medrash was Michel Ber (Pluczer) the beadle (*shamash*). He was a little taller than average, and had a long, white beard. His eyes were hung over by dense, pitch-black eyebrows. He opened and locked up the Beis Medrash. On his order – after a bang on the podium – they began the prayers. At the call of the *shamash* – again after a bang on the podium – the *Baal Tefila* (one who led the prayers) began and allowed his voice to be heard. The *shamash* called individuals up to the Torah reading, and took care of the pledges as well.

In spite of his harsh glare, that sometimes threw fear onto the children, he really had a mild character, played with the children, and told them enjoyable stories. Not once did he remind me that thanks to him I was made a Jew in the right time, on the eighth day after birth. And he told me all the details about this: I was born a weak and thin soul. "Experienced men" said that the circumcision (*bris*) should wait until I had more strength. But Michel Ber, the *shamash*, of blessed memory, ... gave out the order: "Go ahead and cut! He will be a young man with strong bones ..." And that's exactly how it was.

[Page 172]

Outside, on the street, through the walls of the Beis Medrash, one could hear the *gemara* melody of the young boys who were learning, even though in the later years they were small in number. But there were always students who made sure that the voice of learning Torah would be heard.

Directly opposite the entrance of the Beis Medrash was the Rav's home. The first room in this house served as the room for the Jewish court.

Reb Yitzchok Meyer Borenstajn, of blessed memory, was the last Rav of Gostynin. He was of average size, a little bit full, with a handsome dark, wide beard peppered with silver hair. When walking in the street, he would carry a dark brown cane with a metal white handle.

In the *shul* courtyard, when this Rav eulogized the deceased, he tore apart the hearts of the mourning Jews, with tears pouring down everyone's faces. On the Days of Awe, when the Rav led the prayers, the hearts of the congregants were very moved.

His sons, Moshe Mordechai and Gedalia, accompanied him during prayers like a choir. Gedalia had definite musical skill. Moshe Mordechai did not remain in Gostynin, but he tried to live his life in the larger cities.

The Rav's daughters, Chana and Gittel, were both brunettes and very charming. One married Falek Landberg, the editorial official of the Poalei Agudas Yisroel organization and one of its main people. The Rav's daughters would elicit a sigh of longing from the pious young men who were in the *chassidim* room that was part of the Rav's house. The daughters' singing and laughing often mingled with the melodies of those who were learning.

The Shtiebel

As in all the cities and towns in Poland, the Jewish community of Gostynin was also divided into different colors. There were separate groups of the Agudah individuals, Poalei Agudah, and even the more extreme religious people. We had Zionists of all kinds. There were Bundists, Folkists, and even Communists. There was also not a shortage of assimilated Jews and regular Jews from the whole year. But the difficult challenges of the Jews united them all. The various decrees from the Polish government hurt everyone, and danger hung over everyone's head, regardless of what type of Jew he was.

[Page 173]

The *shtiebel* was the natural haven for the *Chassidic* circles. A large majority of them supported the religious party of the Agudas Yisroel. Among the *Chassidim* were also followers of the Mizrachi movement. A portion of the youth were discreet sympathizers of the radical socialist movement. In the *shtiebel*, all were *Chassidim*, and all prayed in the same manner – but they weren't all united when it came to traveling to see the Rebbe. Each group glorified its own Rebbe whom they would visit to seek counsel or ask for a blessing. Before God, these Jews were all of one camp. In the *shtiebel*, Gerer and Alexander *Chassidim* prayed together, as did Sochatchover, Skernewyczer, Strykower, and Ostrowczer.

On Shabbos morning, the Gerer *Chassidim* prayed in two quorums: one at 7:30 AM and the other at 10:00AM.

The entrance to the *shtiebel* was at the front of the house where there was a cement floor. In this foyer of the house there was a door on the right side that opened into the Beis Medrash, and the door on the left led to the Rav's house.

Right at the entrance of the *shtiebel* there was a ladder. One could climb up the ladder to sneak up to the attic.

As you entered the *shtiebel*, on the right side stood a large barrel with water for hand washing, along with a long, hanging towel that was always wet from drying hands. Near the barrel was a small cup in which dirty water collected as people rinsed their hands. Each person washed his hands six times (three times on each hand), bending the body to the right then to the left over the barrel – just to be able to get some water out of it. Most of the water was spilled directly over the wooden floor. If I'm not mistaken, in later years, the barrel was replaced with a sink.

[Page 174]

Along the wall to the right of the barrel, there was a long table and benches. The table was used by the congregants for putting down their daily prayer books, their *chumashim* (printed Torah books), and their holiday prayer books. They also put their *tallis* and *tefillin* bags there. On this same side, the majority of those who prayed there were the "cold" *Chassidim*. These *Chassidim* also traveled to see the Rebbe, but not very often. They did not join in the joyous dancing nor did they participate in the *Chassidic* gatherings. One of these *Chassidim* was Reb Leibish Bender, the grain merchant, a short and stout Jew with a straight beard. His four sons were: Fishel, Yossel, Yakov, and Simcha. He also had several daughters. Simcha, the youngest son, became a scholar in his later years.

The wealthy man in the *shtiebel* was Reb Meyer Brustowski, a handsome Jew with a superbly long, silvered beard. He was one who led the prayers. When he stood before the pulpit leading the prayers, everyone felt as if it was a holiday. His three sons were: Yankel, Yechiel Moshe, and Leybish. He also had four daughters. Reb Yankel Brustowski, also one who led prayers, merited to die a natural death when times were still good.

One should also remember Reb Mendel Vajngarten, an elderly Jew, a *Chassid*, who would study together with Yissoschar Pinczewski, was a scholar of *mishnayos*, and also studied the Zohar (a book of *Kabbalah*, mysticism).

One of the most prominent figures in the *shtiebel* was Reb Avrohom Mordechai Cohen, a wealthy man with a wide, white beard and with a large wart near his eye. He was already in his eighties but he still held his regular position as the leader of the prayers. On the Days of Awe, he led the morning prayers and on Yom Kippur he even led the *mincha* (early evening) prayers. When he banged on the podium for attention, the walls actually trembled.

And now, Reb Avrohom Yitzchok the dye maker. He was a small, thin Jew, but he was the best swimmer in the entire region. He would wade across the mouth of the lake standing up, eating a meal while going one way.

[Page 175]

Then there was Reb Avrohom Meyer Flajshman, the teacher of young children in the *Talmud Torah*. Hundreds of children went through his hands, as he instructed each of them in the *alef bais*. He was known in the *shtiebel* for his deep sighing during the prayers of "The song of ascents, I call to You God from the depths..." said during the Days of Awe. His deep sighing was heard from under his *talis* which covered his head. This was a sign that one had to recite this particular prayer with great earnest.

There was another teacher that was well-known in the town, Reb Avrohom Yitzchok Holczman, a short man with a dark brown, little beard. He was considered a great scholar. He studied *gemara* and its commentaries (*tosefos* and *poskim*) with the young men. When he studied the books of the Torah, particularly the Book of Isaiah, all his limbs trembled. Many students were gripped by fear when this teacher became angry and admonished the students severely with: "Oy, you sinning goy!"

Let us remember a whole line of pious, devout *Chassidim*: There is Reb Shmuel Hersh Fajnzilber and his sons Yisroel Yitzchok and Yoshe; Reb Yisroel Dovid Alberstajn the alderman of Agudas Yisroel, and Reb Yankel Lewi the councilman of the same organization. And there is also Reb Yishai Princz and Reb Chaim Domb. Reb Sholom Alberstajn – a great grandson of the Gostynin Rebbe. Reb Sholom would never leave the *shtiebel* before having completed his reading of the entire Book of Psalms (*tehilim*). Reb Yakov Lomzer, the one who read the Torah, and Reb Elchonon Placzman, a charming, pious leader of prayers. And there was also Reb Efraim Yitzchok Rotenbach, an intense

Chassid, he was able to learn well, had a sharp mind – he was also called "Grinboim." He was the synagogue councilman for the district. He went to the Rebbe for Rosh Hashona and Yom Kippur and then for Shavuos as well. If anyone criticized him for going to the Rebbe and leaving his wife who had just given birth, he gave this answer one Friday night before the Shabbos prayers. He banged on the podium and said in these words: "When a person becomes dangerously ill, and they have to operate immediately, would it occur to anyone to say that the sick person should refuse to have the operation? And what if it is someone in his family who is sick, God forbid? No. I, friends and rabbis, am sick in my soul. When the Days of Awe approach, I feel that I must have an urgent operation on my soul – Do I have to forego this and God forbid, die from this?..."

[Page 176]

Let us end with Reb Shmuel (Shmelke) Zarkowski, the fiery *Chassid*, and Reb Berl Zonshajn. For a time, the community representatives were Reb Motel Hobergricz, the leader of the *mussaf* prayers on Rosh Hashona and Yom Kippur, and Reb Yakov Aryeh Zundman, the one who blew the *shofar*.

* * *

Every city had its Jews. Gostynin was no exception. We loved Gostynin, because there were Jews there. These very Jews left their imprint on the town. And without these very Jews Gostynin would not have been Gostynin. They are no longer here. Gostynin is standing, but Gostynin is without Jews. My city is no longer, it is not the same Gostynin.

[Page 177]

Cultural and Theater Activities

Yakov Gostynski

Translated by Pamela Russ

Yakov Gostynski

The great era of enlightenment in Eastern Europe, the *Haskalah*, infected the Gostynin youth with worldly ideas. A town like all the others, with a tradition of God-fearing and *Chassidus*, it was transformed into a center of advanced thinking and activity.

The Zionist movement in Gostynin caught onto many people, and made a great impression on them. Simkhah Bunim Danciger was the director of the Zionist organization in the town at that time, and the liberal elements and general public grouped themselves around him. Often there would be meetings and lectures with speakers brought in from Warsaw.

The youth at that time was under the influence of the national progressive movement, *Poalei Zion*. Many of the youth moved themselves to the forefront, and one of them was Yosef Keller, the leader of the youth, who contributed greatly to this cause so that Gostynin should be revived, and modern cultural life should be raised to a higher level.

The stocking factories transferred from the great industrial city of Lodz to Gostynin, as to other towns.

[Page 178]

With the evolution of the small industry, the PPS [*Polska Partia Socjalistyczna* (Polish Socialist Part)], the *Bund* [General Jewish Labour Party], and the *Poalei Zion* [Zionist Socialist Workers' Party], were born in Gostynin. They all helped improve the workers' economic conditions.

The heavy burden of earning a livelihood that rested on the fathers' shoulders, forced even the children of *chassidic* families to become stocking makers. The efforts of the religious circles to maintain the old ways were not successful.

It was almost like a wildfire from the large cities had caught onto the smaller cities. The stocking makers snatched up the freedom-catchwords, the revolution songs, the folk songs, and theater songs, and sang them with fire and spirit. When you think about those years, you remember that not only were you young, but also the entire period of Jewish life was still young and blooming.

[Page 179]

At that time, there was already a library in Gostynin. The youth read all kinds of books, including theater literature. This was the first push for the youth to organize a drama circle and perform Yiddish theater. Yosef Keller became the founder of this group. The orchestra leader of the Russian military orchestra, who was Jewish, took upon himself the initiative to perform the first two pieces, "*Hertzele Meyuchas*" ["Special Heart"], and "*Der Wilder Mentch*" ["The Wild Person"]. Yosef Keller played the lead roles in both pieces. Understandably, the performances were primitive.

Years later, various "-ists" grouped themselves around the library. The library administration accepted all political parties. Of the activists around the library, Shlomo Krancz was exceptional in his knowledge and intelligence. He got a lot of merit for the development of the social work. Years later, he moved to Bialystok, worked in his profession as lawyer, and at the same time was busy with social activities.

The Gostynin library had a reading room with newspapers and books. The library held discussions about literary works, and from time to time, brought speakers over from Lodz or Warsaw. The lectures were about various topics, both literary and political. These lectures brought in a lot of life, stirred up and nourished the Jewish youth.

A picture of the Gostynin drama circle in the Gombiner forest

Standing from right: Yakov Leyb Matil, Yakov Gostynski, Dvoire Zajacs, Yakov Czelemenski, Adam Domb, Feige Sarna, Efraim Kofman, Shloime Krancz, Bronka – a Plocker girl.

Kneeling from right: A Gombiner girl, Yissachar Matil, Shmuel Markowicz, Laytche Makowski, Berl Lewi.

Last Row, sitting, from right: Yakov Leyb Pinczewski, Kayle Goldman, Mashe Dzhencjol, Pesse Narwe (Wajczman), Ber Gonsher, Khana Zajacs, Moishe Klajnbard, Khaim-Sender Zandman

Of this group, in America there are: Yakov Gostynski, Yissachar Matil and Yakov Czelemenski, a Gombiner who was one of the fighters in the Warsaw uprising. Khaim-Sender Zandman lives in Israel, and Ber Gonsher died in America in 1944.

My sister Rokhtche and my brother Shlomo, who were also very active in the library, had a tremendous influence over me, and actually because of them I was enticed to the "tree of knowledge" and began reading books. The youth at that time thirsted for knowledge and swallowed up every new book and every new publication. This pushed the youth to participate in this cultural life that was sprouting in Gostynin.

[Page 180]

The Development of the Drama Circle

The movement of the drama circle bloomed in all towns. But Gostynin, in this area, had more good fortune than other towns. The professional actor, Adam Domb, lived in Gostynin at that time and he organized the amateur group in the library.

Adam Domb was an actor with a European manner and demeanor. He performed with Russian and Polish troupes, wore elegant suits, and didn't really have in him the specific Yiddish nuances. He was not able to speak any Yiddish, but with time, through his work and as stage manager with Yiddish amateurs, he learned the Yiddish language.

Aside from his acting profession, he also had a photography studio. His artistic aptitude was renowned in our town. And by the way, Adam Domb performed in Esther Rokhel Kominski's troupe and later with Ida Kaminski in Lemberg. Some time later, he performed in the Astrakhan Russian Theater. In 1943, he died in Russia.[20]

From his great theater experience, we learned how to perform in a theater. We looked up to him as the *chassidim* do to their Rebbe. We had great pleasure from his work. Here I am listing the names of the amateurs who contributed a lot to the success of the group. Thanks to their love and efforts that they put into this very important work, the dramatic circle went from success to success:

Adam Domb, main actor and stage manager; Feige Sarna, Khana Bagno-Keller, Dvoire Salomonowycz, Laya Tabacznik, Yehoshua Noakh Wilner, Khana Zajacs, Yakov-Leyb Matil, Yakov Sarna, Ilenokh Kuczinski, Yisroel Kuczinski, Yissakhar Matil, Ber Gonshor, Regina Matil, Shloime Gostynski, Borukh Matil, Hersh Kruczik, Heczke Sarna, Shmuel Markowycz, Khaim Yehoshua Tabacznik, Mordekhai Moskal, Yekhiel Moshe Pluczer.

---

20. See Yitzkhok Grудberg-Turkow, "Yiddish Theater in Poland," publisher: Yiddish Book – Warsaw, 1951; and Jonas Turkow, *"Verloshene Shteren"* ["Extinguished Stars"], 2nd volume, publisher: Central Union of Polish Jews in Argentina, 1953.

[Page 181]

**"Der Dorf's Jung" [The "Village Youth"],
Yankel Boyle, from Leon Kobrin,**

performed in Gostynin

**Prokop – Yakov Gostynski
Natasha – Feige Sarna
Yankel Boyle – Adam Domb**

Under the direction of Adam Domb, we performed the following repertoire: *"Der Meturef"* ["The Worthless"], *"Gott, Mentch, un Teivel"* ["God, Man, and the Devil"], *"Der Fremder"* ["The Stranger"], (Yakov Gordyn), *"Die Yiden"* ["The Jews"], (Tchirikov), *"Der Dorf's Jung"* [The "Village Youth"], (Leon Kobrin), *"Die Neveila"* ["The Carcass"], (Peretz Hirshbein), *"Gavriel un Zeine Techter"* [Gavriel and His Daughters"], (Dovid Pinski), *"Der Dybbuk"* ["The Dybbuk" (evil spirit that haunts or possesses a living person)], (Sh. Ansky), *"Der Voter"* ["Father"], (Strindberg), *"Die Geister"* ["Ghosts"], (Ibsen), *"Shnei"* ["Snow"], (Przibisewski), *"Kean"* ["Kean", based on the life of the famous English actor Edmund Kean], (Dumas), and many other plays from the better repertoires.

In some of the plays, the Yiddish actress Rose Shoshana performed with us. She now lives in New York. At that time, she performed in the Lodz Yiddish theater, and when she would come home for vacation to her mother, she could not stand by idly, and she performed with us.

The success of the Gostynin amateur group reached into many surrounding cities and towns, and the performances made such a sensation that the group was invited to Plock, Kutno, Gombyn, also by the local cultural institutions, and we performed Kobrin's "The Village Youth," Tchirikov's "The Jews," and Sh. Ansky's "The *Dybbuk*."

[Page 182]

The Jewish populace in all these cities welcomed us with the greatest love and warmth. We felt that the Gostynin amateur group was something substantial. We felt elevated from the recognition of the professional stage managers who offered voluntarily to work with us. The first professional stage manager who was invited to do a play with us was Yakov Wajslycz from the Vilna troupe. Wajslycz presented with us *"Mitten Shtrom"* ["With the Stream"] by Sholom Asch. The play was very successful. And with this performance, the Gostynin amateur troupe wrote another beautiful page in its history.

The Gostynin amateur troupe contributed immensely to Jewish cultural life, and certainly to Yiddish theater in the Polish province. It is not my purpose to describe them and characterize them as a professional critic would, but as a member of the Gostynin amateur troupe, I feel that at this opportunity that they have earned that I briefly qualify their place in performance and go through the roles that they acted.

I will begin with Leon Kobrin's "The Village Youth." Shmuel Keller played the role of Hersh Ber. He made a sensation with his performance. He played the character of the kind-hearted fisherman-Jew Hersh-Ber as an actor who knows what he is doing and knows what he wants. Keller was a moving actor of fine quality and a natural for the stage.

The role of Khatzye was played by Khaim-Sender Zandman (he now lives in Israel). He played the role with understanding, and the main thing is that he took the role with its complete technique of how to frighten the primitive Yankel Boyle with the "beautiful face of Lilith."

Adam Domb's Yankel Boyle presented a magnificent portrait.

[Page 183]

The voice, the body movements and his whole demeanor was not of an imagined figure. Seeing him on stage you believed that he actually was Yankel Boyle.

Feige Sarna, the beauty of Gostynin, played the role of the village girl Natasha, whom Yankel Boyle deeply loved. Her Natasha came out as very gentle.

Zalman the fisherman youth was played by Yehoshua-Noakh Wilner. He thoroughly understood his role. He was very fitting to this role, both in appearance and in form.

Khana Zajacs and Dvoire Salomonowycz played the role of the parents of the unfortunatel Khaike. Both of them were very clever in their roles.

A scene from "The Village Youth" performed by the Gostynin drama circle

<u>**Sitting, from right to left:**</u> Adam Domb, Shmuel Keller, Feige Sarna, Khana Zajacs.

<u>**At the fisherman's net, from right to left:**</u> Herczke Sarna, Hersh Kruczik, Yehoshua-Noakh Wilner, Khaim-Sender Zandman

[Page 184]

Khana Bagno-Keller as Khaike created a character and you believed that she was raised that way, and that she was rooted in this setting.

A very fine role in the play was the farmer Prokop. To play such a role was a feat in acting performance. This role was delegated to me by the stage manager.

In other plays, Mirel Matil and Manja Klajnbard were exceptional, both of them university graduates. They were talented actresses and performed with inner depth, just as seasoned professional actresses, not amateurs at all.

Yakov-Leyb, the "dandy" and intellectual, was the regular prompter. He contributed greatly to the development of the Gostynin amateur troupe. Shlomo Gostynski was the regular stage administrator. With his work, he always helped the performances run smoothly. Hersh Kruczyk-Kraus was exceptional in episode roles. His youthful face had a lot of charm on stage.

Ber Gonshor, my unforgettable friend for many years, performed in Sh. Ansky's "The Dybbuk" in the role of Meyer-*shamash* [beadle]. He played this role with a lot of piety. In the scene where the Rebbe quarreled with the *dybbuk*, and then gave the stick to Meyer-*shamash* and ordered him to go to the Jewish cemetery and call out the deceased for a Jewish trial, there were moments one could never forget. With his performance, Ber Gonshor worked up the audience to believe that the *shamash* had a difficult mission to carry out. When he left the stage, he created the illusion that all those present in the theater were accompanying him to the cemetery...

Yissachar Matil was the busiest social activist. It became his lot to be the guardian of all cultural achievements in Gostynin, and he accomplished his missions to perfection.

From time to time, Wacsman and his troupe would come to perform in Gostynin, along with Ana Jakubowycz and her troupe (Ana Jakubowycz now lives in America and performs from time to time). It is worthwhile to mention one very interesting episode. Once, on the eve of *Shavuos*, Wacsman's troupe came to Gostynin to perform Yakov Gordin's "Shloime's Charlatan" on the two days of the *Shavuos* holiday. The Rav discovered this and put out a prohibition that the Gostynin Jews were not to attend the performance. The youth, that was already carried away with the freedom movement, went to the performance intentionally and even convinced others to go to the theater, and the performances were well attended.

[Page 185]

The theater activity of Gostynin not only refined the artistic taste of the people who participated, but also taught them to see, admire, and take pleasure in a Yiddish theater performance. This activity, with which we in our youth were occupied in our former home, pushed many of us to approach the Yiddish theater in the later years. That's how the author of these lines managed, already in America, to participate in the performances of the

"Artef.[21]" More than once, did our amateur performances of Gostynin come into very good use in my theater activity in America. The theater inheritance of the drama circle in Gostynin did not go to waste.

---

21. Artef is a Yiddish acronym for *Arbeter Teater Farband* (Workers' Theater Union), and the company by that name that entertained, hectored, puzzled, and occasionally infuriated its audience over the course of a decade was a grand experiment in the application of left-wing principles to Yiddish theater. (Project Muse: Yiddish Proletarian Theatre, Jeremy Dauber: American Jewish History Volume 88)

[Page 186]

The History of the Jewish Theatre in Gostynin

by Chaim-Sender Zandman

Translated by Yocheved Klausner

Chaim-Sender Zandman

I would like to relate here an episode from the Jewish past in Gotsynin, which is characteristic of the devotion of the Jewish youth in its quest to improve and enrich the life in town.

How much energy have those young people invested in the establishment of a Drama Group in Gostynin! The first steps were made in 1908. All the lovers of the Yiddish theater converged around this group.

The members of the group were Yosef Keller, Ben-Zion Keller, Rachel Motil, Itke Pintchewski (Glicksberg), Tuvia Yakobowitz and others. The prompter was Isser-Meir Motil.

This amateur group decided to produce a play. They began reading the available works, and they chose the play "the Wild Man" by Jacob Gordin. The group found a director and began the rehearsals and the play was finally ready for the stage.

However, being immersed in work, nobody gave a thought to the question of a place. It turned out that the Polish city-fathers did not agree to lease the City Theater for a Jewish performance. The group was greatly disappointed.

[Page 187]

Soon the group found a solution: they will build their own hall!

It was said and done: The members of the group "pulled up their sleeves" and began working. With the help of the three brothers Mordechai, Hershel and Yakov Motil they soon constructed a hall of wooden boards, brought to the site by Avraham Bressler.

This improvised structure was home for the Drams group in Gostynin. The public came, enjoyed the plays and was proud of the fact that this was the achievement of the young patriots of the Yiddish Theater. A long series of performances took place in this building.

Di Yiden [The Jews] played by the Gostynin Drama Group

Sitting from right to left: Feige Sarne, Yakov-Leib Motil, Shmuel Keller, Adam Domb, Dvora Zayontz, Chone Zayontz
Standing from right to left: Bashe Seideman, Henich Kutchinski, Yakov Sarne, Yehoshua-Noah Vilner, Israel-Zelik Kutchinski, Yakov Gostinski, Chaim-Sender Sandman, Baruch-Meir Motil and Chaim Shiye Tabatchnik

[Page 188]

PROGRAM

przedstawienia amatorskiego
na cel dobroczynny.

Dramat w 4 aktach A. WAJTERA p. t.

NIEMOWA

OSOBY:

Aleksander	—	A. Domb
Ojciec	—	Ch. Zając
Matka	—	M. Dzięciołówna
Nuchim Kapilosz	—	J. Sarna
jego żona	—	L. Makowska
Azja ich córka	—	F. Sarnówna
Wujek	—	I. Apelast
Ciotka jego żona	—	P. Wajemanówna
Reb Łajb	—	H. Kruczek
Gość	—	I. Kac
Przyjaciel	—	Ch. S. Zandman
Purysz	—	J. Sarna
Chasyd	—	I. Kac

Reżyser: ADAM DOMB.

Sufler: J. L. Motyl.

Dekorator: J. Sarna.

Słowo wstępne przez Pinczewskiego.

גאסטינין   שטאדט טעאטער

פּראגראם

שבת ד. 4-טן לושי 1928 קומט פאר א מענטאר-פארשטעלונג
פון די גאסטינער יידישע אמאטארן פאר א וואלמעטיקן צוועק

דער שטומער

א דראמע אין 4 אקטן פון א ווייטער

פערזאנען

א. דאמב	—	אלכסאנדער
ח. זייאץ	—	דער פאטער
מ. דזשענטשאל	—	די מוטער
י. סארנע	—	נחום קאפילאטער
ל. מאקאווסקא	—	זיין פרוי
פ. סארנע	—	אזיא זייר פאטער
י. אפעלאסט	—	דער פעטער
פ. וייצמאן	—	זיין פרוי
ח. קרוטשעק	—	מחותן רב לייב
א. קאץ	—	מחותן
ח. ש. זאנדמאן	—	דתר פרייש
י. סארנע	—	דער פריש
א. קאץ	—	א דר

רעזשיסער אדאם דאמב

סופלער י. ל. מאטיל

דעקאראטער י. סארנע

איינליטונג פון פינטשעווסקי

Performance announcement

[Page 189]

How and What We Used to Read

by Tuvia Yakobowitz

Translated by Yocheved Klausner

Tuvia Yakobowitz

The Gostynin youth, who always felt an attraction to books, went through several stages before the establishment of the library.

The first stage consisted of the books the mothers would buy from the passing Jewish salesmen, and which contained stories and folktales: *The 7 Beggars*, *Three Brothers*, *The Stories of the Baal-Shem-Tov* etc. Other Jewish books were practically unknown. The second stage was the introduction of the *Haskala* [Enlightenment] books, which only several distinguished people could obtain, borrowed from old R'Fishel Tzivye. These were the works of Levinsohn (RIBAL), Y.L. Gordon, Brandstetter, Yitzhak Erter and some others. Then came the romantic literature, books borrowed from Mordechai Moritz: the writings of Avraham Mapu – *Ahavat Zion* [Love of Zion], *Ashmat Shomron* [Guilt of Samaria], *Ayit Tzavua* [Hypocrite Eagle]; some science books, as, for example, history books by Schulman and books on nature by Bernstein, and finally old copies of the newspapers *Hatzefira* and *Hamelitz*.

Later, the "Hebrew Traveling Library" was established in Plock, and books were sent from town to town to responsible subscribers. This library contained scientific as well as modern literature:

[Page 190]

The Complete Works of Y. L. Peretz[22], The Blind Musician by Korolenko, Children of the Ghetto and other books by Israel Zangwill, the essay *Al Parashat Derachim* by Ahad Ha'am etc.

The first transport of books arrived at the Gostynin address of the writer of these lines, with the suggestion that, after all the books had been read, they would be sent to Lubien.

Later we received more books – novels by Shemer, Blostein and Spector. These books were kept by Yitzhak Tcharke the bookbinder. In his possession were also books by Jules Verne, and other novels – The Indian Prince, Gold Miners in California and others. Israel Yitzhak Zimmerman had some books as well, and he lent them for reading, for a small fee. Isser Meir Motil had a small collection of humoristic literature. He distributed an English humoristic weekly as well.

At that time there were no Yiddish newspapers in Gostynin. Then Yona Baruch Katz began to receive the newspaper *Hatzefira*. When it was time for the postman to arrive, a group of people, headed by old R'Fishel Tzivye, would already be waiting in front of the house. The editorial was barely read, and old R'Hersh Leib the *shamash* [synagogue attendant] appeared and claimed the newspaper, as partner to the subscription. After he read it, he would give it to the third partner, R'Yakov Miller, and only after all this wandering the newspaper would finally reach me. A great deal of "book-exchanging" took place in town at that time, just like the barter trade in the old times: "I give

---

Translator's Footnote

22. Reprinted from a publication of the Y.L. Peretz Library in Gostynin, on its 20th anniversary.

you an axe and you give me a bear-skin" – when one wanted to read a book he would first have to acquire another book so he would be able to make the exchange.

Even the rabbi, Rav Unterman z"l, participated in the book exchanges. I would bring him, understandably, books of religious nature, like *Hadat Vehachayim* [Religion and Life] and he would reciprocate with a work by Socrates, for example.

It can certainly be said that the love of books was much stronger then than now. Even though the books were not easy to obtain, we did everything to get them. We even walked to Plock to exchange books. Today, many persons are members of the library not so much for the sake of the books, but in order to have the right to vote for their favorite party.

[Page 191]

The interest in the Jewish book embraced even larger sectors of the Jewish youth after the revolution of 1905. This tendency was initiated by the illegal literature, provided by the party representatives – the Bund, the PPS (Polish Socialist Party) and some others – who came to our town. It should be remarked, that the youth of the above-mentioned political leanings would meet, to discuss the literature of their parties, in the house of one of the Zionists.

[Page 192]

Gostynin, My City

by Chana Bagno-Keller

Translated by Pamela Russ

Chana Keller

In our city of Gostynin, as in the majority of cities in Russian-Poland, the city administration was Russian, but in the year 1914, when war was declared, all Russian locals left the city. Soon a civilian militia was established to maintain order.

Unrest and fear took over the population. Gostynin was not far from the German border. Everyone 's eyes were turned to the western side of the city that was surrounded by mountains.

It was early one morning, when a German vanguard appeared from the Koval direction. They looked around the town, and turned back. But it wasn 't much later when a camp of German soldiers came down from the mountains. They marched through our town all day on their way to Warsaw, leaving a small number of soldiers and officers to take over the city.

Days passed, quiet days, but the silence was pained, unsure, the air smelled of gunpowder.

The military withdrew to the road back to Germany. They marched all day and into the night.

Again, the residents lived with fear. The Germans did frequent searches, made arrests, and took with them many people. Among those was my brother, the wealthy man Aron Bresler, the former German pharmacist Jahne, and a Russian policeman.

[Page 193]

Meanwhile, the Russians began to return to the city. And suddenly we saw them bringing back all kinds of war machinery and wagonloads of many wounded soldiers. We sensed that things were not right in the lines of the Russian army. In fact, soon there was a retreat of the military and an even greater chaos befell them. Suddenly, there was loud cannon shooting.

The shooting became louder and closer. It felt as if it was a few kilometers from our house because the shutters were rattling.

My father, who in the meantime had returned from Kutno and found out that his sons were taken by the Germans, advised our mother and the children to go to our friend Itche Meier Strikowski who lived in the center of the city in a walled stone house where it was safer than staying in our small wooden house. My mother went there with the children, and I stayed with my father because I didn 't want to leave him alone in the house. We sat together, quietly in the dark.

In the middle of the night, we heard how they were smashing the fence around our house. We held our breath, and didn 't move from our place. Quietly, my father whispered a prayer. When they didn 't destroy our house, he gave praise to God. With pounding hearts, we heard the retreating steps of the soldiers; it lasted the entire night.

With the beginning of daylight, we did not hear any more soldiers' steps. It became quieter and quieter. One by one, people began to appear in the streets. Suddenly, we saw riders (on horseback) wearing grey capes, and helmets on their heads. We understood immediately that this was a German vanguard. When they saw the locked stores they politely asked if it was a holiday and then ordered the storekeepers to open their stores.

[Page 194]

The truck in which we went to Gombin to perform "The Dybbuk"

The first by the driver: Yakov Gostinski; the first row that you can see: Yakov Leib Pinczewski, Yakov Leib Motil, Faige Sarna;

The second row: Berl Levi, Pesse Narve;

Third row: Yissocher Motil, Ber Gonshor; fourth row: Shloime Krantc, Chana Zajac.

[Page 195]

The merchants, who were looking through the cracks with fear and saw the friendly behavior of the Germans, immediately left their place of hiding and opened their stores.

Soon the German military marched into the city. They were friendly to the residents, particularly to the children who had already assembled in the streets during that time. The soldiers gave the children cookies and chocolate.

Slowly, life began to quiet down, and all those who moved in with friends in the center of the city, now moved back home. This was the beginning of the German occupation.

Gradually the Germans began to remove products from the villages - products such as wheat, corn, potatoes, chicken, beets, fruit, and more. The farmers did not have anything to bring into the city and sell, and so business came to a halt. There was no work for the workers. Even for the stocking producers, stockings being the largest product made in the city, there was no work.

The atmosphere of the city was very strained. People were going around not knowing what to do with themselves. The youth woke up and energetically undertook community social activity. The first thing they did was to revive the former group "*Linat Hazedek*" with a women 's unit available for overnight stay for the sick, because at that time the typhus epidemic, that eventually took many lives, began to rumble.

The organization "*Hatchiya*" was also established under the administration of Yosel Gonshor, Moishe Pinczewski, Yankel Rusak, Ben-Tzion Keller, Tuvia Jakubowicz, and Yakov Zerkhyn.

Incidentally, it is also worth mentioning that Yakov Zerkhyn had come from Russia and had brought his family along with him, and he worked as a Hebrew teacher in the Gostynin gymnasium. He was an interesting personality and was always involved in important projects. The administration of *Hatchiya* set up a touring club where a few young people joined up with a special gymnastics teacher. They frequently did all kinds of tours in other cities.

[Page 196]

The library was revived again. They organized a reading room and they would often invite a guest writer and cultural activist and have an evening of culture that was attended by almost all the youth.

From the larger cities, where the conditions were even worse, families came to settle in Gostynin. One of these families was Dzhalowski from Lodz. Dzhalowski was very musical. In a short time he became acquainted with the youth and he found out that among them there were talented singers. A singing club was set up with Dzhalowski as the director.

Members of the choir were: Chaim and Rochel Zweighaft, Yehoshua-Noach Wilner, Borucj-Meier Motil, Yankel Sarna, Glike Lewi, Faige Shteynman, Chana Bagno, Yankel Gostinski, Chaim-Yehoshua Tabachnik, Chana Zajac, and Shmuel Keller.

The singing club prepared for a concert with a repertoire of Yiddish, Hebrew, and - because of the German military and the locals - also German songs.

At an administrative meeting, it was decided that at these concerts there should be a reading and recitation. To this end, Chaim Pozner from the city of Koval near Wloclowek helped out. He had come to study in the gymnasium.

Chaim Pozner was a talented writer. He had written a poem titled "*Shoin Vider Finster*" (Dark Again). This poem mirrored the pogroms of the Jews that were taking place at that time. I was the reader for this poem. (Today, Dr. Chaim Pozner is one of the foremost Zionist leaders in Switzerland.)

[Page 197]

Glike Lewi, one of the singers, who was blessed with a beautiful alto voice and a strong desire to sing, joined the singers club only in her older years, because she knew that her father Benyomin Lewi, who was the town 's *shochet* (ritual Slaughterer), would not have allowed her to belong to a singing group.

On the day of the concert, when the excitement in the town was bubbling, and the crowd was preparing for the big evening, everyone knew that Glike would not be part of the evening 's performance. Her father found out about it and locked her up and even took away her shoes. We, in the choir, were very upset about the news that quickly spread across the entire town: first because we would be missing a singer; we were afraid that the Jewish residents would cancel and would certainly not come to the concert.

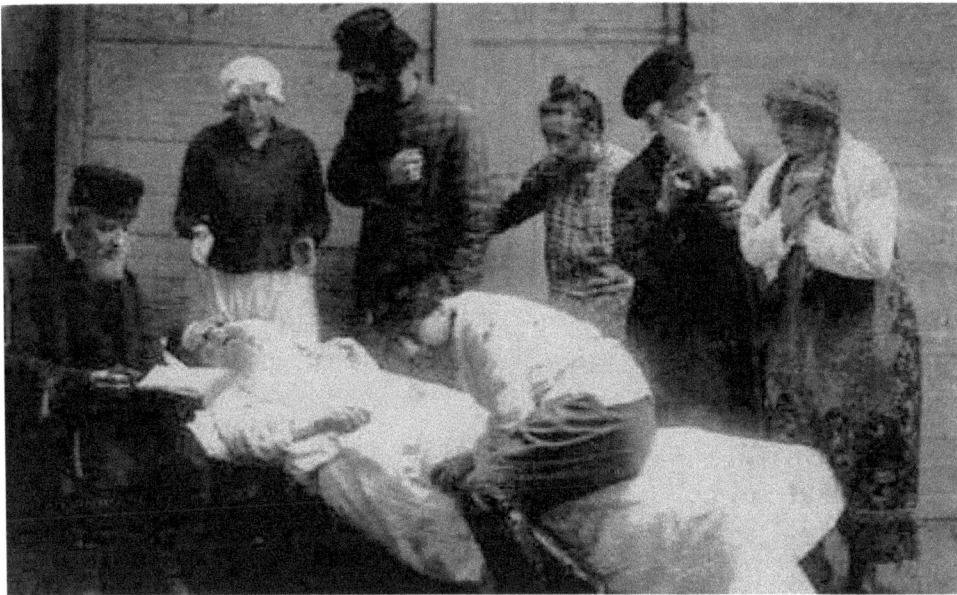

A scene from "Dorf 's Yung" (The Village Youth), performed by the Gostynin drama circle.

Standing from right to left: Faige Sarna, Shmuel Keller, Chana (Bagno) Keller, Chana Zajac, Dvoire (Solomonowicz) Friedman, Chaim-Sender Zandman

Below, sitting on the bed: Adam Domb

Lying down: Yakov Gostinski

[Page 198]

As it turned out, the Gostynin residents did come, and the concert was a great success. The entire purpose of that evening 's event was in order (to raise money) to buy books for the library.

During that time, Adam Domb came to Gostynin to take over the photography studio from his brother Julius. Domb was from Plock. He was a Polish-speaking young man. He had artistic talents. Sometimes he would act on the Polish stage. As soon as he became acquainted with the youth that was involved with the culture and social activities, he noticed their artistic talents. So, Domb decided to establish a drama circle.

The youth was very enthusiastic about this plan and after a brief discussion, it was decided to set up a drama circle with Adam Domb as manager. Domb was not familiar with Yiddish literature, but he began to study Yiddish enthusiastically, read a lot, and became proficient in Yiddish drama.

The first play that they decided to present, was Yakov Gordin 's "God, Man, and the Devil." These were the performers: Yechiel Yehoshua Pluczer, Shmuel Keller, Yakov Sarna, Mordechai Maskel, Mirel Motil, Faige Sarna, Bimtza Motil, Malke Charke, and Adam Domb.

There was a hall with a stage in Gostynin, but there were no seats at that time. The hall belonged to the firemen. The administration received permission to use the hall. When the time for the performance approached, we rented horses and wagons and went from house to house to collect chairs. On each chair, the name of the owner was marked.

The furniture (props) that was needed for the stage was lent by people who had always been sympathetic to our work. We also needed a steel safe on stage, but this was a complicated issue. The administration was taken over by Efraim Motil who was a social activist and always supported our projects. Even though it was almost impossible for him to do, he did not refuse to give us his steel chest.

[Page 199]

The day of the performance was a real holiday. The Gostynin people who filled the theater applauded the performers very enthusiastically.

After the performance, we saw these same people from the audience sharing their impressions about the performance.

This first time, the wealthier townspeople showed their displeasure with this whole thing, but when the administration told them that the money from the upcoming performance would go to various philanthropic causes, they took on a more positive attitude towards the drama circle.

It was decided that the play "God, Man, and the Devil" be performed again with the thinking that if the general public would also come to the theater, then this play would be an appropriate one to perform.

At that time, Yekhiel Yehoshua Pluczer, one of the most important actors, as well as Bimze Motil, left Gostynin. Shmuel Keller took over the role of "Hershele Dubrowner." The director, Adam Domb, told me to take the woman 's role of "Tzipenyu," because they had told him that I had already acted several times. I was happy to take the role and to belong to the drama circle, but I knew that my father would oppose this.

Nonetheless, I tried to talk to my father and explain to him that even the daughter of the well-known, wealthy Nute Motil was participating.

It did not help. My father categorically refused all of it. The administration decided to send a group of well-known youths to my father. These were: Moishe Pinczewski, Yosel Gonshor, and Ben-Tzion Keller.

[Page 200]

They explained to my father that the work the youth was doing was important. The income from the performances went to philanthropic causes. And they also assured him that the representatives from the municipality would come to the performance: those such as Yakov Zerkhin, Mendel Krel, Nute Motil, Moishe Brakman, and Yakov Mendel Keller, my father-in-law, of blessed memory.

My father cautiously listened to the youths and after a brief, silent reflection, he agreed to allow me to perform. It seems that the discussion with the delegation had the desired effect on my father. After some time of rehearsing this drama piece, the actual performance date was set.

It became known in town that the municipal representatives would be coming to the performance. So, others, who would never have come to a theater, also came to the performance and because not everyone was able to fit into the theater because of crowds and space, the play was repeated on a second night.

After that, other plays performed were Yakov Gordin 's "The Madman," "Khasha the Orphan," and "The Stranger"; Sholom Aleichem 's "Only the

Doctor"; Y.L. Peretz 's "After Burial"; Chirakow 's "The Jews"; Strindberg 's "Father"; Ibsen 's "Ghosts"; Alexander Dumas ' "Kean"; and Sholom Asch 's "With the Current."

With this drama circle, Domb also performed Dovid Pinski 's "Gabri and the Women."

Those times in Gostynin presented the well-known contemporary Rose Shoshana. Our director used the opportunity and invited her to play the leading role in Dovid Pinski 's play.

They also prepared to perform Sholom Asch 's "With the Current," but we were stuck with a difficult problem: Where would we find a *shtreimel* (round fur hat) for the Rav? In this small town, who would lend out a *shtreimel*? So, Shmuel, who was playing the role of the Rav, remembered Soro 'le, a daughter of Yishaye Feinzilber, from one of the famous *Chassidic* families of Gostynin, to whom the Kellers were related. He met her secretly, and asked her to help him get her brother-in-law 's *shtreimel*.

[Page 201]

For this naïve daughter, this was a great challenge, but she gave in. The night before the performance, her brother-in-law, Yitzkhok Shtern, a great *Chassid* and God-fearing man, and one who had Rabbinic ordination, left for Warsaw and she, Soro 'le, spent the night with her sister.

That night, when the family was sound asleep, Soro 'le tied the *shtreimel* to a rope, and let it down through a window where we were waiting for it.

Right after the performance, Shmuel and I immediately went to Yitzkhok Shtern 's house where Soro 'le was already waiting for us. That 's how the situation was saved, and no one, not her brother-in-law nor any of the *chassidim* in town, knew anything of this.

It has remained a secret until today.

The story with Glike Lewi, that her father locked her up, and the story of the *shtreimel* were not the only incidents that could have disrupted a concert or play.

There were others too. I am remembering those days when we were preparing to perform the play "The Father," by Strindberg. I played the role of Berta. That same evening, potential in-laws came to our home to "check out" my older sister Hinda. My parents wanted me to be there to welcome the guests. As much as I tried to have them understand that I had to go to the performance, and that without me the performance could not go on, nothing helped. My parents were fixed on me having to stay home. I had no other choice but to sneak out of the house in the last minute.

After the performance, when I went home, everyone was already asleep. I knocked at the door and heard my father 's steps. He was angry, but he let me in. In the morning, I tried to avoid meeting my father 's eye. I was happy that my father left to the synagogue. Later, I was standing in front of our store, and thought about the anger that I had to experience before going to the theater.

[Page 202]

Suddenly, from a distance, I noticed my father returning from the synagogue. My heart began to pound in fear. When he came closer, I saw a satisfied expression on his face, and even a smile. He turned to my mother and said: "You hear, Genendel! I have shame and humiliation from YOUR daughter!" Then my father told her that on his way to the synagogue he met his friend Yakov Linderman. He told him that all the actors had performed well and that I, Chana, excelled in portraying the role of 12-year-old Berta.

Our drama circle became famous in the surrounding cities and towns. Yakov Weislicz, reknowned reciter (reader), also learned of our work. He came to Gostynin and proposed a reading for us of Leon Kobrin 's "The Village Youth."

For amateurs, this was not an easy play to produce, but Adom Domb, our director, was a man of great ambition, so he immediately told us to get to work.

For this specific project, we needed more actors. So, these are the ones who joined the drama circle: Chaim Sender Zandman, Yehoshua Wilner, Hersh Kruczik, and Dvoira Solomonowicz.

Yakov Gostinski played two roles in this play: Yeshiye the store owner, and Prokov.

With heart and soul the actors threw themselves into the work; everyone tried to bring out the personality of the character they played exactly as Yakov Weislicz directed.

The actors from Gombin came with their director Chaim Luria to attend the performance.

There was a dignified atmosphere within the audience. After the performance, the Gostynin and Gombin actors got together with the director in the studio. The guests from Gombin were so enthusiastic about this event, that they decided they too would perform "The Village Youth" in their town.

[Page 203]

The Gombin director, Chaim Luria, began rehearsals for "The Village Youth," but he did not have an appropriate actor for the role of Hersh Ber the Fisherman, and since Shmuel Keller had played this role in Gostynin, he (Chaim Luria) asked him (Shmuel Keller) to play this role in Gombin.

Shmuel accepted the invitation.

On the day of the performance our director went to Gombin with all the actors to attend the performance.

The wagon driver, a cheerful and happy person named Blind Chaim 'el because he was blind in one eye, called out from his wagon 's step: "Actors! Hurry up and get on!" We climbed into the wagon and the wagon driver followed behind us. He slapped the horse and before we knew it, we had left the city behind.

The road from Gostynin to Gombin was very dusty. The speed of the trotting horses raised the dust high up so that it seemed that we were traveling in a fog. However, this did not prevent us from filling the air with song. When we passed through the forests, an echo surrounded us as if there were choirs with many people singing.

The wagon driver told jokes at our expense and we laughed heartily.

As we entered Gombin we felt the holiday atmosphere in the city. We saw big posters that were put up announcing the performance of "The Village Youth" that was to be held that day.

People were looking at the horse and wagon that was bringing in the Gostynin theater lovers. And that 's how we went to the theater.

[Page 204]

"The Village Youth" was also performed twice in Gombin with great success.

This was a trip that one cannot forget.

✳✳✳

Other than these above mentioned groups in which the Gostynin youth participated, there were also other activities, such as work that provided help, and also activities in the area of education, where Jewish students proved themselves outstanding in the gymnasium. They gave free classes to the younger ones who did not have these opportunities, or the opportunity to receive an elementary education.

Part of the drama circle under Adam Domb

<u>**Sitting from the right:**</u> Yakov Sarna, Yakov Gostinski, Adam Domb, Yakov Leyb Motil, Faige Sarna, Manja Klajnbord.

<u>**Standing from the right:**</u> Borukh Meier Motil, Shloime Gostinski, Dvoire (Solomonowicz) Friedman, Bibiczje Motil, M. Zajf (Motil), Hinde Domb, Shmuel Keller, Chana (Bagno) Keller.

[Page 205]

One of these students, Avrohom Zajf, who had come from the city Radziejow Kojowski, was very active in helping young men and women who wanted to leave Poland. (That same Avrohom Zajf later was a teacher in a *Mizrachi* school in Wloclowek, then lived in Danzig, and was connected to the prominent Zionists in the city. He died in Konin in unusual circumstances.)

After the Great Depression in the year 1918, when the German army suffered on the Western front, a revolution broke out in Germany. They overthrew German Kaiser Wilhelm, and the German armies ran away from all occupied countries.

The dream of the Polish people came true - Poland became independent.

But for the Jews, there were new days of fear, pogroms, and unrest. The anti-Semitic General Haller and his group of hooligans and pogrom instigators moved in. It was impossible for Jews to pass through the streets. They beat the Jews and ripped out their beards; they attacked Jews in trains, and they did not permit Jewish youth to study in the universities.

The youth saw that they could not build their future existence in Poland, and they began to emigrate. I, too, decided to leave Poland in 1920.

Thanks to the help of the social activist Avrohom Zajf, I was able to board a small ship in Danzig that was going to Swinemunde, Germany. From Germany I went to Belgium where my brother Shmuel Borukh had already been for a long time. One year later, I arrived in America.

[Page 206]

My yearning for Gostynin never abated. Even though when we lived there, it was always with the fear for tomorrow, it still pulled me to see my dear and close ones.

After a period of thirteen years, I decided to go back to Gostynin, so in 1934, I and my 10-year-old daughter Ita Fraide'le went to visit my place of birth, Gostynin.

I found a new youth, and recognized only a few of them who resembled their parents. This youth also had a drama circle. Their director was a younger brother of Yechiel Yehoshua Pluczer.

By that time, Adam Domb was no longer in Gostynin. He was now part of a professional acting troupe in Warsaw.

During the time that I was in Gostynin, the drama circle was preparing for their performance of "Thieves," by Fishel Bimko. On the day of the performance, there was the same holiday feeling as in the former years.

I sat in the theater and looked over at audience and at their enthusiasm for the curtain to rise.

The performance was as I expected - superbly presented by the entire troupe. I went behind the stage to congratulate the actors, enthusiastic about their acting abilities.

As I was sitting in the theater in 1934, all kinds of images and memories went through my mind about the former life and activities in Gostynin.

Who would have imagined that a few years later there would be a massive destruction in which the beautiful Jewish capital of Gostynin would be erased.

[Page 207]

Pictures and Types from Gostynin

by Meyer and Yakov Gostynski

Translated by Pamela Russ

Dedicated to the holy memory of our sister Zisse, may she rest in peace

Our town of Gostynin was situated in an area of fields, woods, rivers, mountains and valleys, windmills, watermills, brickyards, sugar factories, distilleries, and also peat storehouses, since the peat was a cheap combustible material that the residents – particularly the poorer class of residents – used to heat their homes.

Years later Epstajn's sawmill was set up on the Plock highway. There they chopped wood for lumber and transported it across the Vistula River to Danzig and other cities.

Our city of birth, Gostynin, was on the way between Plock and Kutno. One side was three miles from Gombyn, and the other was three miles from Koval.

The center of Gostynin was the four–cornered marketplace that was paved with cobblestones, flat and smooth. On all four sides around the marketplace there were nice sidewalks lined with pretty trees. Almost all the shops and stores were in this marketplace. The two eyesores were the two water pumps from which the water–carriers would take water and then on a yolk [with hanging buckets] would distribute the water across the town. In the marketplace there was also city hall, the police station, and the "*kozeh*" (that's what they called the city police).

I remember once when suddenly there were loud cries and shouts in the marketplace that came from the *kozeh*. The police said that this was coming from a boy who was arrested because it was thought that he belonged to a revolutionary party. The police wanted to get the names of the party heads from him. But the boy withstood all the punishments and did not reveal any names. Later it was found out that the boy was Zelig Hode's.

[Page 208]

On the other side of the market, just opposite city hall, stood Ristow's hotel–bourse. Right nearby was Meir Burak's inn, that also served as the depot for all the wagon drivers and their carriages, carts, covered wagons, and coaches, that would drive passengers to other cities and into Gostynin.

On the sides of the market, were the two mains streets of Gostynin: Plock and Kutno Streets. The two streets went lengthwise through the city and were the main promenades for the Gostynin youth. At the end of Kutno Street, there was the pleasure garden and the long garden. On the Russian holidays, there would be entertainment and the military orchestra would play in the pleasure gardens and in the long garden.

The house in which we lived was on Plock Street, not far from the Polish church where poor peasants would kneel and pray in front of the church. On the side of our house, there was an orchard where all kinds of fruit grew: apples, plums, gooseberries, and "hazelnuts." In general, Gostynin had the fragrance of fruit orchards. Both the Jews and the Christians did business with fruit.

In the summertime, the orchard would be rented to a lessee, who would live in the orchard the entire summer until the fruit season ended. When the fruit was already picked, and the lessee had left, then the orchard became available for us young boys. We would climb the trees and tear or shake off the remaining fruit – some with our hands, some with sticks, and some with large rocks. This was our greatest fun.

Our family – the Kellers, the Epstajns, Reb Leibish Lipsycz, and the "black Freide" with her sons lived on Plock Street. When the Polish holiday "Green Thursday" arrived, it usually occurs around Shavuot time [end of May], we children had to stay indoors; we were afraid to go out in the streets because at that time the Polaks took out the "icons" (religious pictures) from the church and carried them in a procession through the streets of Gostynin.

[Page 209]

On Koval Street, there was the German church; on Kutno Street were the Russian church, the gymnasium, the post office, and the military barracks. The Rav lived on Gombyn Street. On that street was the *shul*, the *Beis Medrash* [study hall], and the *mikva* [ritual baths].

***

Many years have passed, summers and winters, that we have not seen our town, and yet we still can see the *shul* courtyard where the young school–age boys had their "wars," one school against another, and then having "losses" and "victories"!.... We loved to watch the *shul*'s pulpit where we little boys used to celebrate on *Simchas Torah* with the *hakofos* [dancing in celebration with the Torah scrolls]; to see the *Beis Medrash* with its large bookcases, and, to make a distinction, see the mountain of all mountains (the oaks), of which every person from Gostynin has memories; of the Jeziero Lake, where we would swim in the summers; and of other places that are deeply etched in our memories.

I remember when our town welcomed its first automobile (*samochodt* [trans: goes by itself]). Crowds of Jewish men and women, boys and girls, surrounded this "bird," staring at it and touching it, trying to find out the secret of where it had the horsepower to make this automobile go as fast as a train and yet without a horse ... and when the car began to shake violently and a white plume of smoke exploded out of the back and then the automobile took off in a gallop, the men and women farmers crossed themselves and the Jews muttered: "Miracles of the Creator!" Daring Jewish young boys took part in a contest to see who would be able to run faster: they or the automobile. Understandably, the automobile came out the winner... But one thing we didn't understand and that puzzled our brains was the driver of the automobile. He sat himself inside, turned a crank several times, and the car made a noise and jumped up and down. The driver pushed a button and in the front two torches lit up and gave the automobile a whole other appearance. Many times did the automobile cause great disturbances. When it went through the streets, the horses, harnessed to wagons, became frightened and began to kick, as they would go up on their hind legs and then run so wildly that it was impossible to control them. For the people it was actually life threatening.

[Page 210]

***

I remember how they tried out "incandescent" lamps in the marketplace. The light from these lamps gave the impression of gaslights. Groups of people surrounded the lamp poles, gazed in wonder at the new lights, and speculated at how these lamps were lit without "*zapalkes*" (matches). The farmers from around Gostynin came to town with their children to look at these wonders. Years later, Gostynin already had electric lights on almost all the streets. The city's residents were proud that the city of Gostynin became a city likened to any other.

***

It comes to mind those times when we were still young boys and our fathers sent us to Avrohom Meyer, the teacher of young children, and he began to drill the first bits of Hebrew. He is standing before my eyes – our teacher – when he would say: "Children, it will soon be *Lag b'Omer*. * Prepare yourselves with your weapons [bows and arrows]. We're going into the forest to celebrate the holiday!"

This is a holiday celebrating the anniversary of the passing of the great sage and mystic Rabbi Shimon bar Yochai, author of the kabbalistic text, the Zohar. It also commemorates another day. In the weeks between Passover and Shavuot, a plague raged amongst the disciples of the great sage Rabbi Akiva. On the day of Lag BaOmer, the dying ceased, causing great celebration.

When the eve of *Lag b'Omer* had arrived, he would repeat: "Children, tomorrow is *Lag b'Omer*. Go home and tell your mothers that they should prepare pouches of food for you because we will be spending the entire day in the forest, and don't forget to bring *Lag b'Omer* money!" ...

The following day, the day of *Lag b'Omer*, the teacher came with us into the forest to celebrate the holiday. We boys were carrying our weapons – wooden bows with stretched out string attached, pouches with all kinds of foods, hardboiled eggs, egg cookies, and other snacks. And we really stayed in the forest until the sun went down...

[Page 211]

When we were a little older, grown up, our father moved us from Avrohom Meyer and gave us to Reb Leibele *melamed* [the teacher]. With Reb Leibele, we began learning *Chumash* [five books of the Torah] and *Rashi* [commentary], and later on *gemara* [Talmud].

Reb Leibele *melamed* lived in one room which was also the classroom. In the middle of the room, there was a long, narrow table, and on either side of the table – there were two long benches where the children sat. A little deeper in the room were two beds where the Rebbe and the Rebbetzen [his wife] slept. The beds were hidden behind curtains – a sign that that place was no longer part of the classroom. ... On the side of the room there was an oven and a kitchen for cooking, and a little niche behind the oven that served as a place for sleeping in the winter. Near to that niche, a little on the side, there was a large barrel of water onto which was hooked a copper cup that rested on a board which covered the barrel. A little farther, closer to the door, was a – slop pail [for garbage or food scraps]...

Reb Leibele *melamed* was of average size, with a wide, disheveled, graying beard. By nature, he was quieter, and though even in his demeanor, his idleness was very evident, nonetheless, he was very able to understand a concept and whatever he expressed was clearly understood.

Every morning, we would study the Torah portion of the week. According to his mood, Reb Leibele would punish the boys for not knowing the Torah portions. If he was in a foul mood, he would rip the boys by the ears, poke them in their sides, hit them on their backs, and so on... For not looking into their Torah books, he would beat the boys.

Every morning, when his wife Shprintze would set down his breakfast on the table, we boys would love to see how he would behave with his food. He would go towards the barrel of water, fill up the copper cup, and wash his hands maybe ten times, switching the cup from his right hand to his left, and from his left hand to his right. After washing his hands, he would replace the cup, grab the right side of his long, black coat, and dry his hands, then say "*se'u yedeichem...*" [Verse recited when washing hands before eating bread: "Lift your hands to the Sanctuary and bless God].

[Page 212]

This blessing over a piece of bread would go on for a long time because he repeated one word five times. During his meal, he would sway back and forth, and rub the thumb of his left hand on the edge of the table. When reciting the grace after the meal, he would repeat a word ten times and rub his hands together so strongly that his fingers were replete with peeled spots. He would also rub his head with his cap and then spit on the floor.

In the winter days, the Rebbe would recite the afternoon prayers [*mincha*] and evening prayers [*maariv*] in the room. He would begin his prayers very slowly, and then sway back and forth slowly as well. Gently, he would go into a state of ecstasy and would recite the words more and more quickly, strike his hand onto his heart, rub his *yarmulke* [skullcap] onto his head, raise one leg above the knee, and with all kinds of gestures, would recite the verses of the prayers. These types of scenes went on repeatedly in front of us boys in the *cheder*.

Shprintze, the Rebbetzen [Rebbe's wife], of small size and bent over, wore a bonnet [*kupke*] over her head, and then a headscarf covering that. She watched over the Rebbe as if he were an eye in her head. Every morning at the same time, his breakfast was already prepared for him on the table.

In her free time, the Rebbetzen would busy herself by mending stockings and knitting many things. On a stool that stood near the oven, she would sit with her feet resting on a small chair and she would have the small ball of black thread on her lap. From the ball she would always pull out some thread and put it through the large wooden needle. That's how the Rebbetzen would sit and knit for hours, and not even for one minute allow the stocking to leave her hands.

Once, it happened that the ball of black thread slipped out of her hands, fell onto the floor, and then began to roll across the room. Even before the Rebbetzen started to bend over to pick up the ball of thread, the cat, that was lying on the oven shelf warming himself, saw something black running across the floor, so she awoke briskly, perked up her ears, set out her lightening eyes, pounced off the oven, and then chased after the ball of thread. When the boys saw this, it became lively around the table.... We began to poke one another, with one glance into the *gemara* and another glance at the cat, and another glance at the Rebbetzen – and then we choked on our laughter....

[Page 213]

"What's this?" the Rebbe raged. "Scoundrels! Respect!" and then immediately went to get his belt in order to teach the wise guys a lesson for their impudence in the middle of the learning session. At that very minute, it happened that the Rebbetzen bent over to retrieve the ball of thread, but the cat got there first and grabbed the ball between her two feet and began to roll the ball across the floor. The Rebbetzen, still leaning over, ready to grab the ball of thread, fell over with an outstretched hand, and let out a cry: "Leibel! The cat!"

The Rebbe remained standing with the belt in his hand, confused. All the boys immediately broke out in laughter. The Rebbe, a little lost, placed the belt on the table, went over to the Rebbetzen, lifted her up, seated her on the stool, and then himself went to grab the cat. He took the ball of thread away from the cat and then gave it to the Rebbetzen.

When the Rebbe came back to the table, he was already cooled and calmed down. But he threw angry eyes at the pupils, as one says: It's your luck that it happened just so. Any longer, and I would have thrashed you all!"

[Page 214]

***

As all cities and towns, Gostynin had many types and characters of people. There were four water carriers in Gostynin, four different types, each with his unique Jewish behaviors. Each had his own areas, his streets, to bring those residents their water. Who does not remember their comments, their curses? ...

Among the Gostynin coachmen, who were all strong, sturdy young men, was one who was called Yakov the coachman [*Furman*]. This Yakov *Furman* lived on Plock Street where Reb Leybish, the son of the Gostynin Rebbe, lived. Yakov *Furman* never used the whip on his horses. He was a man of great compassion for living things....

It happened often that the wagon was filled with passengers and so one or two of the passengers had to sit with Yakov *Furman* on the coachman's seat. Once, a passenger who was sitting on the seat noticed how the horse was always pulling to one side. The passenger asked the coachman: "What's wrong with your horse? Is he a little short–sighted?" ...

"Oho! Better you shouldn't ask," the coachman replied.

"What, is the horse really blind?" the passenger asked again.

"Once, I went to the railway station with my wagon, and just at that moment, the devil brought in the speed train and a spark from the locomotive lodged itself in the right eye of this horse," the coachman recounted. "But you just show him some oats, and he'll see that much better with one eye than other horses with two," the coachman ended with laughter.

***

[Page 215]

Gostynin did not have a permanent music band; there was only one musician in town who played the flute. And that's why the townspeople called him "*turleteh*" ... When there was a wedding in town, they would bring over a band of musicians along with an entertainer [a *badchan* (entertainer) specializes in humorous and sentimental rhymes that he sings as entertainment at weddings].

Gostynin did not have an old age home. Because of that, Osher Meroz, the perpetual drunk of the town, kept himself in the house for the needy of the *Chassidim shtiebel* [small synagogue], and on the cold winter nights he would go behind the tiled oven of the *Beis Medrash*. The *Beis Medrash* and the *Chassidim shtiebel* were located in the same building.

It was a beautiful tradition for Jews to have guests for *Shabbos*. When a poor man would come to town from somewhere else for *Shabbos*, and through him one was able to fulfill the mitzvah of hosting guest, he was very welcomed by the Jews. When a poor man would come to Gostynin, he would go to the Jewish stores and receive very handsome donations. When a guest would appear in the *Beis Medrash* or the *Chassidim shtiebel* on Friday night, all the congregants would busy themselves with him. They would almost take him apart.

Our father, may he rest in peace, when he was lucky enough to have a guest for *Shabbos*, would tend to him as if to the Kaiser, and would not let him go without giving him a handsome donation and giving him the best of the best for his trip.

***

Every Tuesday and Friday there was the fair in Gostynin. Farmers from the surrounding villages brought in by wagonload all kinds of food products: corn, wheat, eggs, butter, cheese, chickens, sacks of potatoes, bundles of wood for burning, and all kinds of fruit. The farmers set out their wagons in the marketplace, and customers would come around and look at and touch the produce, would negotiate and haggle, according to their means.

[Page 216]

For the yearly fair, small merchants from other cities and towns would come to Gostynin with their merchandise and the marketplace became filled with people from all different regions.

Other than the shops that were on all sides of the marketplace, tables were also set out with all kinds of material merchandise, colonial articles, haberdashery, men's and women's clothing, shoe ware, stockings, hats, earthenware, pots, baskets, steel beds, tin ovens, lime, rope, noodle boards [for rolling out dough], graters, herring, soap, bread, cake, twisted bagels, children's toys, and many other things. There was a happy tumult, a lively hoo–ha and noise, as is usual for a fair. The farmers began to bring out the products that they brought: a calf, a heifer, a foal, a mare, geese, ducks, barley, millet, dried mushrooms, raw skins, wooden dishes, brooms, and other things. The entire marketplace was topsy–turvy. Tailors patched up the farmers' shirts and coats; shoemakers fixed old boots and felt–boots; customers were standing head to head. Women peasants, young and old, tore the displayed merchandise right out of their hands, bought remnants of velvet and fleece. The young peasants bought ribbons, beads, silvered earrings, and rings.

And then suddenly, the crowd all moved over to one side. The city officer arrived, and on each yearly fair day, he would drum on his drum in all the corners of the marketplace and would call out the new "decrees" of what one was permitted to do and what one was not permitted to do. At the same time, he would announce that so–and–so had lost a pig, the other person lost a goat, and so on. People gathered around him and to hear him out. When the "man and his drum" as they called him, finished his job, the crowd disbanded.

The marketplace was not only for fairs, annual fair day, and for haggling, but was also often used for political activities. Around 1905, when the Czarist government delivered a list of independence decrees, the Polish and Jewish population of Gostynin put forth a great push for Poland's independence. May First demonstrations in our town, according to our memories, were never legal, but they took place anyway. That's the way it was until after World War One when Poland once again became an independent country.

[Page 217]

***

With the onset of spring, with the awakening of nature, the youth's longing to be part of the free, fresh, blossoming outdoors awoke as well. Who doesn't remember the May strolls in Gostynin? The Jewish residents, and particularly the youth of that time, went out into the Gostynin pathways in groups into the villages, as the young boys and girls, the loving couples, absorbed the refreshing air of the month of May – the air that smelled of lilacs, with a sweet fragrance that Mother Nature bestowed with an open hand. And when we would finally get tired from the long hours of strolling around, then we would soothe our hearts in the villages with some black bread and butter and buttermilk and sour cream and other good foods that we negotiated from the farmers in the villages. When we finished eating and were rested, we left to ride on the swings. Such happiness! Such fun was this for the Jewish youth of Gostynin!

And when the hot days of summer arrived, we left for the Kutno–Sosnow woods to pick red and blue berries, cranberries, and mushrooms.

Not once did the "cuckoo" with her cawing steer us wrong, and not once did we get lost on our way back. Many times, instead of coming back into town, we saw large meadows where calmly and gently the animals were grazing. The shepherd was sitting near a small fire, and was throwing in pieces of wood and dried twigs that crackled in the fire along with the aroma of roasting potatoes. The shepherd's flute and the Polish songs that he sang so heartily were pieces of the Jewish panorama that spilled organically into our town's way of life....

[Page 218]

***

Wintertime in Gostynin was exactly like in any other city. Every house was transformed into a palace with a silver roof. The town became lit up from the white snow; the air is cold and invigorating; people were dressed in warm clothes, the farmers in their fur coats, pelts made of skins, and cotton padded pants. The store owners in the market were sitting on the fire buckets, wrapped in their heavy shawls, wearing thick gloves. The storekeepers were wearing fur coats, boots, and galoshes, and they were doing business, in the usual manner.

For the *cheder* boys, winter was a wondrous time. They made snowmen and threw snowballs. Whenever there was a free minute from *cheder*, they were playing in the snow.

When the lakes and narrow gutters would freeze over, then the bunch would go skating. It was the older boys, the bigger ones, who did this. The younger boys got together for skating on the frozen puddles around the two water pumps that were in the market. The older boys, who skated with ice skates on, did "*kutzke*" (this was a different trick, that involved sitting down and "skating" while sitting.)

On the heavy snow that lay for many weeks on the streets and open highways like a silver tapestry, blinding the eyes with its whiteness, other groups went out with some sleds, some with rented sleds, at a gallop ... the lightness of the sleds that slid across the Plock highway, the white, snowy pines with the frozen "*tzapenes*" [trans: "braids" referring to pine cones] on the branches that stood on both sides of the roadway, led us into a dream world. The bells, that hung from the horses' necks, rang happily, as frost exhaled from the coachman's mouth, and we sat in the sleigh with our heads wrapped in warm cowls and we were so happy that no one could compare themselves to us ...

[Page 219]

***

The stocking industry distributed its production in many larger cities, such as Plock, Kutno, Wloclawek, and also in a list of many smaller cities. Making stockings on a hand machine was not such complicated work. There were many techniques and grades in this work. Everyone worked in his own way – quickly, slowly, easier, more difficult.

The stocking makers were mood–people. They worked according to their mood. Singing at work was also an expression of their mood.

Songs such as Morris Rosenfeld's *"Mein Yingele"* [trans: "My Little Boy"], Dovid Edelstadt's *"Mir Wehren Gehast un Getriben"* [trans: "We Are Hated and Chased"], or the folksongs *"Fonye, Fonye, Ganif"* [trans: "Fonye, Fonye, Thief"], *"Feierdike Liebe Titt in Hartzen Brennen"* ["A Fiery Love Burns in the Heart"], *"Direh Gelt"* [trans: "Rent"], *"Ott Azoi Neyt a Shneider"* [trans: "That's How a Tailor Sews"], or the lullabies with which the mothers and grandmothers used to put us to sleep: "When you, my child, will get older, you will know the difference between poverty and wealth." – Those were the songs that were sung from the depths of the heart. All the stocking manufacturers in the Gostynin factories sang while they worked.

Our small stocking factory was made up of seven journeymen: our four brothers – Shloime, Meyer, Yakov, and Yosef, and three others. The first to become a stocking manufacturer was Yosef. He very much preferred to work rather than to sit and study Talmud. Our parents, may they rest in peace, understood this and then made peace with it. Meyer, Shloime, and Yakov were also very anxious to become workers – because to become workers at that time meant to liberate oneself from the fanatically religious environment. Of all the four brothers who were stocking manufacturers, Yosef was the best worker. His stockings were exceptional, like pearls. Meyer was the machine specialist. He understood the mechanics well, and was an expert at knotting a fly so that the needles should work well, and could also set up the machines so that they could produce dyed stockings that came out of the machine imperfect. Our dear sister made the patterns or ironed the stockings and our father often helped her with this work.

[Page 220]

The stocking manufacturers did not work long in the factories. They would change their place of work almost each season. As a result, we often worked with many types of stocking manufacturers. One of these "types" who left a deep impression in our minds was Efraim Borscht.

Efraim Borscht, as we remember him, was a bit of a stiff figure. Because of that, he would sit at work straight as a string [of an instrument]. He was a very slow worker. As stiff as he was physically, that's how soft was his character. For example, he could converse with a seven- or eight-year-old child not using "you" [in informal direct form], but with "Listen, you," [using the formal "you" in Yiddish, "zie"]. His mother made her living from delivering milk and selling borscht [beet soup] to the homemakers in Gostynin. Every morning she brought her Efraim breakfast to the factory. Breakfast consisted of a bowl of small boiled potatoes with sauerkraut borscht and a piece of bread and butter.

At our home, for breakfast we would have a roll with butter and a drink of coffee. There was no cooked food prepared to eat in the mornings because it was felt that eating cooked food in the mornings was just too uncouth. Nonetheless, we children looked on with envy at the shiny small potatoes with sauerkraut borscht, and our mouths actually drooled.

Sitting opposite Efraim Borscht was Motel Mikhalski, a quick worker. The stockings almost fell out of his hands, one after the other, without stop. There he sat, it appeared, at his work, and he saw no one around him. But suddenly, an impulsive thought struck him. He stood up counted the stockings, got dressed, and rushed out to bathe in the Jeziero Lake. And before anyone could say one word to him, he was already gone! And with that he ended his day's work. (Motel Mikhalski is no longer among the living. During the First World War, he registered in the Jewish Legion in Israel. On the way back to America, he died in Marseilles, France.)

[Page 221]

***

Even though we children were busy producing stockings in our home, from time to time we tried to entertain ourselves in a civilized manner. When our father would be on the road with his business trips, our dear sister would invite our neighboring friends – boys and girls – to our home and we would celebrate with great partying. To this kind of party, the Keller daughters would come – Chava and Pesse. Pesse was a sprite – a fiery beautiful girl. She sang and danced beautifully. Everyone loved her. Among the invited guests were also Simcha Bunim Danziger's daughters, Soro and Feige. Tauba Chaya's children were also among the guest. It was lively in the house. We sang and we danced. The crowd delighted in home baked oil cookies, drank a little wine, sang songs, and told stories and anecdotes until late into the night. That's how we spent our Friday nights when our father did not come home for Shabbath.

Our mother, may she rest in peace, was very friendly with Mrs. Epstajn. It was, in fact, that my sister Rochtche and I, Yakov, would often go to their [Epstajn] house. I remember back to my childhood years, when we were at the Epstajns for a Chanuka party, where there were many other invited friends and acquaintances. I remember how the group was seated around a large, set up table, where all kinds of drinks and foods were laid out. It was bright in the house, warm – a pleasure! I sat on the side where the sofa stood.

[Page 222]

The Epstajns were wealthy and a much respected family in Gostynin. They helped the needy with a generous hand and gave to the charitable organizations.

***

The military conscription (or "*Los*" as it was called) in Gostynin, evokes a lot of memories. Gostynin was a prefecture. The smaller cities, such as Gombyn, Sanik, and the villages and regions in the area, belonged to the jurisdiction of the conscription commission in Gostynin.

Each year, around *Sukos* time [late September, early October], the city was filled with young men who had to present themselves for military conscription. These "conscripts" planted themselves in the streets and there was a joyous mood. At the same time, however, the Jewish residents of the town lived in fear of the village recruits. Knowing that they already were enlisted soldiers, they would assault the Jewish residents, beat them, and then make fun of them.

The only one in the town who stood watch to protect the Jewish population in a time of danger was Shloime Blecher's son, Shmuel Mikholski. He was a sturdily built young man and strong as steel. He would have with him several of the other strong and sturdy wagon drivers who put up resistance to the village hoodlums and broke their bones, so that the others were more careful in the future ...

For the Jews to serve "Fonje" was a forbidden sin – like eating pork. So many of the Jewish conscripts went to the *Beis Medrash* every evening to recite Psalms ... These "Psalm reciters" held gatherings in the *Beis Medrash* and decided that everyone who was reprieved from serving "Fonje" – particularly the wealthier boys – should contribute to the fund for the poorer recruits. This decision was given over to the freed young men in the form of an ultimatum. Against these freed men who declined to give this contribution, in the middle of the night there were "punishment expeditions" .... From one of these, they removed the wooden steps from their house; from another they removed the shutters from the windows; from many others they removed the signs from their stores; and then did other antics. Since it was a tradition in Gostynin to take the enlisted soldiers to the synagogue and have them deliver an oath, the recruits already remained in the synagogue until late at night, and from there they went to carry out the "punishment" ...

[Page 223]

***

Our family was blessed with a lot of earnings. So here is a description of a curious episode in our business deals.

We also had a store of soap, vinegar, and wine. When it was Purim time, we began to make the preparations for making Passover wine. We made the barrels or "tubs" kosher for Passover with red hot stones, soaked the sacks of raisins, and made other preparations for the kosher–for–Passover wine.

Our grandmother Baila lived in the marketplace. There was a cellar in her house, half of which was rented to the lame Avrom Aron for his winter fruits, and the other half was for our small factory. All of us children wanted very badly to accompany our father into the wine cellar and watch how the raisin wine was made. With my childish intelligence, I couldn't understand at that time that in order for the wine to come out crystal clean and clear, you had to first distil it. I was just curious to know how it was made and what was the "distilling" all about.

We were all standing near our father and looking on. Our father took a specially made sack, stretched it over a large tub, put a hoop over it to hold the sack down, and then he rubbed the sack with broken up charcoal made of wood cinders and something else like that. Through the sack, he poured the raisin wine into the tub – and that's how the wine became clean and clear.

[Page 224]

We children were told not to "touch" any of the fruits that were in the other half of the cellar, and we actually never stole any apples or pears from there.

When the lame Avrom Aron would come into the cellar to rearrange the fruit so that they wouldn't rot, he would always sing a song as he worked. Each apple that he took into his hand, he first spat onto it. And then rubbed it and shined it in the back of his pants and thereby appraised and stored away a prize: "A six–coin! A six–coin!" and a satisfied smile would show on his face.

***

That's how we lived and grew up in our town Gostynin. Everything that our senses experienced, they absorbed in the prime of our childhood years. These memories live within us to this day, even though decades have passed and much water has flowed by, and oceans of blood have been spilled. We still live with our Gostynin of long ago.

[Page 225]

From My Childhood[23]

by Florence Keller-Malmeth

Translated by Pamela Russ

Florence Keller-Malmeth

My eight-year-old daughter has just come in, full of enthusiasm. She is becoming a member of a club. "Mother," she says to me, "can we have the club meeting at our home? Will you put out refreshments so that the meeting will really become like a party for the club?"

"Certainly," I answered, looking at her shining face and realizing that my little girl was already a grown-up young lady. As in so many other instances, I began to think about my own childhood.

The sheaves of the calendar suddenly turn back and it is the year 1934. I was a ten-year-old girl, a little older than my own daughter Baila Genendel, and I was then about to join my first club. But this is where the similarity ends. My club was organized to meet on a sunny summer day in the Polish town of Gostynin.

---

25. Translated from English

God works in mysterious ways. People like to think that they control their fates, but with time they begin to understand that maybe they should stop and rethink this. In the early 1920s, there was a mass exodus from the European countries to the large country of greater opportunity, the United States. The woman with the torch in the New York harbor stretched out her welcoming arms to my parents, Shmuel and Chana Keller. Just as others, they left their country of birth, their families, and their friends. Many came, but more than six million remained behind.

[Page 226]

In 1934, after thirteen years in America, my mother felt a deep longing, and maybe this was an unknown foreshadowing of what was to come, to see her beloved town of Gostynin. When school was over for me, my mother and I went to Poland to her hometown, for a vacation. This experience has remained in my memory until today.

I will never forget these happy times that I spent in Gostynin. Since I was born and grew up in the tall tenements of New York, at first glance I felt strange, as someone living in a story or in a magical tale.

The small houses, the large marketplace, the horses and wagons, gave the town the feeling of olden times.

We arrived in Gostynin on a Sunday morning. The entire city was still wrapped in a deep sleep, when we arrived at the house of my grandmother, Genendel Bagno. Laughter and tears, hugs and kisses - what a welcome greeted us! Soon, all kinds of people streamed in to see the Americans. I felt the warmth of my grandmother's hands when she embraced me close to her. I felt that she couldn't hold me close enough to her. What can be more beloved for a grandchild's heart? A mother is a mother, but there is still room in a little girl's heart for a grandmother.... It is God's gift that my children were fortunate to have this at the first moment of their lives, when I was only given this gift at the age of ten.

Soon there were other experiences. One of the most exciting moments of that morning was when I met my other grandmother, my father's mother. Looking through the window, I saw an elegant woman walking towards us through the crooked, small streets. "This is my father's mother," my mother informed me, whispering in my ear. Oh, I knew quite well who she was. I remembered all the stories that my father told us about his beloved mother whom he described as a Jewish queen. With an instinctive love that only very young children can feel, I ran to meet her. Her grandchild was with her, my cousin Yisroel Itche, whom she had raised. That's how the first few days went, filled with joy to have met relatives and friends.

[Page 227]

As everything else in life, our visit to Gostynin fell into a routine. I wanted ice cream, so my mother bought *"lody"* (Polish word for ice-cream), but it didn't taste like ice-cream back home and I expressed that openly. I didn't think that my words would offend the vendor, but he took this to heart. The next morning, he gave me a portion of ice cream with pride, calling it "American *lody*." That hit the spot. From that time on I was able to taste the full flavor of the Gostynin ice cream.

Days and weeks passed. I saw places, met people about whom my father had talked about. I saw my parents' home where they had hours of pleasure and joy. I went swimming in the Ratei Lake, and went to *shul* (synagogue) where my grandfathers used to pray. I experienced the market days in town, and on those days the town was full of activity. My grandmothers' and uncles' stores were filled with noise and business. Then my grandmother, Baila Faiga, took me to her home where it was calm and peaceful.

As I was holding my dearest doll in my arms, which was to me as if alive, I passed through the streets and the marketplace on the way to her home. The peasants saw this kind of doll for the first time and thought that it was a living child. On those days, my grandmother would tell me and my young cousin all kinds of stories about kings and princes from a faraway land, and open photo albums and show us all kinds of pictures and photos ....

[Page 228]

I met many people about whom I had heard in New York, and among them was the "dark" Fraida. It was actually through her that I met her grandchild Franja Bender who became my closest friend. Franja Bender and her family took me in as their own. I ate there, played there in her father's wheat, and played on Plock Street. Fraida, then 106 years old, sat in front of Franja's house and watched out for us with her eyes that sparkled with the wisdom of generations. Franja and I thought about organizing a girls' club in Gostynin. With childish simplicity, we prepared the initial work of the organization. Since I was the initiator of this idea, I automatically became the president, and she, the vice-president. Our membership fee was one penny (*groshen*) a day. Our group had a total of eight girls. Even though our finances were meager, our plans were grand. We planned a picnic. But it seemed that our slim taxes did not amount to a significant sum. We were very upset.

My uncle Efraim Motel came to the rescue, and he gave us five zlotys. Great joy! Our picnic took place and our club was saved.

The highlight each evening was our trip to the cinema. One *Motzei Shabbat* (Saturday night), my mother and I took my uncle Leibish Bagno to the theater. The theater usher was a different one than we were used to seeing. He was probably a temporary one. In the back, there were tables with baked goods and sweets. Between scenes, there were breaks where the lights were turned on. People went over to the tables to eat and socialize. Even though the atmosphere was foreign to me, nonetheless, I probably enjoyed myself at least somewhat, because they were showing an American film with Polish subtitles.

[Page 229]

A treasured memory that will remain the dearest and most sentimental for me, was the day I left Gostynin. Years later, I understood Shakespeare, who said "Parting is such sweet sorrow."

Our departure began like a *yom tov* (holiday). The train was to leave Kutno in the middle of the night. That night, people came and left. Even though we had said our good-byes, that had not left the impact of actually separating. Finally, my friends came. Franja and her family gave me a small autograph book as a gift. Everyone wrote something in it - some in Yiddish, some in Polish. It didn't really matter how long the inscription was, there was so much warmth in each letter. Among all my personal mementos that I have, I will most treasure this Gostynin memory. I kissed Franja, we promised one another to write. We were certain that we would see each other in the future.

Suddenly, the time came. In front of the small house on Koval Street there was a special bus that would take the entire families Keller and Bagno to Kutno. My father's brothers Moishe, Yekhiel Meyer, Sholom, Aron, their wives, dear Aunt Charna, my mother's brother Leibish, all of them, all of them wanted to be with us until the final moments when we would be seated on the international train on our way home.

Standing in the small window of the train, I saw our Gostynin family that was a sea of faces, with hands that waved with hankies, escorting us with the finest of blessings.

[Page 230]

Memories

by Rivka Danziger – Fundak (Israel)

Translated by Pamela Russ

We can't forget those days, when we wandered across the paths and climbed the mountains. Who doesn't remember those mountains that were overgrown with trees and greenery, and that intoxicated the air with fragrant smells? During the spring and summertime, in the shade of the trees, we would spend time strolling there. In that magic of nature we found tranquility against our broiling youth, as we threw off all our worries of home. In winter, we, the youth, went sledding across the snowy mountains, downhill, with joy and excitement – how beautiful were the mountains in winter!

I remember those fresh days of our youth, when we, a gang of children, left our houses with pots to go into the woods and pick blueberries. Who can forget our joy as we wandered through the fragrant pine trees and heard the birds singing all around? But clouds spread over our town. In 1939 I left my hometown and went with the illegal *Aliyah* to Israel.

[Page 231]

Two World Wars

by Sh. B. Bagno (Belgium)

Translated by Pamela Russ

Shmuel Borukh Bagno

In the year 1914, at the outbreak of World War I, the German armies began to take over Poland. The first army marched across our city Gostynin on the way to Warsaw, but a few days later the German army retreated to the German border. Their marching back through our town went until nighttime.

On one particular day, my father was not at home. He had gone with other merchants to Kutno. At nightfall, our mother became restless. We heard the loud noise of the soldiers, the clang of the horseshoes, and the clattering of the cannon wheels. Suddenly, we heard a loud banging. We heard an order for us to open the door, and if we would be resisting, they would break down the door. My mother, trembling with fear, unlocked the door. There stood German soldiers with bayonets aimed at us.

"Where is the owner of this house?"

When my mother explained that my father had gone away, the senior officer ordered to search the house from attic to cellar. When they didn't find my father, the officer ordered that they take me, a nineteen-year-old boy, and my brother, thirteen years old.

[Page 232]

When we went outside, I became very confused. The street was filled with military. They put us among the horsemen and took us on the road to Koval. When we crossed the little bridge, I heard a soldier say to my brother that he could go home; he was just too young.

After an entire night of splashing through mud puddles, we entered the town of Koval where the military had stopped off for a few minutes. There I saw a few other people from Gostynin: Aron Bresler, the wealthiest man in the city, Jahne the pharmacist, and a Russian policeman.

We were forbidden to speak to one another, so we communicated with looks of all kinds, and then soon once again dragged ourselves back on the road. We passed through Wloclawek, Aleksandrow, and other towns.

On the third day, we arrived in the German city of Toruń where they took us directly to prison. The first welcome we received was from an official who told us to undress fully. Two doctors examined us, and after that we put on the prison clothes.

In the prison there were civilian prisoners along with criminals. The German thugs made fun of our embittered situation, with ugly comments. In a few days, they brought in more men; among them were three from Gostynin: Leizer Schneider's son, and Yekhiel Zalman Motel and his brother-in-law (I've forgotten his name). We spent a dark few weeks in prison, and we lost hope that we would ever be freed.

One day, they took us and put us into closed wagons and took us to the big camp Schneidermuhl. Aron Bresler and Jahne remained behind.

There were thousands of Russian prisoners in Schneidermuhl, along with many Poles and Jews.

The conditions were intolerable. The Germans even at that time were murderers. They beat us mercilessly for the slightest thing. Many men remained crippled from these beatings.

[Page 233]

Those of us from Gostynin were afraid to ask for a piece of bread, so we starved. On top of that, there was terrible cold. We slept on the cold, hard floor, and insects of all sorts swarmed around us.

That's how we suffered all winter. In spring of 1915, the Germans removed all the civilian prisoners to the Havelberg camp. It was even worse there. Typhus was rampant and swallowed up new victims each day. That camp was the worst one in terms of hygiene. We lived in constant fear that the disease should not swallow us up as well. Those who weren't sick were taken to work in the fields. We were still hungry, but it was better than being locked up all day in the dirty camp.

After a few days of working in the fields, my Gostynin friends did not return. A rumor that they had escaped circulated around the camp. My thoughts also turned around such a plan, but they guarded us closely, and in the meantime, any thought of escaping was impossible.

They stopped sending us into the fields. There were very difficult days, without an end, until one morning they took us to work not far from the Belgian border.

The hard labor under the burning sun was unbearable. We dropped from weakness. I decided that now was the time to escape. I secretly told the plan to a young man by the name of Braverman, from Lodz. He agreed to take the daring step with me.

We hid until it was dark. Then we began to crawl across fields and hills. Just at daybreak, we noticed that we were close to a town. Since we didn't know if this was still Germany or if it was Belgium, we entered the town. We sneaked through the streets, when our ears caught the sounds of the Yiddish language. We approached with great joy, and then saw that these were actually our Jewish brothers.

[Page 234]

We told them from where we had come. They were frightened, and they took us in and calmed our hunger. After we finished eating, they urged us to leave this small Belgian town and told us to go to the large city of Brussels, where we should go ask for help from the organization "Ezra."

That same day, we arrived in Brussels. When we saw German officers and military in the streets, we were terrified. We went from one street to another. Everyone who even glanced at us, made us shudder.

Suddenly, at a distance, we noticed a *shul*(synagogue), and a Jew was going over there and unlocking the door. We went into the *shul* and told the Jews what had happened and what our situation was. The *shamash* (synagogue attendant) promised to help us.

Meanwhile, more Jews arrived, and they began their prayers. The *shamash* brought us a *siddur* (prayer book), and I felt that it had been two years since I last held a *siddur* in my hands. After *mincha* and *maariv* (the evening prayers), the *shamash* took us over to "Ezra." He presented us to the Ezra workers, and when one heard my name and that I came from Gostynin, he was very excited because he too was from Gostynin, from the Kruk family.

I will never forget how he welcomed us. He helped us along with hundreds of other Jews by hiding us for about one year.

In the year 1918, the German army suffered one of their worst defeats on the French front. This was the end of the German rule and also the end of World War I. The German military, in the greatest confusion, began their retreat from all their occupied countries. Belgium became a free, quiet country again. Hundreds of Polish Jews remained in Belgium, and I among them. We rebuilt our lives in this free land. Almost everyone brought relatives over from anti-Semitic Poland. From Gostynin, there was: a son of Moishe Brakman, a son of Henokh Makowski, Efraim Kaufman with his sister Khavtche, my three brothers - Yosef, Yakov, Sholom, and my sister Hinde and her husband.

[Page 235]

One by one, the Jews settled down, and conducted a quiet life, until the year 1939 when the Germans once again set the world on fire.

Already at the beginning of World War II, the Jews in Belgium were uneasy. Their fear grew daily. In May 1940, Hitler began a lightening attack (*blitzkrieg*) on Belgium. The Germans bombed Brussels. People were running from the city, Jewish families were running to hide, and in particular Jewish men were running to cross the border to France. I and my two brothers Yosef and Sholom were among these men.

They caught all three of us at the border and separated us immediately. I never saw my brothers again.

The Gestapo assumed that I was French because of my name, which was a French name, and because of my fluent French, and they packed me along with hundreds of other Frenchmen into cattlecars. There was nothing to sit on. They stuffed us all together like herring in a barrel. They took us to Mathausen in Austria.

The very first day in the camp, we went through hellish tortures. The food was very meager and foul. When it was already late in the evening, the SS moved us into barracks, where we fell onto sacks from hay in total exhaustion.

One morning, the chief of the Gestapo came in along with two SS men, and they told us to stand in rows. They took out some men from each row, I was one of those. They took us through dark hallways and when we came outside they stuffed us into cargo trucks. We were taken to the camp Wiener Neustadt.

[Page 236]

There we found many internees, and among them were Jews from Austria, Poland, and Germany.

We were counted, sorted, some sent to the right, some to the left. I, the Frenchmen, and the Belgians, were sent to the right. After that we were all sent to wooden barracks. A hell began - sadistic tortures, very heavy, physical, forced labor. Daily, the food became less and less, and worse and worse. We were in this camp for more than a year, and went through the seven gates of hell. Then we were sent to a third camp, Nagaike.

Everyone in the Gestapo carried a revolver and rod which he used at every opportunity, whether it was necessary or not. Very often, the internees were hanged there. Every time they hanged someone, the murderers made a whole show of it.

One thing was clear: If not for the extraordinary will to live and survive, it would have been impossible for anyone to survive the first few months of 1945. Of course there were victims, but the majority survived even the worst tortures and punishments...

In April 1945, there was news that the American army was already battling on the European continent.

In a few days' time, we already heard the shooting of cannons.

In the camps, everything continued as before with German precision, but we saw that at night the SS kept the entire camp in the dark.

A few more days passed. We began hearing louder shooting. We saw American air bombers flying over the camp. We thought they would soon start dropping bombs over our heads and that we would all die.

[Page 237]

We lived through many difficult hours in fear. There was chaos among the Gestapo and the SS. We had to be very careful that they shouldn't see our rage. Our terror grew with each minute, hoping that in these final minutes they would not kill us all before our liberation.

But still on that same day, everyone began to shout that the Americans had broken into our camp. All the internees, comprised of sick, starved, and half-dead people, suddenly acquired super-human strength and began jumping through doorways and from windows in order to meet our liberators and saviors as quickly as possible.

The camp guards soon hung out white flags.

That was in May 1945, when the American army liberated us from Hitler's hell. The entire camp was soon filled with liberated people who kissed and hugged for joy.

For me, the joy lasted only a few minutes. I remembered my wife and child, my mother, and my brother Leibish and his family from Gostynin, my three sisters and their families, and three brothers and their families.

Are they still alive? I asked myself, and I cried bitterly...

The American army treated us very well, showed us friendship, gave us good food, clothing, and even cigarettes. I will be thankful to them all my life.

That same month, May 25, the American pilots from Linz sent us over to France by airplane.

When we arrived at the Paris station, the French officers gave everyone papers with questions to answer: name, place of birth, religion, and where we were going.

When they took back the papers, I heard my name being called. With great fear, I barely came forward to the table where a young man was sitting, wearing a French uniform. When he asked me if my name was Bagno, I became very upset. I began to shake. One more second and I would have fallen to the ground, if the Frenchman would not have caught me and led me to a chair. He sat down next to me and said that he too is a Bagno. His father Avrohom and his grandfather Yekhezkel Bagno were also from Gostynin.

[Page 238]

Tears ran from his eyes. From our conversation we discovered that we were close relatives.

In all my wanderings and experiences, during World War I and World War II, in all the roads and steps, I found Jews from Gostynin .... We recognized one another, helped, and carried the love for one another deep inside....

[Page 239]

The Matil Family

by Rivka Matil–Margolit (Israel)

Translated by Pamela Russ

Rivkah Matil–Margolit

The family Matil in Gostynin was branched out for generations. Friends and family knew that the Matils were extraordinary with their excellent character traits and self–sacrifice. Our home served as an inn for all the Zionist activists who came to town to dispense propaganda for the Land of Israel. My father, Reb Isser Meyer, was someone renowned in Gostynin. He was beloved in all the Jewish circles and was also popular among the Christians in the town. If he appeared in the street, there was immediately a circle of Jews around him who wanted to hear from his mouth a witticism, a happy story that evoked a cheering up and laughter from the crowd. They loved to hear his numerology and initial letter [i.e., how initials stood for something deeper or more interesting than the actual words they represented] theories. As an activist in the Zionist organization and in other city institutions, he was in contact with all types of circles of the population. He was the founder of the *Gemilas Chesed* funds [free loan funds] in Gostynin, and he was also in the management of *Linat Tzedek* [organization that attended to the sick at night]. My mother, Henne, of blessed memory, was also active in social work, and particularly, she was most active with the work of WIZO [World International Zionist Organization], where she was treasurer for many years.

[Page 240]

My grandmother, my father's mother, was the "Black Freide." She was renowned in the town and her name was associated with the Polish January uprising of 1863. The old woman had a long life and died at 106. In the times of the Polish revolt, in the year 1863, she risked her life and hid several rebels in her cellar. Fifty years later, when the Polish government put up a memorial in memory of those heroes of the year 1863, the *voivode* [the military commander] mentioned the name of "Black Freide" as one of the heroes of that time. In his speech, he emphasized that her son and family should be proud that they bear the name of Matil as the name of the elderly heroine.

My grandmother Freide was a religious and God–fearing woman, and she believed and had faith in other people just as she had perfect faith in God in Heaven, Who gave her many rich years of life. She remembered her young years very well, those times when the Polish nationalist heroes wanted to liberate the Polish ground from its Czarist occupants and Cossack battalions. She used to tell us stories of old legends that to us children appeared distant and wrapped in secrets. Just as she had things to tell us about her experiences during the historical period of the year 1863, she also told us the wondrous events of her father's life, our great–grandfather, of blessed memory, who had told us stories about how Napoleon and his army marched through Poland, going through Moscow. *Bubbe* Freide was very careful about going to the gravesites of her parents each year in the old cemetery in Gostynin. She had plenty to complain about to her father or to her mother at their gravesites, or at the gravesite of her husband who died as a young man at the age of 46. Once, my father tells, he accompanied my *Bubbe* [grandmother] to her parents' gravesites, and while she was pouring out her heart and praying, my father dropped a $100 banknote from his hand over *Bubbe's* head. The *Bubbe*, who was standing there with her head bowed, suddenly saw a $100 floating past her. There was no doubt in her mind – that this was being sent to her from Heaven. She later told everyone of this miracle, how great are God's kind acts – so we should all give thanks and praise to the Creator and follow in His generous ways.

A group of football players in Gostynin in 1925

Standing from right to left: Klajnbard, Burak, Dovid Matil, Wowe Morycz, Meyer Matil, Bolek Epstajn

Second row, from right to left: Yisochor Bressler, Avrohom Hersh Matil, Moshe Katz, Moshe Goldman, Lasman

Third row: Lasman, Manjek Jakubowycz, Bressler

[Page 241]

* * *

Regardless that the military commander swore patriotism to the Poland of our *Bubbe*, the Black Freide, and of more similar heroic grandmothers and grandfathers who sacrificed themselves for the Polish Fatherland, yet the anti–Semitism in Gostynin – as in all other cities in Poland – was very great. The drive for education and knowledge penetrated wide–reaching classes of the Jewish population, not wanting to remain behind the Christian segment of the population that had free access to the wellsprings of education. Jews wanted to see themselves as equal citizens in the country – and specifically in the area of education, they might even surpass their Christian neighbors. With that said, my father made efforts to raise his children in the nationalist spirit and gave us a gymnasium education. The majority of the above mentioned parents were not satisfied with the teachings of the *cheder* [religious elementary school] or *Folksshul* [public elementary school]. Everyone tried to register his child in the gymnasium, and this is also how it was in our home. For us, the children, the emphasis on "gymnasium" was enticing. To study in a gymnasium was like being part of a cult. To dress in the single uniform of the gymnasium, the beautiful celebrations, all this entwined and attracted us Jewish children.

[Page 242]

* * *

In Gostynin, there were two government gymnasiums, one for boys and another for girls. We Jewish students were hardly even six percent of the total general number of students. On the Polish national holidays we students were taken in a set format to participate in the religious services for the glory of the Polish republic. We went lengthwise along Kutner Street and through the marketplace. We were grouped according to our religion. After the Catholics came the Protestants – and at the end, marched the Jewish students. As we approached the end of the market, at Kowalska and Gombiner Streets, each group went off in different directions to their respective churches. We Jewish students became busy in the synagogue. Mixed feelings awoke in our hearts; the red–white flags, the music of the Polish nationalist anthem, and in general, the complete celebration, was not such a holiday for us. In the synagogue, they said prayers for peace in the country – and in our hearts, along with that we prayed for the Jewish old–new homeland. And characteristically, in the Polish gymnasium a longing for Jewish nationalism, Zionism, awoke in our hearts. We used to meet in secret (the students who attended the gymnasium were not permitted to belong to an organization) several times in the week, and read Zionist literature, and listened to reports with Zionist themes. Our longing for Zion became more earnest and stronger. Meanwhile, we studied diligently in order to receive our final diplomas. We, the gymnasium students, were very helpful in the activities of the Zionist organizations. Our Christian teachers in the gymnasium, directly, it seems, assisted us in realizing our longings and dreams – to immigrate to the Land of Israel and live in our own country. And, truly, thanks to the diploma [of completion of studies] it was possible to be taken into the Hebrew University on Mount Scopus, and in due time receive a ticket to be able to leave for Israel; so some of the youth of Gostynin successfully were able to come to this country [Israel] – and they were saved from falling into the murderous hands of the Nazi beasts.

[Page 247]

In the Years of Destruction

The first Jewish victims of Nazi terror in Gostynin who were murdered along with another 24 Christian intellectuals, in a forest not far from Gostynin, on November 27, 1939

Left: Rafael Burak, President of the Jewish bank in Gostynin

Right: Yakov Leyb Pinciewski, Chairman of the Bundist organization

Left: Yechiel Meir Keller, co–founder of the Jewish Froebel school*in Gostynin

Right: Avrohom Zajacs, Bundist councilman in Gostynin

[Page 248]

After the liberation, the victims were brought to "Kever Yisroel", the Jewish cemetery in Gostynin

The surviving Gostyniners stand at the gravesites

* Follows German educator Froebel, who created the concept of "kindergarten," recognizing children's unique needs and capabilities

[Page 249]

Years of Suffering and Danger

by Moshe Szajewicz (Israel)

Translated by Pamela Russ

Moshe Szajewicz

When the Nazis marched into Gostynin, Yom Kippur 1939, they herded all the Jews, men, to the market place and ordered everyone to kneel down on the ground. The SS soldiers surrounded them and terrorized them with their machine guns. Soon, groups of Nazis went to Jewish homes and emptied them of every valuable item they could find. They stole money, jewels, and valuable things.

Then the Jews were chased into the Polish church and locked up there for the entire night. The following morning, the Germans released from the church the more important workers in the food business, such as bakers, butchers, and small food store owners. My father and my older brother, who were registered as meat merchants, were also let go. The city was taken over by a hope that now they were finally beginning to free the Jews and soon all the others in the Polish church would also be let go. Apparently, the Gostynin Jews were very naïve. They couldn't imagine what kind of terrible fate was about to pour itself over their heads.

My father, Shaul, a professional butcher, was working with meat in his butcher shop as usual. Even Germans came to him to buy meat. German patrols often went through the food stores and butchers, and for the smallest misdemeanor, and even without misdemeanors, they murderously beat the people they found, Jews and Polaks alike.

[Page 250]

The Family Szajewicz

Shaul Szajewicz and family

[Page 251]

Once, a civilian German came into our butcher store, and sniffed out each corner. He went to the door, gave a lash in the air with his whip, and said: "Keep this place clean, Jew. I've already closed up many stores."

It seemed that this German was the county leader of Gostynin, who demonstrated much cruelty towards the Jews and committed countless murders. The next time he came to us in the store, he was already wearing a military uniform, and a huge dog did not leave his side. Who knows what type of merits supported us, so that this German gave my father a note so that he would be able to get animals on Gombiner Street to slaughter.

After that, it became known to all the Jews that this county leader was the
worst sadist who satisfied himself with spilled Jewish blood. With his leather
whip in hand, and in the company of his huge dog, he would rip into Jewish
homes and murderously beat every Jew that he encountered. The worst was that
he spent his fiercest rage onto Jewish women. He forced the women to stretch out
on the ground and that's how he beat them until he saw that blood was gushing
from these tragic women. Until that point, he did not leave his victim.

The situation for the Jews became continually worse. The order was given
that every Jew must wear a yellow patch – one on the right sleeve and one on the
back. Jews were forbidden from using the sidewalk – they were only allowed to
walk on the street. Whoever disobeyed the Nazi orders was severely punished.

They began to snatch Jews from the streets for work – and this caused a
panic in the town. Those who were taken, worked very hard and as a "benefit"
were given terrible beatings.

People decided to leave the city and go to the Polish border areas that had
been taken over by Soviet Russia. Everyone sold everything they had. With a
small bag in hand, they took to the long road. It was a road of hundreds of
kilometers, and a road fraught with all kinds of dangers. Jews could not travel
by train, and not always were they able to get a horse and wagon. But only
very few could leave their homes, wives, and children. So the majority of Jews
remained in their places.

[Page 252]

Our butcher shop was the only one that remained open. So, at the same
time we sold bread and other products that were given out with ration cards.
At that point, you could still buy meat for free, without cards. That's why the
people actually did eat mainly meat then. My father gathered together all the
butchers of the town, whose shops had been closed by the Nazis, and told
them to unite together so that the earnings would be divided equally among
them. You could still get animals for slaughtering, especially since the
Germans who were occupied with giving out the permits for these animals
were all being bribed.

Suddenly, an order from the Nazis came to the Gostynin ghetto that all the
Jews had to go to a confined area. Several streets up to the Bug River were
enclosed with barbed wire. A gate was put up on the side of the market. The
entrance to the newly set up ghetto was over there. Soon, a community council
was set up with Jewish police who had to maintain order. The total overseer of

this council was Asher Zweiboim. They established a worker's department whose job it was to send Jews to work. The Germans no longer had to grab Jews off the streets. They would come into the ghetto to the people, and the council had already collected the number of Jews that they ordered.

[Page 253]

Every Jew had to work three times a week. Even though I was still too young to go to work, I voluntarily lined up for work to take the place of my father. I worked with other Jews in the school on Kutno Street. The German military was located there. From five to seven o'clock you were permitted to go out of the ghetto with a note from the community council in order to get water, since there was none in the ghetto. Often, I would take off the yellow patches, go through the barbed wire, and out into the market. There I bought eggs, butter, chickens, and in the Polish stores I traded for bread and cigarettes. You could go back into the ghetto until nine o'clock. If anyone was caught in the streets after this time, he would be beaten murderously by the Germans. Often the SS men would sneak into the ghetto and any Jew they would meet would be severely beaten.

It was the first time that there was a free trade going on in the ghetto. Anyone who had money could buy what he wished. Everyone thought that life would now go on like that in the walled–in ghetto, but suddenly everything changed. All at once, there was an uproar among the Jews in the ghetto. The Germans put out a demand of the council in the ghetto that they assemble 150 Jews to be sent out to work. The Jewish police distributed notes to the houses that the men should be present on a specific day with their packs, to be sent off to work. Women and children wailed and cried: How could they let their husbands go, not knowing where they were going, and remain without earnings and with hardly anything for themselves or for the children who are losing their fathers? No one presented himself at the set time.

The Jewish police approached the Germans, telling them that without the Germans, they would be able to do nothing. Then, some Nazis went with them, with shotguns in their hands. The Jewish police went from house to house, and everyone who refused to go to work received deathly beatings from the Germans. This made it appear that it was the Jews who had put themselves into this situation.

[Page 254]

The entire ghetto population was assembled in the square. Soon the trucks arrived and all 150 men were loaded up as oxen. As we found out later, the people were transported to a camp near Posen. From there, families received letters saying that the men were well and were working. You could even send packages to them. The days passed, and those who remained in the city spoke incessantly of the men who were sent to work.

One fine day, posters were put up in the ghetto, calling all Jews to go before the community council to register in the worker's bureau. In these announcements, it was promised that the workers would be paid for their labor. Everyone believed this. My two brothers were working from before, taking apart Jewish houses in the market (such as Alberstajn's house near the pharmacy). Jews worked there together with Polaks and were paid for their work. Many Jews went, therefore, to register. My father was among them.

I went out in the morning to see what would happen with the registration. I myself was too young to register. When everyone was already assembled at the municipality, suddenly, from all corners, the evil Gestapo police ran out with gunshots in their hands. They surrounded all of us, and with screams they warned us that whoever would try to run away would be shot. The Germans released only the older people and a few foremen. They also let my father go.

After that, they led all of us out of the ghetto, me included. The took us to the Russian church. It happened that Yitzchok Kreuczer was the first to cross the threshold of the church – and I went in right after him. I turn around and see that Yitzchok jumped to the widow, opened it up, and so – he was outside. I wanted to do the same thing, and now I was in the street too. But to my misfortune, a German policeman noticed me, and captured me. Now they had to carry me back to the church, since I was so beaten up. For long hours, I lay in faint. Later, when I got up on my feet, I saw that the church was packed with Jews, and they were continuing to bring in more and more. The municipality people arrived with Zweiboim at the head. They demanded money from the captives. Whoever could buy themselves off with money – was released, and in his place a poor man was brought in. The Gestapo continued to drag in fresh groups of Jews into the church.

[Page 255]

Wajland showed up, accompanied by the municipality people. He was the head of the German worker's unit. He assured everyone that they did not have to be afraid because they were taking us all to a work place where there would be plenty to eat and also money would be paid for work. The German noticed me and I saw that he was whispering something secretly to Zweiboim of the Jewish municipality, gesturing with his hand toward me. Zweiboim whispered something into his ear. I did not hear what they were talking about. Probably that I looked like a child who should not be sent with the transport.

I saw my mother crying, and she called to me: "You're still a child. You'll get lost in the world." Soon my father arrived and comforted me from a distance, saying that he spoke to the municipality people to release me – and they promised to do so. But meanwhile, the Gestapo people arrived again and they chased in all those who had gathered outside. They brought more Jews in two more trucks – one from Gombyn, and another from Sonik – everyone was stuffed into the church. It became so crowded there, that one was actually standing on top of another. The night passed. Exhausted, we lay down on the concrete floor, and in the narrowness, we slept through the night.

The following morning, my father brought me a sack with a few things and some money. They did not allow my mother to go out of the ghetto to see me. When I asked my father what was happening with my being released, he cried bitterly and answered that if they released me then they would take my brother.

[Page 256]

Soon the trucks came to get us. I said goodbye to my father who was standing with me near the window. We kissed each other and cried bitterly. The policemen began to take the people outside. The Gestapo, with arms in hand, surrounded us – and with them, we were taken to the trucks. Sixty men were told to get into a truck. I went into the second truck. We left soon after that. A Nazi police rode behind each truck making sure that no one would jump out while the truck was driving. We passed by the market. I saw my two brothers working near the buildings. From a distance, they waved their hands at me. Now we are riding past the gate to the ghetto. Crowds of people were standing there waving to us and crying. I also saw my mother. The entire Kowalier Street until the Bug was inside the ghetto. Everywhere, people were standing and crying as we passed. The barbed wire of the ghetto with the people disappeared from our eyes, and outside of the city, the trucks started to speed up. Now we could only see the edge of the church, and everything disappeared from our eyes. Would I ever see Gostynin again? I thought to myself, and that's probably what all my companions were thinking as well.

Away from Gostynin

The trucks took us to the Bug River where we washed ourselves very well. There we were guarded by the Wloclaw [Wraclaw] police who came to take us with them. We came to Wloclawek and from a distance we noticed that the local Jews were wearing the yellow patches. The trucks then took us to the station. We were loaded up into the wagons, and very soon the train moved from its place.

[Page 257]

In about an hour, we arrived in Torun. From there we went to Inowroclaw, and we stayed there for a few hours under guard of Gestapo police. It started to get dark – then the train resumed its journey. Half an hour later, the train stopped and they told us to get off.

After counting us, they set us out to five men in a row and they took us to the side where they had set up barracks. When we went inside, we saw about 200 men. These people had been brought from Kolo and Sampolne, near Wloclawek. They were already here for a few days and they had put up the barracks.

The camp commander arrived, a young Gestapo man in a black uniform, and said to us that here we would have to dig canals 20 kilometers in length, because here they would be putting in water pipes. Now we were in Amsee (under Poland, this area was called Janiekowo). The camp director told us to obey the rules or else we would be walled in with barbed wire. We would get up at four in the morning, have some bread and coffee. At five, we would go to the train and from there we would be taken to Inowroclaw. There we would work, he told us, from seven in the morning until four in the evening.

After the speech of the camp elder, we went to the kitchen to get food. Everyone was holding a bowl in their hands. The cook poured a liter of soup into the bowl. The cook was a Polak from Posen [Poznan]. Whoever did not hold his bowl properly received a smack with the ladle. They started beating us already at the first meal. We complained to the camp elder about the cook's treatment towards us. The elder cold–bloodedly replied: "It is not his fault. You should hold the bowl straight."

For sleeping we were given cots and covers. There were 80 men sleeping in each barrack.

The following day, Sunday, we did not go to work – but we worked in the place we were. For lunch were given a soup made of kohlrabi, that one feeds to animals. In honor of Sunday, there were small pieces of horsemeat cut into the soup. For the evening meal, we were given watery cabbage.

[Page 258]

The following day, at four in the morning, the bell woke us from sleep. There was hardly any water with which to wash. After a very meager breakfast, at five we were already taken to the train. Under guard of the Gestapo, we were shut in the wagons, and were forced to stand on our feet all the way to the place, passing out from the cold of the fall dawn.

In the Work Camp

At the place, we were given shovels and spades and we were ordered to dig three meters down in length, 1.80 in width, and 2.70 deep. The ground was hard. Civilian Germans kept us under guard. Whoever didn't do the work right was immediately beaten.

For breakfast and lunch we were given breaks of half an hour, but there was nothing to eat. We finished working at four but we had to wait for the train until seven. When we arrived back at the camp, it was already very late, and now we got food that consisted of potatoes and a watery soup. We were exhausted from a hard day's hunger and purposeless work. The camp elder went to give out the food and screamed that we should move faster to get the food. Whoever did not move fast enough to get the food from the cook was beaten by the camp elder and the cook assisted him with that. Many people forfeited getting their food and went to sleep without food instead.

In addition, each evening – each time it was people from another room – we had to work in the kitchen: peeling potatoes, washing pots and plates. This work went on until 12 or one o'clock at night. At four o'clock exactly, the bell already went off to wake us up.

[Page 259]

Once it happened in the middle of the night, right in the middle of our sleep, that Gestapo police crashed into our room with truncheons in hand and with their dogs. They began beating left and right, and chased everyone out into the yard. In only our underclothing, we had to run around the yard, and they hit us with their truncheons wherever they could. For an hour we had to run like that under the shouts and beatings of the Gestapo. Only when we went back into the barracks did we find out that this had been a punishment for two of our people had run away. These were the two from Gostynin, Alberstajn and Rosenberg, the rope maker. After this happened, the Germans walled in the camp. Their treatment of us became worse.

We wrote to our families to send us food stuffs. The packages that we later received from our homes were opened and the goods were taken out by our German guards and Polish overseers – left were worthless remnants.

Once, when we came back from work, we found a new 120 men in the camp, all had come from Gostynin, Gombyn, and Sanok. The news that these newcomers gave us was bitter: They were sending the men of Gostynin out to work.

I, and some of the younger ones, could not tolerate the hard labor of digging the canals. I went to the supervisor to ask if he could get us some easier work, since our strength could not keep up. He promised that he would ask in the worker's department about our request. Only two weeks later, they told us to register and tell them our age. The next day, the camp director let us know that all those who had registered should not go out to work. We were thirteen boys. From Gostynin were: Shmuel Etinger, Meyer Jesyn, Yakov Srebnagora, Zenik Tabacznik, Lipe Rosenberg, and I. Incidentally, Rosenberg was very tall, and he was afraid that he would fail to look like part of us, who were smaller. When the camp commander called out our names, we took in Lipe Rosenberg in the middle of this, and he crouched over slightly. In short, we all passed through peacefully.

[Page 260]

Across Villages and Farms

Soon, a Polak with a horse and wagon arrived. The camp commandant told us that we would be going to work on a farm. We were very happy to hear this news. When we were already sitting in the wagon, we asked the Polak what it was like with the food, he answered us: "You will explode from the food, and you will not work too hard with potatoes and beets."

When the wagon began to move from its spot, we practically cried for joy, and the farther we got from the camp, the happier was our mood, to such an extent that we started to sing.

We arrived to the place. A fatty soup with a lot of grease was cooking in the pot. We were so starved that each of us ate 10 or twelve bowls of soup. The Polaks who were watching the way we wolfishly swallowed all these bowls of soup, crossed themselves in terrible wonder at how children were able to eat so much.

The following day, we went out to work. The labor was heavy and went on from the morning until it was pitch dark. Some worked at gathering potatoes, some with the horses. But we were able to get through the work because we had enough to eat.

Winter was approaching. One time, Tabacznik said to me that he had to leave for a while, but he would be back soon. Suddenly, I saw at a distance how he threw himself down on the earth. At that moment I did not understand what had happened to him, I thought he was playing at something. But I saw that it didn't stop. I ran over to him and saw how he was thrashing about in convulsions with his face down towards the ground and there was foam around his mouth. I lifted him up and carried him to the closest pool of water. I washed him and led him to the working field. The following morning he did not come to work. He received a discharge permit and went home to Gostynin by train.

[Page 261]

From the letters that were written to me from home, I found out that in Gombyn they captured my brother Pesakh, and Shmaye Zajacs, and many others – and they were sent away to Germany.

When we finished working at the farm, they sent us to another farm. There they did not guard us at all and we were able to move around freely. In that whole area there were camps for men and women, but these were under guard. I longed to meet the people from Gostynin, and therefore, once on a Sunday, on a cold, snowy day, when we were free of work, I and another young Wloclawa boy went on the road to try to find people from our town who were in the camps. After about 20 kilometers, already being good and tired, we went into a Polak's hut to warm up. He welcomed us with something warm to eat and something to drink. From him we learned that four kilometers from where we were there was a women's camp. When we heard this, we quickly got up from our place and, in a good mood, we went on our way. Suddenly, at a distance, we saw a girl. How excited I got when, as we got closer to her, I actually recognized the girl. It was Brastowska from Plocker Street, a neighbor on that street. Our joy was without end. She was going – she told us – to work in the village as a seamstress. On this free Sunday, she got food to eat for this. Three kilometers further on, there was a camp, and over there were other girls from Gostynin – she told me. Of course, we went directly over there.

[Page 262]

As we opened the door of the large house, a group of Gostynin girls separated themselves from the others girls. We immediately recognized the girls [from Gostynin]. They cried with joy – it was not a small thing, to see a young man from your own town of Gostynin in these circumstances. To this day, I still remember many of them: a daughter of Shloime Zalantcz, Chaytchke Tabacznik, Mudzhe Glancz, and others. The camp commandant appeared, an elderly man in a uniform. After a brief talk with him, he permitted us to have more conversation with the girls. They told me that they were working very hard paving roads. They got very little to eat. Eight kilometers from here – they said – there was another women's camp and there were more Gostynin girls there, namely: Rute Faige Szatan, Chana Tabacznik, Baile Neiman, and others. It got late, and we promised that we would come again the following week.

The next week, we brought food along. When we arrived to the camp to see the girls, they were overjoyed. We also visited the other camp and met the other girls from Gostynin.

I received mail. My mother wrote that they had taken away all the young men and women from the ghetto. They also took away the municipality people and the Jewish police – my father and older brother Pinkhas as well. Only elderly Jewish men and women remained. All the younger ones were taken to Konin near Posen [Poznan].

Our work on the farm was completed again. There is little work to be done in the fields during winter. They sent us to a "resting camp" until the end of the winter. There were girls there who had also worked on farms. We found ourselves in a church surrounded by a tall fence of barbed wire. The city was called Mogilno, not far from the historic city of Gniezno. They sent us into the city to clear the streets from snow. January 1942, I received a letter from my mother. She wrote that she wanted to send out all her belongings because they [the people] were going to be transported – she did not know where to. I did not receive any more news from my mother.

[Page 263]

In the spring, the work department sent us to different farms. We were all together – they even added 40 girls who were from various cities in Poland, such as: Warsaw, Lodz, Wloclawek, Czekoczynek, Krusniewycz, and others. We worked in the villages.

I received mail from Konin from my father and brothers. They wrote that they traveled 60 kilometers to work. The labor was difficult, it was on the railway, and that the food was terrible. They also had not received any mail from our mother.

We worked in the village for more than a year. One clear, bright morning, some Gestapo men arrived and ordered us to get up onto the huge trucks. Under a hail of dirt and beatings, we climbed up and left for Inowroclaw. From there we were taken on foot to a camp.

In a New Camp

As soon as we arrived, I heard someone shout out my name: Moshe Sajewicz! When I ran in the direction that the voice had come from, I saw before me the Matil brothers – Shmulek and Gershon. Also, Hershel Szwarcz, and others. We hugged and kissed each other out of joy. They told us that my father and my brothers were working at the railway. My brother Pinkhas was hit by a wagon [from the train] – and was no longer able to work. He remained behind in the camp as a sick person. Later they registered all the sick people to send them away. My father also registered himself as a sick person. They were both sent away to Jezow.

A little while later, a transport of Gostynin girls arrived from their camp. We spent the night under the open sky.

[Page 264]

Very early the next morning, they took us to the train, and we were loaded onto the wagons, men and women separately. Each wagon was overcrowded with people, beyond the limits, without food or drink. That's how we went, shut in without even a little air. We had no idea where we were going. Some knew enough to tell us that the Germans had set up ovens to burn people to death. We rode all day, until the train stopped. Finally, the doors of the wagons were thrown open and the SS soldiers with the truncheons in hand, screamed and chased us out, and did not permit us to take our packages.

"Thieves out!" they shouted and beat us with their truncheons. The chaos among the people was unimaginable. They set us out five in a row, men and women separately. The square was huge and was lit up by reflectors [light beams]. We found ourselves in Auschwitz.

In Auschwitz

Soon they chose people who were capable for work – those who could not, were set aside separately. The fate of those people was only too well known. Then we were loaded onto trucks and driven away. As we drove, I said my farewells from a distance to the Gostynin girls – that was the last time I ever saw them. The SS soldiers on motorcycles followed behind us. In the truck I was in, were also the Matil brothers, Lipe Rozenberg, and others. Finally, we came to a camp. There we got off, and again were set out five in a row. We were about 800 men. We marched, and were taken to a bathing barrack. There was such crowding there, that one practically stood on the other. We were ordered to strip naked, and to only keep our belts with us. The heat was so bad that we could not catch our breath.

[Page 265]

So, they are going to gas us – we thought – they told us to keep our belts with an intention, so that they could carry us more easily out of here.

We looked up at the ceiling from where the gas should have streamed out. Out of fear, many Jews recited their confessions. Suddenly, there was a spray of water. Can anyone even imagine the wave of joy that the water brought along with it?

After bathing ourselves, we went outside. Everyone got their shoes back. Naked, we were forced to march across the square. The cold was unbearable. That's how we were taken into the camp's infirmary where we were marched around and each one was given a number tattooed on the arm. Then they gave us all clothing.

The following morning, after a sleepless night, everyone received a piece of material on which was written the number that was on the person's hand, with an addition of a Star of David. We had to sew this onto our jackets and onto our pants. In these unusual clothes with our belts on, we looked like clowns. We slept 800 men in the barrack, and were given 350 grams of bread and soup twice a day. At 5:30 AM we were given tea or coffee and a portion of bread with margarine or marmalade. Our cots were three tiered. When the Kapo beat awake those sleeping on the bottom, the ones on the top had time to run away – I always slept on the top bunk.

When the bell began to ring, we had to be in the roll–call square in a flash. There we were counted. There were 22,000 people in the camp, from all nations of the world. Then we marched to the gate, to go to work. An orchestra of 40 men was playing there. We had to march to the rhythm of the military orchestra. The Kapo yelled out: "Caps off!" In one move, everyone had to take off their hats – and stamp with their right foot. And that's how we marched out through the gate where the SS men counted us, to see how many of us were going to work. We came back from work with the same ceremony, and the orchestra again played marches for us, and the SS men counted us again to see if anyone was missing.

[Page 266]

One day, when we returned from work, the bell was ringing. This was a sign that the SS men were taking the "sinners" to their hanging. According to the number of gallows that were set up in the square, we knew the number of people who were to be hanged on that day. We had to wait in the square until all the commandos came back from work. Deathly starved, we had to wait for hours until they would carry out the executions of the innocent people. After marching before the elders, we went into the block to receive food.

From Shabbath noon until Sunday morning we did not go to work.

Life in the camp brought with it some tragic–comic moments. On the free days, the unfortunates, under the worst conditions, undertook all sorts of boxing matches, football games, and theatrical presentations. At the same time, the chimneys from the crematoria did not stop spitting out thick balls of black smoke.... In the shadow of death, pathetic life continued on. I remember that in Auschwitz, they put a filling into my tooth that had gone bad...

I was in the camp from 1943 until 1945. We had to leave the German concentration camp in January, because the Russians were getting closer to the camp. The sick people in the hospital did not want to be left behind since they were afraid that they would be shot when we would be gone.

When the Russians Were Approaching

I remember that Sunday afternoon when we left the camp. There was a terrible frost. What a tragic picture my eyes saw: The sick people were wrapped in blankets (they had no clothing on), and they went on the way with us. Of course, not all survived the difficult conditions. Many of them actually froze to death from the cold.

[Page 267]

We marched for about 40 kilometers. At night, we came to Glejwicz [Gliwice]. There were several camps there. They crowded in more people into every camp. The difficulties had so exhausted us that we slept deeply under the open sky in the snow. There we were loaded onto wagons. In my wagon I met the brothers Shmulek and Gershon Matil, and Beryl Szwarcz. We took up a wooden beam and set it up by the wall – and on that, set out some straw so that it would be softer to sit on. In each wagon, they pushed in about 90 to 100 men. We, the Gostyniner, stayed together. We covered ourselves with our blankets, and since we were exhausted from the difficult roads, we fell asleep right away.

The following day, when we awoke from sleep, half the wagon was covered in snow. We washed ourselves with snow. We were hungry and no food was provided. When we got up in the evening, we became very frightened: In the wagon, there were several frozen people. Every day, we removed dead bodies of those who froze on the way. We, the four Gostyniners, managed to maintain ourselves.

When we came to the Czechoslovakian city of Baden, the residents there helped us with food. When we stopped in a station, they threw food into the wagons. The SS soldiers forced the people away with shots, and did not allow them to throw the food up [into the wagons]. But the Czechs continued to throw food up to us, until the SS men opened fire. We were able to successfully catch a lot of the food, and we shared it among ourselves. We continued like that in the open wagons for five weeks, until we came to Buchenwald.

[Page 268]

When they opened the wagons in Buchenwald and they told us to get down – no one was able to get up. The people from that camp had to come up into the wagons and physically take us down. From each wagon, 20 to 30 barely breathing people were taken down. The rest had died from hunger and cold. They quickly put us into a warm bath. Two people carried me. I did not feel my feet and felt that I would pass out at any moment. When the warm water started to flow – I felt as if a new soul had entered me. The water was steaming hot – and no one felt the heat. We came back to our senses. Soon we received fresh clothing. We were taken to a block where there were 2,500 people. We got food only in the evening. You can only imagine how long it took to give food to all these people and to count them in the roll–call square. We were standing outside in the cold for a few hours – until the counting came out evenly.

When the order came to go to the block, the pushing was unimaginable. The block elders began to beat and spray with hoses of water. The clothing was frozen with frost, and many died from becoming sick from the cold. These scenes repeated themselves each day – until finally you managed to get into the block.

Eighteen men slept on each cot. It was very difficult to turn over. One person warmed himself on the exhausted body of the other person, in the terrible cold. When one person went outside for his personal needs, he couldn't get back into his cot and had to suffer until morning.

Breakfast was given out to 2,500 people: bread and coffee. This took hours. The camp was overflowing with people and there was terrible hunger. People slept in the washrooms. The blocks were overflowing.

One Brother Searches for the Other

[Page 269]

In one of the rooms, I found a Gostyniner, Wladek Laski, and he gave me regards from my brother Pesakh. He was in Block 51. They had sent him to another camp. I was sorry that I didn't have the good fortune to meet my brother after years of wandering. I visited the block, maybe I would meet other acquaintances who were with my brother. All at once, I saw a familiar face – Binyomin Dancziger, a carpenter from Plocker Street. Surely he knew about my brother – he even showed me the bed where my brother used to sleep. He moved to another camp only two days ago – to which one, Wladek did not know. We spoke for a while about our hometown, and about acquaintances and people from the town...

There was an uproar in the block. The block elder let everyone know that tomorrow morning a transport would be leaving for work – they [the workers] would be given food. All those who wanted to go with this transport should be at the gate tomorrow morning. I, the Matil brothers, and other acquaintances decided to leave the camp. Anyway, here, more than once a day we did not receive any food.

We traveled to the second camp for two days – about 80 kilometers. There were ongoing bombings all along the way. At night, we came to the camp Ohrdruf, but it seemed that we still had to go farther. But meanwhile, we received warm soup. We spent the night in horses' stalls on the bare concrete floor, without any covers. Early the next morning, we were chased on foot for about 30 kilometers until we came to the camp Krawinkel, that was located in a forest. We slept in bunkers deep in the ground. We got up at dawn and went to work. We worked hard loading cement, steel, and other heavy loads onto the wagons. The conditions were very bad.

In the camp, I met a familiar young man from Warsaw, who used to come often to his family in Gostynin – he told me that the day before, in the evening, when he came back from work, he recognized my brother. He even tried to call out his name. My brother turned around and waved. But it was impossible to approach him – because they were under guard. The camp was about seven kilometers from here, and was called Zeltlager.

[Page 270]

Two weeks later, we had to leave the camp because the Russians were approaching. The Germans took us back to Buchenwald. People escaped on the way. Many were shot during this time. I didn't want to run away because I had my brother in my mind. When we came to Buchenwald, the loudspeaker announced which transport was coming in. With all my strength, I called out the name of my brother, Monjek Szajewicz! I called out and asked of each new person that came in. All at once, a man approached me in a straw hat on his head and a French coat and wooden clogs on his feet. I recognized him immediately. We embraced and cried like children. What joy … what joy! We kissed and kissed each other and couldn't tear ourselves apart. We had plenty to tell each other. My brother Monjek, looked terrible. I gave him some of the food that I had saved up.

Where We Spent the Day, We Did Not Spend the Night …

March 1945. It was very dark before sunrise. I don't remember the exact date. A few thousand men were taken out of the camp. The Matil brothers joined me and my brother. We waited outside for several hours. The SS men and their huge dogs arrived. We were surrounded and guarded by them. They ordered us to march. We left – where to, we did not know. There were many SS men, approximately one German for every four Jews. It was pouring rain, and that's how we marched for 50 to 60 kilometers a day. In the beginning, every group of four men received a loaf bread, and later even that was not given. Whatever we found on the road was a prize. Our "good fortune" was that we went through backroads, and so we would pass through villages and would find potatoes, beets, sometimes rotten, on the roads. We would eat these, picking them right up from the ground. We spent the nights in stables where sometimes we would find some oats, barley – we would eat all kinds of grains.

[Page 271]

A feeling always enveloped us that our end was near. People stopped in the middle of the way, feeling they could not go on. The SS men shot these people on the spot. And not only these: Often, they would simply remove 30 or 40 men from the rows, take them into the forest, and there end their lives. From day to day, our strength was more and more drained. Every day, the SS head would inform his officer how many Jews were shot that day. And the superior officer would give him further instructions about how many Jews should be shot the following day. We heard these reports ourselves.

We continued to march – and saw how every day the rows were becoming more and more sparse. In the middle of one such bloody day, my brother calls out to me that he is stopping – he has no more strength to continue going, and he wants to run away. "It will be whatever it will be," he justified himself to me. "Let them shoot me. You can only be shot once." And once again he called out to me, "You are stronger than I am, you're still fine."

"If you run away," I said to him, "then we both run away." My brother did not support this plan. If one person runs away, then he might still be lucky, it's easier for him to hide. I did not allow my brother to run away by himself. I held him up and supported him so that we could go together.

[Page 272]

People fell like flies, some from weakness and exhaustion, and others from German bullets. My brother did not stop thinking about his plan. Okay, let it be that both of us should escape together. Finally he agreed. We decided that we would run away. We would hide separately, spend the night separately, and if possible, sustain ourselves wherever we would find provisions. Then we would meet in the forest, when the group would already have marched off.

I left to sleep in a stall, and that's what my brother was supposed to do as well. Under the hay, I felt a bag of oats – it was a treasure! Suddenly, I heard that they were ordering everyone to assemble. I quickly filled my pockets with oats and went outside. We all felt that something different was happening. SS men and German people were talking among each other, that the Americans were not far from here. We were overtaken with joy, but the Germans – with a terror. They decided to continue with the marching, and actually to do so at night. Now they were not afraid that we would run away. The SS men recruited German civilians from the local mayor to help move out this transport. The civilian Germans wore white armbands on their sleeves – and also carried weapons.

I did not see my brother. Apparently, he remained there as we had discussed. We marched through a city and I could easily have run away. I saw German women and children run away. They were afraid of the American military marching in. What joy it was to live and see such a picture! The German soldiers let their dogs loose from their leashes and we repeatedly heard shooting in the forest and the barking of the dogs. It seems that the Germans had not yet ended their acts of slaughtering and murdering.

The entire time, I was tormented by thoughts of my brother. I searched for him without end. When the Germans ordered us to sit and rest – they themselves were exhausted from these long treks – I did not stop looking for him. But all for nothing. I thought that maybe he suffered the fate of all the others whom the dogs had captured, and that he was no longer among the living.

[Page 273]

The chaos of those escaping was getting greater. The SS men themselves were beginning to desert. Among our leaders were also Ukrainians, Hungarians, Romanians, Lithuanians, and they too began to leave. We went over to a camp that was called Flossenberg. I was very happy, because my strength was completely gone. The camp, however, was overcrowded, and they did not let us in. They told us to go to a nearby field and lie down there. The night was dark and cold. We looked forward to the morning. There was no notion that anyone could sleep.

Again, we took to the road. Across the skies, there were airplanes flying – English, American, and Russian, which bombed the area. Later, they flew down low, over our heads. The rescue was near, but life for us had become ugly. Smashed up trucks and cars littered the roads.

The war was ending. But we were still prisoners and did not see even a sliver of light. Every minute was life-threatening. Soon a new day would dawn across the world – and in our moods, under the whip of the German truncheons, ruled more dark nights.

We could not suffer any more. I decided to run away. I and someone else decided to escape. Soon, once again we were in stables. It was nighttime and we got up to go out into the field. We'd run about 20 meters, and suddenly the spitting of a machine gun hit us. We ran back into the stable. It passed, but we were prisoners again.

I ran away a second time to a village, in the middle of the day. I hid in an oven where they baked bread – and to my luck, there was an SS man hiding there too. He was sleeping. Near him was his dog who smelled me and started barking. I left quickly and went back to the transport. This also passed, and again I did not escape, but I was still alive. It was difficult for me to walk, my feet were raw and wounded. I bared my feet – and that's how I went in the deep cold. Some sort of extraordinary strength pushed me. I myself was already like a fettered wild animal.

[Page 274]

From several thousand men, a group of about 150 remained. I saw that the SS chief was giving his men more bullets. He pointed with his hand to the nearby forest, about five kilometers from us, no more than that. They would shoot all of us in that forest. It began to pour rain. Drenched to the bone, we went. We simply didn't care anymore what would happen to us. Suddenly, from the forest, a company of German policemen on horses appeared. We were ordered to sit on the ground. There were puddles on the ground because of the rain. We sat in the mud. For a long time, the policemen argued with the SS men. We did not know what had happened here. Finally, they ordered us to get up and they took us to the forest. Deep in the forest, a gate opened – and we went in. Once again, the SS men beat us murderously and yelled: "You cursed dogs! You are lucky!"

In their rage, we felt that something fateful had happened. We went to a large house. We saw women looking out of the barred windows.

Salvation Arrived

Suddenly, the women opened the windows and began to scream in all languages: "Keep your heads up high! The Americans are coming soon!"

[Page 275]

When I heard the overwhelming news, I felt as if my hair was standing on edge and all my pains disappeared. We saw how the SS head ran away. The camp commandant came to us with the news that he was taking over and would give us over to the Americans. Right before they left, the SS men took out two men and shot them. These were two brothers who allegedly had wanted to run away.

It seemed that the SS men and our other overseers did not want to leave us here. There was a fight with renewed energy that came along with the approach of the end of the war. In the end, the German police got their way, and we stayed in this camp and every minute we waited for the American army.

We actually did not even have the strength to celebrate. We lay on the beds, sick and broken. The camp commander came to us in the block and explained that now we were under his responsibility and no more bad would happen to us. We asked him for candles. He gave us some. We lit the candles and all together we recited the *kaddish* [prayer in memory of the deceased] for all those who died or were shot by murderous German hands. I cried, not knowing how I could have had so many tears. My heart was in pain because I couldn't understand why my brother could not have been freed along with me.

I fell asleep. When I awoke, I no longer heard anyone speaking German.

What did I see? Walking around were Negroes, American soldiers, who were distributing packages to the survivors in the beds. Another soldier explained to us in Yiddish that we should not eat what was in the packages too quickly, but eat slowly – or else the food could harm us. I have to confess that I did not have the strength the open the five kilo package. I fell asleep again. I only opened my package the following day, others had had already eaten much of theirs. The food in the package hurt me. Bu the help that we received from the Americans put us on our feet.

[Page 276]

And so, here is the tragic statistic of our final march: We were a few thousand men when we marched out under the guard of the SS murderers. In about six weeks, we covered 2,000 kilometers. At the very end, with the liberation by the Americans, we were left with only 147 men. Under the murderous regime of the SS camps, from hunger and pain, I became tough, and no disease was able to take control of me. And now, at the moment of liberation, when I tasted some good food and refreshed myself with normal behavior – I became sick with typhus fever. For months I lay in a hospital and in a rehabilitation place. They wanted to send me over to England or Sweden. But I decided to go around to all the camps – as many others did – because maybe I would find someone from my family who was still alive.

Through the Camps to Find Gostyniner

A rumor spread that there was a large camp not far from Munich. It was called Feldafing and it was full of Jews. I went there, and as soon as I got off the train I met a Gostyniner, Moshe Brostowski Understandably, we were overjoyed. There was another person from Gostynin, he said, Nakhman Zeideman. I noted the number of the block. When I came into the block, I found Zeideman lying in bed. I recognized him immediately, but he did not recognize me. But it did not take long, and soon we were spending brotherly time together as compatriots who had so much to tell one another. He also told me that there was another person form Gostynin here, Leybish Todeles. Of course, I ran to see Todeles. How great was the joy when people who saved themselves from such a world's furnace, met one another. It is unimaginable, one cannot describe it.

[Page 277]

Now, I often came to see my Gostynin friends in this Feldafing camp. There was a closeness among all of us. How excited I became once when I came to the camp and, under a torrential rain, soaked, I opened the door to my compatriot Todeles' block, and who did I see before my eyes? There sat my brother Monjek! Resurrected from the dead!

"You're alive?" I screamed almost in a faint.

This is a welcome I did not expect.

My brother told me that Zeideman went to Poland and he met him there and told him that I was in this camp – and that he could find me with Todeles in this camp, where I often come.

That evening, my brother told his story. Every Jew who was saved has his own story. My brother and another person left the rows and fled into the forest. They heard how the dogs were running after them with frightening barks. The two men held hands and ran in the dark between the trees. They stopped by a tree, and my brother stayed there while his friend continued running. The shooting did not stop. When the transport moved away, my brother Monjek lay down by the tree.

When day was breaking, he awoke and saw that there was someone lying not far from him. When he got closer, he soon recognized that it was his friend – but sadly, he was dead. The dogs had torn him apart. For a few more days, Monjek hid in the forest, until the Americans found him and freed him.

***

My brother and I left for Poland. We left, cursing the dirty German ground. We left Poland voluntarily, and enlisted in the fighting Jewish army that was already in a war before the liberation of the Jewish Land.

***

[Page 278]

These memories were written "with blood and not with pencil." A people died in horror and in tragedy. These are not only memories of personal experiences, but they are characteristic – maybe with some changes – of hundreds of thousands. But in front of my eyes, my Gostynin never ceased to hover.

[Page 279]

Gostynin Jews in
the Shadow of the Gallows

by Shimon Rumer

Translated by Pamela Russ

Shimon Rumer

When the Germans entered Poland, the immediately began to exterminate the Jews. Their demonic plan was calculated with hatred towards the Jews. The Polaks excelled at this hatred. They knew very well that with the local Polish population they would have no difficulties in carrying out their monster plan, because in the course of twenty years of their renewed independence the Polaks themselves were interested in getting rid of their Jewish neighbors. The Polaks made the Jews' lives miserable. The Germans took away the Jews' lives.

At the very beginning of their barbaric occupation the Germans sought to demoralize the Jewish masses and their leaders. All their anti-Jewish laws struck at the heart of Jewish life. They set up new leaders of the Jewish communities, the so-called "*Judenrat*," who obediently and punitively carried out all that their German bosses ordered them to do. First they applied new taxes one higher than the next, and the new community heads pumped out monies from the poor and rich, amassing the required sums. The *Judenrat* went to great lengths to carry out the orders of the Germans. Many times, in these leadership positions, there were people who had never before worked in any fashion in social or community activities. Now, in this dreadful time, they diligently undertook to help out the Nazi murderers, and using these circumstances they reaped personal good from these great tragedies. Often, these persons were murderous towards their brothers and did things that even the Germans themselves would not have done. They hoped that their extraordinary devotion would save them personally.

[Page 280]

The *Judenrat* received an order from the Germans each time to gather up contingencies of Jews that were designated for specific work. They fulfilled these quotas until the very last individual. In this way, the Jews were transformed into slaves. They were chased to work, not paid for the work, beaten, and very abused at work as well.

The Germans confiscated the Jewish businesses, not permitting Jews to carry on their work. Their warehouses were closed that's how they Jews were left without any means to sustain themselves. They were morally and physically broken, but the *Judenrat* who actively helped the Germans, threw these Jews into the ghetto. They gathered up families and put them into inhumanly cramped conditions that were completely surrounded by barbed wire and guarded by German or Polish police. In the ghetto itself, the *Judenrat* was given the right to have its own Jewish police that tormented the Jews even more. That's how the Jewish population was left without rights, impoverished, and entirely torn apart from the rest of the world.

However, this was not yet enough for the murderers. The organized labor camps where men and women were sent. These people worked under frightful conditions of hunger, cold, inhumanity, and terror for bare life. Despite all this, everyone's will to live was tremendous. Nobody wanted to voluntarily give up hope that in the end Hitler would get his dues and the sun would shine again for everyone and for each individual. Jews worked in every situation labored, and looked to survive, to make it to the end of the war. Heavy clouds of worry, fear, and danger spread everywhere, yet with that all, there was still that spark of hope that we would survive.

[Page 281]

Because the Germans set up death camps, of those who didn't end up there, none knew of them for a long time.

With all of this, all that was said until now, is only a broad description of what happened of what the Germans did to the Jews of Poland. And every detail of this also befell the Jews from my own beloved town: Gostynin.

***

I came to Janikowo with a transport of Jews from Gostynin. This was a camp not far from Posen. In German, this place was called Amsee. The majority of the population there sustained itself with work in the city's sugar factory. The camp director was from the Gestapo, by the name of Malinowski. In the camp there were many Jews from Gostynin, Gombyn, and a small number from Lodz.

The oldest people in the camp were: Avrohom Belfer, Sender Ring, and my unforgettable father Yechiel Hersh Rumer. I worked in the camp doing all kinds of illegal tasks, and at the same time as a barber and a medical orderly. There were 505 people in the camp. The suffered terribly, labored mercilessly, and the hygiene was horrific. There was very little help for the sick and wounded. The Germans permitted the orderly to help the sick and wounded only after many hours of their suffering, after the invalid was practically consumed by insects and doused in dirt. Every day people were injured at work. Every day the German torturers and their assistants beat their Jewish slaves on their sides and cut off complete limbs. The sick couldn't expect immediate help, and even when the help did come, it was seriously limited. There was practically no medicine available.

[Page 282]

The camp supervisor was surrounded by assistants that carried out the most brutal acts on innocent people. The main assistant was most vicious and cruel his name was Alphonse Hillel. He was a non-Jew from the Posen area, an anti-Semite who couldn't even look at a Jew.

Among these assistants, was unfortunately also a Jew from Lodz, who with his flattery towards the Germans and animal behavior towards his brothers, worked himself up in the camp and reaped all kinds of privileges. Kalman Dovid was his name. That's how he was called, and he was the terror of the entire camp. Many innocent Jews died by his filthy hands.

One of the finest people in the camp was Volf Zilber, born in Brisk-Kujawski. He was a young man. He was the son-in-law of the well-known Zionist activist Herman Levi from Wloclowek. He, along with his father-in-law and his family, came to Gostynin when the war broke out where they hoped to live through the war because their hometown was absorbed into the Third Reich right at the beginning of the war, and Jews there were treated in the most horrific manner. Volf Zilber was an educated person and refined too. In the camp, he had the job of camp recorder. He put himself out for everyone and tried to make each person's situation better. Understandably, there was precious little he could do. The evil of the Germans dominated everywhere.

There was a very heavy discipline in the camp. The provisions were very meagre so much so that there was nothing for the living and nothing for the dying. There was surely nothing for those people who used their physical strength for every day, physically taxing labor. The sadism of the German camp staff was infinite.

***

[Page 283]

I will relate one of the thousands of incidents that took place:

This happened on a Sabbath afternoon. The biggest surprises were saved for the eve of the rest day, Sunday. The exhausted and starved Jews had returned to the camp from work. As they entered, they heard a scream from Kalman Dovid, may his name be erased. We immediately understood that something again had happened. It wasn't long when we saw that they were taking out Avrohom Belfer from the barracks. It was difficult to recognize him. He was as pale as the walls, his body was trembling and his face showed an indescribable pain. Soon, Malinowski brought out the familiar benches that were used for corporal punishments in the camp, in front of everyone's eyes. Kalman Dovid positioned himself with his stick in his hand, and exclaimed: "This Jew committed a crime. He tried to smuggle bread into the camp. Therefore, he deserves to be beaten." He continued by instructing each of us to pass by and beat the guilty one. The beatings were done with a rubber stick, with wire woven through it. Each of us had to approach and beat him. Malinowski was not satisfied with the way the beatings were going, so he took of his black uniform, rolled up his shirt sleeves, and showed us all how we had to do the beatings. Kalman Dovid followed. Avrohom Belfer was beaten so terribly, that he fell unconscious across the bench. Kalman Dovid poured a bucket of water over him to revive him, and then he was dragged, bloodied and soaked, into the barracks. Everyone else dispersed.

I, the orderly, had to bring help to this tragic victim. Menashe Wajsbard and Wajnrajch, Jews from Gostynin, who worked in the laundry, helped out with piece of old but clean clothes that I used to stop the bleeding. Only the exceptional patience and the outstanding will to live gave Belfer the superhuman capacity to live through these agonies. He lay in the barracks for many long weeks and wasn't able to go to work.

[Page 284]

One morning, when a rumor spread through the camp that the Gestapo was going to evacuate all the sick, and probably be murdered, Belfer picked himself up off the bed and decided to go to work with us. That's how he was saved. According to my memory, I can also say that Sender Ring, Avrohom Lopski, Yosef Stajnman, Dzhiganski, and Laski were also saved this way.

***

Once again, it's the Sabbath afternoon. The exhausted and starved slaves had returned from their daily work. Suddenly, a terrible shouting was heard from the murderous camp supervisor Malinowski: "Everyone stay in your places outside!"

The order was clear.

"Tomorrow, no one will be going to work. The camp is going to be cleaned. Visitors will be coming. Tomorrow we will show you what will happen to those who will try to escape from the camp."

We were already used to the brutal behavior of the Germans. Every word of theirs was inciteful, every wink was dangerous, and every movement a game with a Jewish life. Because of that, we didn't place any unusual significance on the words of this devil. Nevertheless, his words did not allow us to remain at ease. We went into the filthy barracks and everyone crawled into his cot. Suddenly Volf Zilber bursts in and informs us of a tragic piece of information: Eight Jews wanted to escape from the camp, but the German bandits caught them. Who knows what the Germans are preparing for us for the next day.

A shudder went through us. We did not yet know who the eight Jews were. The German murderers had isolated them in a separate barrack. Not one of us closed an eye that entire night.

[Page 285]

From our hard cots we heard moaning, and here and there, we heard a whispering prayer.

Sunday morning, as soon as the sun appeared, we heard the fearful voice of the night guard, and in one wink everyone got up.

***

Soon, Alfonse Hillel appeared, tall, good-looking, broad-boned, and well-fed, with thick blond hair on his head, a murderous person, a Jew devourer. Next to him was his wolf-dog, with its tongue foaming and hanging out. Everyone was trembling. Not only into one person had the sharp teeth of this dog already sunk its teeth. With his coarse voice, he informed us that today the camp has to sparkle with cleanliness. Gestapo officers were coming, and they very much loved cleanliness and precision. He completed his words with the usual: "We will destroy you!"

A very strained mood reigned over the camp. The people were already depressed and starved, and fear was already no novelty. There was a veil of despair everywhere, but the words of the murderer did not make any new impression. People were already used to this.

Outside, there was the loud noise of cars. Quietly we approached the windows and saw how two large cars had stopped in front of the camp building. Gestapo men got out of the first car, dressed in their black uniforms of evil men, with white arm bands, decorated with swastikas. Wildly, these men got out of the car, each carrying a rubber truncheon or a sharpened stick in his hand. They had weapons in their holsters. From the second car, five people got out, dressed in civilian clothing, with coarse, fat, raw-looking faces. Later we found out that these were Ukrainian assistants. Each of them had the appearance of a murderer.

[Page 286]

These five men went to work immediately. They threw down their coats (probably stolen from their Jewish victims), and they unloaded pieces of wood and boards from the car, and amused themselves with harsh laughter, pushing one another and calling out all kinds of things.

They did not allow us to think too long about what was going on. Soon, the camp supervisor appeared, surrounded by his attendants, and ordered us to go out of the barracks and stand five in a row.

All the camp slaves went into this format of the letter "*ches,*" and in that manner, it was possible to see everything and everyone. In the middle of the camp courtyard, there was already a scaffold set up actually from the beams that were just brought and from the top beam, there were five thick ropes hanging. We all understood that these were for a hanging. But who was going to be hanged here and for what crimes? One of the Gestapo men tore into the silence. He went to stand on the base of the scaffold, and then he said with curt, abrupt, and brutal sentences. This type of talk can also kill people without revolvers and without hangings. They robbed us of the little worth and dignity we Jews still had. He said, among other things: "You Jews wanted this war! So now you have a war. You will all be murdered before this war is over. Whoever tries to tax the discipline of a German camp, whoever tries to run away from here, will pay with his life on this scaffold!"

He hardly finished his terrifying words, when the five Ukrainian henchmen marched out five men with hands tied into the courtyard. It was hard to recognize them. They had been murderously beaten. Their faces were like a ruined mass of flesh. The Ukrainians dragged these men to the scaffold and placed the ropes around their necks. We strained to recognize the victims. One of them was Dovid, the son of Zerach Wilner, and two cousins of Boruch and Berel Najman. There were two other Jews that were from Gombyn who were also hanged. The tragic execution took place.

[Page 287]

Soon, the Ukrainians brought two more victims. Three of those who were hanging were taken down in order to make place for the three new victims. Among these three were two Jews form Gombyn and a son of Berel Najman, Mendel Meyer. Mendel Meyer's father was with us in the camp, he was Dovid Najman, as well as a cousin Boruch's Najman's son.

The nooses were tossed down. Mendel Meyer Najman tossed his head in the ropes, and with one final glance, took in the entire court with all his camp brothers who were watching the tragic events. His quiet look was so very expressive but we could do nothing to help. Every desire within us was suffocated. All our capacity had atrophied. Mendel Meyer glanced at the ground where his brother and cousin were laying dead. With his last energies, he shouted out in Polish: "Long live freedom!" He could not get out the last line. The rope broke his neck.

The Gestapo hangman did not understand what his victim had shouted, so the hooligan from Posen, Alfonse Hillel, laughingly translated it for him. With might and rage, the Gestapo devil took an axe into his hand and split open his victim's head. "Now you are free," he called out and spit onto the ground.

Another Hitlerist went to play around in the shadow of the scaffold, and asked for someone of the interned who would be interested in saying a prayer for the dead ones. There was one Jew who volunteered. He was from Lodz. His name was Schneur. He dragged his swollen feet and emaciated body, And then presented himself. The echo of his voice haunts me to this very day. His voice took on a metallic sound, but the camp carried the prayer far: "God Who is full of mercy, Who dwells on high..." (first line of the *Yizkor* memorial prayer).

[Page 288]

The Gestapo men did not allow Schneur to complete his prayer. Irritated by the silence, they ordered their slaves to run around the scaffold and around the dead men.

This was a macabre death dance. People fell, were beaten, tripped over each other. Those who miraculously survived that horrific death dance, will remember forever that "*shtube* #8" where 35 people lay but could not die ...

[Page 289]

In Fear and in Pain

by Yitzhak Krajcer (Israel)

Translated by Pamela Russ

I am the only one of my family that has survived. The family Krajcer lived in Gostynin on Kutno Street opposite the Russian church. We were three brothers – I, the oldest, and the younger two brothers, Michel and Yehoshua. We studied in the government public school and were *chaverim* [members "friends"] in the *Hechalutz Hatzair* [the Young Pioneers]. Before the outbreak of the bloody war, we had a calm, quiet life. My father, Eliezer ben Aron, was a merchant. My mother, Golde, originally from Zychlin, was a quiet woman, devoted to her home, and we studied and then spent our free time in the *Hechalutz* movement.

In one sudden moment, there was an upheaval. When the Nazis marched into Gostynin, a tumult and terrible fear awoke among the Jews. We were terrified by the slightest rustle. They began to snatch Jews from the streets for work. Those who were locked in the church withered from the beatings they were given by the Nazis. After that, the Jews were no longer permitted to live on all the streets – until the time that they were closed into a locked ghetto. We went over to live in the house of Yehoshua Motil, near the river. Along with us, lived the family of our grandfather Aron.

From day to day the situation in the ghetto became increasingly worse. The crowdedness, the lack of means and lack of food was pressing on everyone. The cruelties of the Nazis became more gruesome every day. The *Kreisleiter* [Nazi Party county leader] and his huge dog set themselves brutally on the Jews. I myself received his beatings because I did not remove my hat for him.

Those who survived remember the garden in the ghetto that the youth worked in. There was great danger, and in our naiveté, we brought the flowers and grass in order, as well as the benches and the playground, where they chased the ball.

[Page 290]

Every day, the forced community-elected people mobilized Jews for public works and brought forth contingencies for the Germans. It didn't even occur to anyone to think about the liquidation of the ghetto. Across the streets of the ghetto, you could see groups of children busy with their games. The adults, however, were busy looking for ways to get more food products; they whole-heartedly believed that anyone who has the means to survive these difficult times will live to the end of the war.

There were rumors in the ghetto that there was a hunger in the other ghettos. By us, for a lot of money, you were still able to get marginal supplies of food. So we got as much as possible, so as not to pass out from hunger. Of course there were those in the ghetto who were hungry, but no one died of hunger...

Gostynin Jews go to work on Kutno Street, 1941.
The sidewalk was forbidden to the Jews.

Jews were snatched for work and then transported to labor camps in Inowroclaw and later to Emzej. I was also in this transport. There were other young children with me. I decided to escape. I quickly jumped through the window and ran to Zychlin to my grandfather. After a few days, I returned to Gostynin.

But the Germans did not stop, and once again snatched up Jews for work. They took my father, my uncle Itche, and me. This time they guarded us closely in the church, and we considered ourselves doomed. Trucks arrived and people began to get on. My Uncle Itche went up onto the truck – but he was able to jump down, and he disappeared. My father also went up, and when it came to my turn, I went over to the German Wiland, and begged him to let my father go – and I would gladly go in his place. He didn't want to hear and told me to get up onto the truck. I resisted, so he beat me badly with his whip. I was stubborn, and held on to myself, and he beat me again, until he finally let my father go. Beaten, I then went up onto the truck.

A German who held a loaded gun in his hand came along with us. He said he would shoot anyone who tried to escape. I sat down at the other end of the truck. We passed Kowalska Street. In front of the ghetto walls stood the relatives of those who had been taken away, with parcels in their hands. We heard cries and screams. I saw my mother. At that moment, I decided to run away and return home. When we passed Rolnyk, I jumped down off the truck and, unnoticed by the German, began to run through the field, and I reached the ghetto wall. When I got closer to our yard, I heard wailing. It seemed that they also took Sender Ring with his son and several others.

[Page 292]

Once, at the ghetto wall I noticed Jews whom I did not know. It became clear that they were from Zdunska Wola. From them we learned about the horror of Chelmno. A Jew ran away from there and told them the gruesome truth about that death factory.

We felt that the same bitter fate awaited our little town. From the labor camp Emzej several people escaped and were hiding in the Gostynin ghetto. In the middle of the night, the Gestapo did a manhunt – probably because of some information from the ghetto – and they captured the people and sent them back to camp. The letters from the camps were very tragic.

In a short time, they began to snatch up girls for work. Among them was my cousin Dvoira Trojanowski. Once, when we were sitting *shiva* [seven day mourning period] for my grandfather Aron, may he rest in peace, the Nazis tore into the ghetto and began to snatch up people for work. Almost half naked, I ran out of the house – and the Germans after me. Running with me were our neighbors Kova Pinczewski and Salek Gliksberg. In an enclosed court, we began to climb across roofs and hid all night. The Germans also looked for us on the roofs, but did not find us.

That night, the Germans went with lists from house to house and beat murderously whoever they found. The screams from all sides assaulted us. That's when they took my father, and my uncles Itche and Moishe. They beat them. My mother also received beatings. My uncles ran from the transport, but my father I never saw again. At the beginning we received letters from him, but they later stopped coming.

They stopped forcing people to get onto the transports. To the camp in Konin, we already went on our own, particularly when the members of the *Judenrat* and their relatives were also in the transport.

[Page 293]

The ghetto was almost empty of people. My brothers and a large number of people from my big family were also gone. The letters that came from Konin were horrendous. I remember a letter from my brother Michel in which he begged us to send him a few slices of bread...

The rest of the family came to live in our house. The days ran with fear for the remaining people in the ghetto. We felt that our end was near. Polaks would appear outside and buy up all kinds of valuable things practically for free. There were no longer any young people in the ghetto. If someone was there, then he was in hiding. That's how I and my Uncle Itche lay in a hiding place.

But we knew that this could not go on for long. So my uncle and I went on the road and came to Strzegowa. My mother stayed back home along with my little brother. It was bitterly difficult to part from them. Even my little brother intuitively felt that we were seeing each other for the last time...

Life in the Strzegowa ghetto was very difficult. We also met people from Gostynin there. There was nowhere to live. There was a terrible lacking. We were very beaten down because of the rumor that reached us, that the Gostynin ghetto was to be liquidated. Yehuda Shatan was there to get his sister out. When he came back to Strzegowa, he told us that the Nazis had carried out a mass murder of Jews and that full trucks of Jews were transported to Chelmno.

We learned that the two brothers Glas had escaped from Konin. The older one was shot by the Germans in Dobrzyn, and the younger one came to Strzegowa. Here they were also snatching up people for work – and I was also among those captured.

To my good fortune, I worked for a Polak, producing peat. Others worked in a sugar factory. After work, this Polak took us back to the ghetto. We knew that our turn would come for Strzegowa as well.

[Page 294]

One day, the Germans attacked the ghetto and shot many people. There was chaos and a lot of running. Not all ran, however. My Uncle Itche and I decided to go back on the road, but where to? – No one knew. Pesach Kwint, who also wanted to go, changed his mind in the last minute. He gave us money and a golden necklace. Izbicki also gave us money and a gold ring. They knew we were left without a *groshen* [penny]. I will never forget the expression on their faces, and their words: "Do not forget us, and if we do not survive to avenge this, then tell everyone what happened to us and our families."

In the dark of night, we searched for a place where we could sneak out of the ghetto; we should leave while it was dark. Itche went first – I followed him. Suddenly, we saw about 50 Germans marching. We managed to evade them and then ran across the fields. We stayed for a few days with a Polak not far from Dobrzyn. He knew we were Jews. He offered to send me to Germany as a Polak to work. I agreed. My uncle said goodbye to me and left in the direction of Gostynin. Soon it became apparent that I could not go to Germany. The Polak tried all kinds of other means for me, but without success. I decided to try my own luck. I left in the direction of Warsaw. Maybe I would still find Jews there. But it was a very dangerous and difficult way, and one had to get past a border. I was lucky to cross the Narew River with the help of smugglers. They thought I was a Polish young boy. Together with them, I got onto a train for Warsaw.

In the wagons of the train, the Christians sang, laughed, and told anecdotes at the expense of the Jews. I had to laugh along with them. Oh, how heavy my heart was then!

[Page 295]

When we arrived in Warsaw, I left to go in the direction of the ghetto. I saw high walls. The streets were guarded by Polish and German policemen. Every bit of time, they demanded papers from anyone who went by. I was lucky: Not once was I asked to identify myself. After a few days in Warsaw, without money and without papers, I saw that I wouldn't be able to get into the ghetto. Upset, I started to think of ways to get back to Gostynin. Maybe I would also find my Uncle Itche there, maybe he was hiding by Christians.

When I arrived by train to Lowicz, I heard that a transport of Polish workers was going to Germany. I also heard that they were looking for substitutes for those who did not want to go. They were also prepared to pay. I located a Polak that was looking for someone to replace his son. Of course, I agreed. We left to the employment office and got me papers in his son's name – and I went to the transport camp.

The Germans took us to Germany. In that transport I saw a Polak from Gostynin, Wladek Molkawski. My heart was gripped with fear that he would recognize me. In the passing train stations in Germany, I noticed Jews who working were wearing yellow Jewish stars on their clothing.

At the end of 1942, I arrived to work in "*Porta Westp.*" [Westphalia] in Germany. After working for a few weeks on the railway, we were sent to "*Minden Westp.*" I worked in that train station for the rest of the years of the war. I lived through very difficult times there, afraid that Heaven forbid neither the Germans nor the Polaks should discover that I was Jewish. Not once did they ask me why I did not receive any mail from anywhere as they used to … Often I would moan heavily in my sleep and my camp friends would ask me about it, what had happened to me … It seems that it didn't occur to them that I was Jewish. I befriended one of them and they helped me. Who knows how they would have reacted had they found out I was a Jew. They would talk about Jews very often. At those times, I became silent, looking for an excuse to leave …

[Page 296]

About the Warsaw ghetto uprising I learned in the letters that the imprisoned Polaks received from their homes. How bitter was my situation! I couldn't even cry about the fate of my fighting brothers! Just by chance, I recognized a Gostynin letter carrier, but he did not recognize me. Probably, I was not recognizable. We spoke of Christian holidays, of church, of the priest … He did not recognize me, even though he would often come to us and bring us the mail.

That's how I lived a disguised life until the Allied military forces found us between Hanover and Dusseldorf. The first Jew I met – an English soldier, came from Tarnow. He spoke Polish to me. I had almost forgotten the Yiddish language. The Polaks standing around crossed themselves. They did not believe their eyes. There was a Jew among them the entire time...

After the war, when I came to Israel, my compatriots [*landsleit*] who miraculously survived, told me that my Uncle Itche was hiding in Gostynin by a Polak, and shortly before the Russian army marched in, the German murderers killed him.

***

That's how a young Jewish boy saved himself. The most frightening fantasy could not have contrived such a horrific story. That's how individuals were saved – in anguish and in pain. But millions died in blood and in tragedy.

[Page 297]

Those Frightful Days

by Avraham Danziger (Israel)

Translated by Yocheved Klausner

The German occupation in Gostynin was a terrible one. The purpose of the Nazis was to take from the Jews everything they had – their property and their life. They did that, as always, in a very organized manner: in order to rob their property they allowed the victims to live for a while. Cheating and misleading, they promised every time that the demands they issued "this time" will be the last, and that as soon as the Jews would obey they will not have to endure new decrees. The Jews believed them, because deep in their hearts they hoped that wickedness and evil must fail, that cruelty must be defeated and that a day will come when the power of justice will win. They hoped that if only they survived the difficult times, better times must and will come. Most importantly – to survive.

But the Germans had other plans. Their intention was not only to take all that the Jews had; their aim was to take even what they did not have. The "contributions" that the Germans demanded day after day left the Jews empty of all their possessions. When the "Judenrat" returned to the Germans with the reply that the ghetto was not able to meet the demands, they sent a delegation from the Gostynin ghetto to Warsaw, to find the means to cover the payments.

A delegation of the "Judenrat", accompanied by policemen, went to Warsaw. Members of the delegation were Motel Tzavier, Asher Zweibom, Yakov Zhichlinski, Israel-Meir Russak and Avraham Danziger. The delegation returned with a sum of one thousand Marks.

This sum was immediately taken by the Germans, of course. But even this did not help the Gostynin Jews. In a very short time, Gostynin has become "Judenrein"...

[Page 298]

From the Gostynin Ghetto
– with the Transport to a Labor-Camp

by M. Brustovski (Israel)

Translated by Yocheved Klausner

M. Brustovski

On a Friday in August 1941, the Germans issued an order that all the Jews report to the transport to be sent to the labor camp. No one arrived, however, since nobody would volunteer to such a "project." So the German soldiers began to seize the Jews from the streets, allegedly to take them to work in town, but, instead, all were taken to the church on Kutner Street. Since the number of people did not match the needs and expectations of the Germans, they entered the Ghetto and began calling the Jews and seizing all those who came out. A great panic fell upon the ghetto and people began to run to the hiding places. I fled, with a group of Jews, to the nearby forest, to the pitch-makers. When night came we walked back to the ghetto, from the other side, through the road where the families Alberstein and Librak had once lived. When I arrived home, the Sabbath had already begun. The candles on the table were lit, but the entire house was weeping – my brother Yechiel-Baruch has been taken to the "transport." As soon as I reached home my parents hid me in a little secret room we had in our courtyard.

Next day, all the captured Jews were loaded on trucks and driven alongside the ghetto. The Jews inside the ghetto, seeing the sad picture, burst into bitter tears; they cried for their husbands and their grown sons – who knows where they were being taken and what their fate would be... They cried for themselves as well – the livelihood earners and the food providers have been taken away. To this day the desperate words of my dear mother resound in my ears: "Who knows if I will ever see you again in my life?" Unfortunately, to our great sorrow, her words became true – her heart sensed the danger.

[Page 299]

After the trucks departed, the ghetto calmed down and became silent; people began to emerge from their hiding places, hoping that the Germans will leave them alone. But all felt fear in their hearts and concern for those who had been sent away.

The body of Yitzhak Kreitzer, who was murdered by the Nazis in Gostynin in 1943, brought to *Kever Israel* (Jewish burial) in Israel

From right to left: Avraham Hersh Motil, his wife, Leibik Motil, Danziger, Ide Motil, Djiganski, Leibish Bagna, Moshe Goldman, Ribek Motil.

[Page 300]

Soon letters began to arrive from the workers, telling us that they were in the labor camp in Posen. They were working at laying water pipes for the "Continental" company. The feeling in the ghetto improved a little, as the families realized that their dear ones were in a known place, and alive. In the letters they described their journey: From Gostynin they went to Wloclawek, there they were taken to a public bath to wash up – they must be sparkling clean to be fit to serve the "master-nation." From there they continued the journey by train.

We tried to make peace with our fate. For us, locked up in the ghetto, one day seemed like a year. Time seemed always longer than it was in reality. And then the German murderers reminded us that they needed new victims.

The scenario repeated itself. Again they demanded a certain number of men for work and I was among the men, too. This time they asked for women as well. It was clear that the same fate awaited us, as the first transport. We were divided into two groups – first the men were taken through the gates of the ghetto, then the women. When the women realized that they were to be part of the transport as well, they began fleeing in all directions, until not one of them remained.

The men were much better guarded by soldiers, on all sides. As with the previous transport, we were taken to the church and we waited there for about two hours, then we were loaded on trucks. While we waited, our families brought us packages with clothes and some food.

The journey from Gostynin to Wroclawek was not easy. Some of the Jews jumped off the trucks and disappeared in the forest, among them was Yitzhak Kreitzer. It was already night when we arrived at the camp in Emzey. We met the Jews of the first transport when they returned from work. I saw my brother – we met in total silence. Neither of us uttered a word, as if we were made of stone. One of the veterans in camp approached and helped us familiarize ourselves with the routine of the camp.

[Page 301]

We went to sleep on hard wooden boards. Before we could fall asleep after the day's many experiences, we were already awakened by the guards. The first day we were not sent to work; instead, the managers of the firm, together with the well-known sadist Hugo Brasch, came to register us. Our surnames were entirely ignored – they did not exist; we were given numbers and we were registered as 1, 2, 3 etc. One of the clerks who wrote down the details said: people have names, all of you we will have to remember by your numbers – you are not people...

We felt beaten and depressed, and in this mood we were sent to prepare the working tools. We were 50 men from Gostynin and our job was to lay water pipes between Goflo and Inowroclaw, a distance of 15 kilometers.

First we dug ditches 60 centimeters deep; some of us were not physically strong enough for this labor, and the stronger among us helped to finish the assigned task. Our food was 300 grams of bread a day and one liter soup – boiled water with unpeeled potatoes. In the evening we returned from work frozen and broken. Not to go to work was a severe crime. Even the sick, with high fever, were forced to leave the camp and go to work. Many men died at the workplace.

[Page 302]

At the end of the working day we were tired out, bleeding and full of mud. Washing up was out of the question – there was no water for that. Our clothes were torn. We were miserable and we longed for a letter from home, in which we hoped to find some comfort. But life in Gostynin was not much better – they had sent the women to another camp.

The situation became worse, when, one day a Nazi committee appeared in camp. Their task was to register and control the number of the healthy and the sick workers. Some of us were so naïve, that they imagined that the sick will be sent back to Gostynin, to recover! The truth was, however, that all the sick workers were sent to the punishment camp "Blanje" and there they were shot. When this sad news reached us, we began to considering a plan to escape from camp, at any price.

[Page 303]

The Resistance in the Koniner Camp

by Shmulik Ben-Tzion Matil (Israel)

Translated by Pamela Russ

Shmulik Matil

Shabbath *Shuva* [the Shabbath between Rosh Hashana and Yom Kippur] of the year 1939, is a tragic date on the calendar for Gostynin Jews. On that fearful day, hordes of German occupiers marched into the town, captured Gostynin, and all at once Jewish life was shaken up. What happened to the diversified Jewry of Gostynin? All differences among the youth disappeared. Vehement party conflicts [with each other] quietened and were extinguished. In one swoop, the catastrophe hit every single Jew. Daily Jewish life in Gostynin became a slave life. The human being lost his own "image of God." Often, one neighbor betrayed another. One brother snatched away a piece of bread from the other in order to save himself, and later he shared the same fate as the martyr.

Nonetheless, at the beginning of this difficult period, life went on with its old, established rhythm. It seems that in Gostynin the conditions were much easier, because tens of refugees came into the city from other cities hoping to live out the rest of the difficult war years here. And they thought that despite all of the blows of war, they would be able to survive. Then my father died, on the 25th day of the month of Adar [March], in his own bed, and was taken for burial. It did not occur to anyone to do anything other than to carry out the time-established, traditional burial. In the course of an entire year, they prayed in our house. [This is the traditional mourning period for the loss of a parent.] Of course, there was someone always standing in front of our house to watch out for any oncoming Nazis.

[Page 304]

The Gostynin youth felt that along with everything else, the Nazis were preparing for gruesome murder. They couldn't figure out all the details of the murderous plan. There were no newspapers, no radio. But instinctively, they drew back with distrust from every German visit and from each German as well. The youth got together very often. Many times, they would also get together with the Polish radical circles who were considering resistance.

At the same time, Yitzkhok Zukerman (Antek) came to Gostynin several times as a representative of *"Hechalutz Hatzair"* [the Young Pioneers youth group that trained for Aliyah, or moving to Israel, then Palestine], and I was even with him at several meetings. It could be that the quiet meetings and preparations that went on in Gostynin and nowhere else lit the spark for revolt that later flamed up in the Koniner camp that was guarded by the SS men. There, in the Koniner camp, our brave children from Gostynin and Gombyn demonstrated heroism. With a shiver of holiness and awe, I remember the names of Avrohom Zajf, of Filip, of Avrohom Tabacznik, of Getzel Klajnut and Komlozh, may their blood be avenged. These few Gostyniner Jews organized the resistance and set the SS camp aflame.

***

The bloody nightmare of that experience will follow me all my life. The Gestapo received the alarm of the fiery chaos. After the firemen put out the fire, we miraculously remained alive and were surrounded by a tight guard. The Germans ordered us to collect all the dead, burned, and hanged bodies from the camp – and I and another elderly Jew from Gombyn were ordered to search the bodies (that was the first time in my life that I was involved with a dead body). As it happened, the first body was of a childhood friend, Shlomo Mikholski; my brother released him from the rope, hiding the rope for himself – to hang himself. It was this type of suicidal mentality that held onto us on that day. It became evident that we had taken the rope off him too soon because he was still alive. An SS man then shot a bullet into his eye. Now I approached the dead body, and odd ... despite all this, that he had been hanged, then shot, and even though he had always been a frail young boy, to my great fear and shock, he opened his other eye and recognized me... I could not tolerate this pain. I went to the Gestapo man and pleaded with him to shoot me. As always, he would not fulfil my request.

[Page 305]

Again, I remained alive ...

The bloody ghost of those terrible days in the Koniner camp still follows me everywhere, like a shadow. Wherever I go, wherever I turn.

✳✳✳

After two years of a tortured life in the Gostynin ghetto, they sent us out, 850 able-bodied men, from the Gostynin province to the camp in Konin, where we arrived on March 15, 1942.

The Gestapo was already waiting for us at the train station in Konin. And very soon, they let us feel their brutality. They welcomed us with murderous beatings. The camp was not yet completely finished. There was no water, and we slept on the ground. In the first two days, they gave us nothing to eat. Since we were on the "building site" the first day, we already saw our tragic "future." We had to build a railway line. Jendeczki, the chief of the East German firm, showed us how to do the work. He said how many persons should carry a rail, and each person could hardly take a step. And if someone fell on the way, then this person no longer got up as a whole person ...

[Page 306]

The SS men took care of that. Every day, the dead and wounded fell from these beatings.

On the third day, another 150 Jews arrived from the Jaksyczer camp. We were now about 1,000 men. In a few weeks' time, more Jews arrived from Podzhebycz. The Gestapo received an official order to murder Jews. Winter time, in the frost, we were ordered to undress and stand for hours outside. Our food consisted in the mornings of 250 grams of black bread with black, bitter coffee. At eight o'clock at night, "lunch" was given out, a little bit of hot water with turnips – nothing else.

Understandably, such "nourishment" had its price on our health. People dropped from hunger. Everyone's feet were swollen. The nurses were not able to help us. But the Gestapo came up with an idea for us. The *Sonderkomando* [a group composed almost entirely of Jews who were forced, on threat of their own deaths, to assist with the disposal of gas chamber victims] was a frequent visitor to us. Whoever remained lying sick in the camps was soon transported to Chelmno – an extermination camp, where tens of thousands of Jews from the Kuyawer and surrounding areas died sanctifying the Name of God. Many of them tried to escape but the majority of them were captured. The Jew had no value. For trivialities, the "guilty person" was immediately hanged.

The food became worse and worse. In winter, people froze to death in the barracks. Within 14 months, only 60 Jews were left in the camp. Earlier, 150 men were sent from here to a camp near Lodz. The 60 remaining Jews now fared much better. It was at that time that we heard news about the crematoria in Auschwitz. From the Polish train workers we also found out about the Warsaw ghetto uprising. That heroic act of Jewish courage completely strengthened us.

August 7, 1943, once again the Gestapo tax was put onto us – and we quickly understood that once again there would be a selection [*selektzia*]. We knew very well what this meant: It meant tortures once again, suffering and death. We all decided that we would not allow ourselves to be led like sheep to the slaughter, and as a last resort, when it would be clear to us that the end was near, and that we would have to die in sanctity of God's name, that along with us the camp should be burned down at the same time.

[Page 307]

The resistance broke out on August 9. Tobaczinski and Klajnut from Gostynin, and Komlozh from Gombyn were the first to set the workshops on fire with coals – and then they hanged themselves in the burning fire. In the main barrack, after that, Zajf from Gostynin and Filip from Gombyn also hanged themselves. Nisinowycz and Shlomo Mikholski from Gostynin, and Dr. Kropf, a Jew from Germany, took the same fate upon themselves.

This tragic event made a huge impact on the city. We, those who by chanced remained alive, stood before our heroes with heads bowed. These heroes did not allow the name "Jew" to be shamed. After two weeks of pain and suffering, the rest of those who were still alive were sent to Auschwitz.

[Page 308]

A Tragic Document from the Konin Camp

(The Will of Avraham Seiff, may he rest in peace)
The document is located at the Archives of
Kibbutz Lochamei Hagetaot in the State of Israel

Following is a facsimile of part of the document – ed.

by Avraham Seiff
Translated by Yocheved Klausner

Avraham Seiff

The document below is the last will of Avraham Seiff, may God avenge his blood. Avraham Seiff was in his youth a student at the Gostynin Gymnasium (High School) and later married a Gostynin girl. For a time he lived in Danzig, where he was involved in extensive Zionist activity.

With the outbreak of the war, Avraham Seiff relocated with his family to Gostynin; his activity in the Gostynin ghetto is described in three articles in the *Pinkas*. He was deported by the Germans to the forced labor camp in Konin. He was praised, in the *Pinkas*, for his outstanding devotion to his fellow workers in the camp.

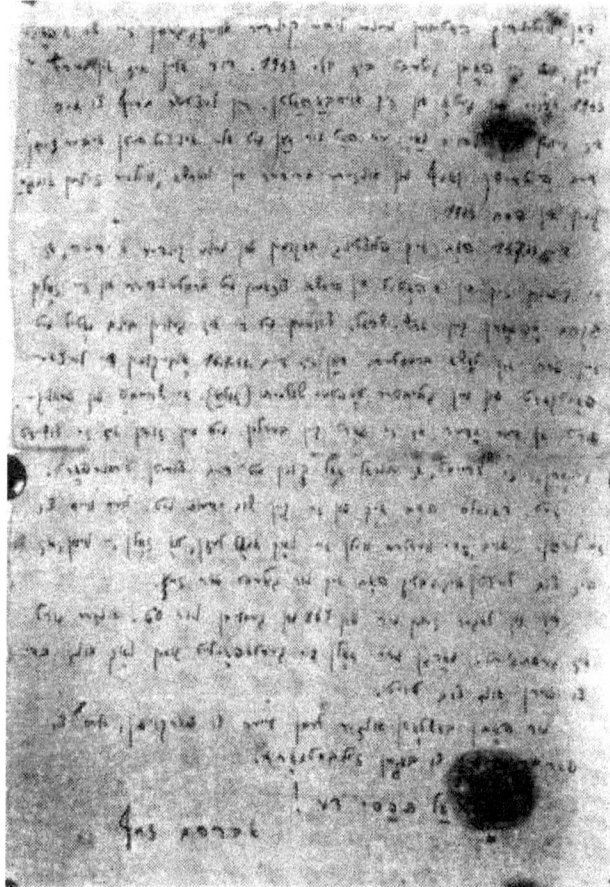

Facsimile of part of the document

Avraham Seiff wrote his ***Last will***, reprinted here, one day before the uprising in the camp. He gave the document to a Polish man who worked there, and after the war it was sent to his sister-in-law in Eretz Israel.

[Page 309]

Konin, 12 August 1943

My last wish:

I request to inform the following persons: 1. My brother Azriel Seiff, high-school teacher in Tel Aviv, 2. My sister Miriam (Marila), the wife of Heinrich Bloch in Jerusalem, 3. My sister-in-law Dr. Tzelina Stadter, nee Matil, dentist in Haifa.

My very dear ones,

I would like you to know how my family and I perished:

On the 9th of March 1942, I was torn out of my home and sent off to this labor camp together with other Gostynin Jews. More than half were tormented to death during the hard work; many were shot for taking a few potatoes, or for other such crimes.

On the night between 16-17 April, my dear wife Minia and my 4 year old Ilana Naomi and my mother-in-law Salia Matil, together with the entire Jewish population of Gostynin were sent to their deaths. We know only that they were taken first to Krasniewic and from there, we assume, they were driven to Chlemno to the slaughter.

I never heard from them again. My dear little children Immanuel and Shulamit escaped from Gostynin and managed to arrive to David and Rivka in Warsaw. My father-in-law Note Matil was in Warsaw as well. He died 4 November 1941.

By the end of July 1942, the tragedy began in Warsaw. On 6 August 1942 Rivka was captured and sent to her death. David was seized on 19 January 1943. However he managed to escape and after three days returned to the ghetto in Warsaw. Then, hoping to save my children, he gave them to a Polish family, and they lived with them until July 1943. In March 1943, David left the ghetto and lived in several hiding places. His last letter was from May. In it he described to me in detail our brothers' heroic battle in the Warsaw ghetto. The ghetto fell on Pesach (Passover) 1943.

On 14 July 1943 I suddenly received news from my children, that they were in a hotel in Warsaw together with some foreigners and they were hoping to leave soon for Eretz Israel. With them were also Binem Matil with his wife and Tasha Bressler. On 17 July I received the last postcard from my dear daughter Shulamit (Zulia). It was from Frankfurt am Oder and she wrote that she will be going to Berlin. She was separated from her brother, my son. She wrote that Imanuel will probably go with the next transport. Since then I had no news from them. Who knows whether they are alive. If they ever read these words, I would like them to know that until my last moment I have lived only for them.

[Page 310]

Here in camp, from 687 men we remained only 60. Our fate is sealed. Tomorrow morning, the Gestapo people will come to lead us to our deaths.

We have decided, however, not to sell our lives cheap. We shall burn everything and commit suicide.

Earth, do not cover our blood!

[Page 311]

Chelmno

by the Esteemed Rabbi Yehoshua Moshe Aronson (Israel)

Translated by Pamela Russ

In November 1941, Yisochor Cohen's son from Gostynin came to me in the Szenic ghetto. He was a religious young man, very competent. He conducted trade among the various ghettos, going without permission, without the yellow patch, and without the "Jewish star." Because of these frequent travels, he had first-hand information about all the laws in the Reich and in the protectorate. From him I learned about everything that was going on in the other ghettos.

With great discretion, he told me that in Chelmno, near Kohl (in German Kulmhof, and in Polish Kolo), the Germans had set up a huge slaughter-house that they disguised as a bathhouse. Since the eve of Yom Kippur, 1940 – he said – Jewish souls were being murdered in large numbers in a brutal manner. He listed tens of communities that had already been killed there. Each ghetto received an order a few weeks in advance to pay two or four Marks as a head tax, that is to say for injections; in this manner this money would certainly cover the expenses of extermination operations in that specific ghetto.

It happened often that Chelmno was overcrowded, so the victims would be locked up for a few days in the Kolo *Beis Medrash* [House of Study]. Until their turn would come.

Cohen also told me that even before the Chelmno period, the Germans murdered many Jews in the Karzhmerske woods.

All this information, understandably, made a terrifying impact. But in some places, there was even a doubt: Can this really be true?

In the middle of January 1942, the veracity of all this news was confirmed and the phrase: "Where are the transports being sent?" became familiar and real.

[Page 312]

A certain Jew from Kolo, Mikhel Podkhlebnik, who until the outbreak of the war lived in Bugoj, a village in the Kolo circle, delivered the following news:

"On January 9, 1942, the Gestapo arrived in Bugoj, and demanded 15 strong men to work for a few days. Podkhlebnik was taken along with this group. They also took 15 men from Izbica-Kujawska. The following day they were taken by car to Chelmno, a large court between Kohl and Dombje. There they threw the 30 men into a cellar. This took place on the day of Shabbath.

"On the walls of the cellar, they noticed all kinds of writing, such as: 'Jews! Be aware that no one comes out of here alive!' and so on. They immediately understood that they were now in hell. Later they overheard that in another cellar there was another group of Jews also locked in. They made contact with them through the walls. From these contacts they learned exactly what was going on there. It was quiet all day Sunday. The following day, Monday morning, 20 of those men were removed. The other ten remained in the cellar. He, Podkhlebnik, was among these remaining ten in the cellar."

Podkhlebnik continued: "From time to time, we heard the noise of an oncoming car. The Gestapo welcomed the arrival with wild screams: 'Faster, louse! Faster!' We heard the steps of bare feet and soon thereafter, cries to the heavens: '*Shema Yisroel*!' wretched, breathless, wild voices. This horrifying scene would continue for about ten minutes, and then a deathly silence would settle all around.

"Each time after the screaming chaos, the *Sonderkomando* from the Gestapo would come to us and bring us up from the cellar with a wild rush, and we would see a shocking sight before our eyes:

[Page 313]

"In a large room all kinds of clothing was thrown around. Men's clothing, women's and children's, under garments and outer wear. The Gestapo would order us to carry over everything into a nearby larger room. There we found countless heaps of clothing, garments, shoes, and so on. Everything was mixed together. When we finished our job of emptying the first room and wiping away all the traces, they sent us back to the cellar. This is what went on several times a day."

The next day, Tuesday, the others remained in the cellar and Podkhlebnik was taken into a truck by the Gestapo, under heavy guard. After driving for about ten minutes out of Chelmno, the truck stopped in the nearby woods. Large ditches were dug out there, slanted deep, wide at the top, and narrow at the bottom. Approximately every half hour, the truck came with the victims. A *Sonderkomando* was already waiting for the truck, and the cellar Jews immediately opened the doors of the truck, from which a light, black smoke came out. When the truck had aired out, they took out the still warm, naked bodies of the fresh victims. They spread out the bodies on the ground. The Gestapo men went around with pliers in hand and walked around among the dead rows of the newly suffocated. They thoroughly searched through each body and took whatever they found. They also ripped the teeth out of the mouths of the martyrs' bodies. After this deplorable procedure and brutal theft, a second group of the cellar Jews arrived and threw the bodies into the ditch. A third group of Jews was already standing there, that covered up the corpses.

Meanwhile, the truck went back to Chelmno to bring fresh bodies. This went on all day. In the evening, they covered up the ditch with a thin layer of earth, and the cellar Jews were taken back to their Chelmno cellars.

April 7, 1942, the Jews were evacuated to Chelmno from Gostynin and from Gombyn. On April 18, that same year, the Jews from Szanik were also taken there.

[Page 314]

***

The above events I described in my diary in 1942, when I was in the Koniner camp.

I would like to describe another episode from this bloody history of those tragic times:

At the end of 1941, when the Jews from our area were still in their towns, we found out that in Bendzin-Sosnowicz there was a *Judeneltster* ["Elder of the Jews"], Munik Merin, and he was in charge of the ghettos from eastern Upper Silesia. News reached us that this very Merin received an extraordinary letter from Himmler himself, and was highly regarded by the Germans.

It occurred to us that we should go to Munik Merin and tell him about the horrifying events in Chelmno, and maybe he would be willing to help us. A delegate left for Sosnowicz under the supervision of Avrohom Zajf from Danzig, who recently, as a son-in-law of a Gostyniner, lived in Gostynin. After great difficulty, the delegation arrived in Zaglembie and met with Merin, telling him that thousands of Jews were being murdered in Chelmno. Merin declared that he knew nothing about this. He did know that in Auschwitz, criminals were being murdered. He did not speak too much with the Gostyniner representatives. He directed them to his secretary who called a council meeting together to hear about the story of Chelmno.

The delegation was very upset by their visit to Sosnowicz. Merin gave the impression of being a Gestapo man. He suggested they organize workshops and warehouses for the German military to make themselves useful for the German war machine, and in that way be able to save themselves.

[Page 317]

There Once Was

Gostynin

by Meier Gostynski

Translated by Pamela Russ

Meier Gostynski

Roads and paths
Wound their way through Gostynin.
On those roads and steps
Something once happened to us.

The mornings were spent in the House of Study
And not far from there was a windmill,
And we all yearned for her.
A step led up to the tall mountain
And as youths we went dancing there.
Couples captured their love there
And the air was filled with song.

Gostynin, a town with Jews of all types,
Shoemakers, tailors, Jews of toil,

And wealthy Jews, and Jews that were merchants,
The one who went to the villages, Moshe Lublin –
Awoke with the morning star, and went to the House of Study.
And right after morning prayers, left the village.
Kerosene and threads the peasants sold,
And for that they took potatoes and eggs.

Brought home the wages
With a few rubbed out coins.
And Izak the book peddler –
His strength was without bound,
He carried a bundle of six,
Of which others could only have carried four...

The beadle Mikhel Ber:
His beard parted in two,
A fiery Jew, running to and fro,
With his frock coat blowing, open so wide.
He was very sad, when a child was born,
And the birthing glow was lost.
And now he's at the podium:
And he is selling aliyas [blessings during Torah reading portions].
A bang on the table,
Two gildens for shelishi [the third portion]
He searched through the crowd,
A distinguished person for shishi [the sixth portion]...

The ritual slaughterer, my uncle Binyomin,
A studious learner, of exceptional ancestry,
With respect and greatness always behaving,
The Rav of Sieradz was his grandfather,
And the ritual slaughterer was the other,
The cantor Reb Yakov Miller,
Beloved in the city.
His loud voice rang warmly.
Everyone loved his prayers
His praying held everyone's
Hearts and minds:
Oh cantor! Cantor! All the strength to you!

The Jews in the town recounted to each other:
My great-grandfather, the Rav of Sieradz,
Was a Rav in our town before that.
But there were rumors about him that happened.
An argument was going on because of him.
So he said:
"I don't want to buy my rabbinic position
Even with the Torah.
I'd rather run away from this place.
I'm afraid of arguments."

And over and above everything else,
The spirit spread itself out,
Of the rabbi, the Gostynin rabbi.
Famed in the world,
As the Jew of Psalms.
Fathers would repeat the rabbi's words:
"Everyone can become a good Jew
Through his own good deeds."

That's how the Jews in our town lived,
In those former years.
Everyone in his little world
Wove his own dreams…

***

Roads and paths,
Wound through the town of Gostynin:
And on these very roads and paths
They took all our beloved ones to the slaughter…

[Page 320]

A Meeting at the Old Cemetery

by Josef Keller

Translated by Pamela Russ

The cemetery of Gostynin stretched from the Bug River to the Kutno highway. The Bug, which flowed along the length of the city from north to south, ran much farther west than did the Kutno highway, so that the area of the cemetery appeared to be vast.

Quite close to the water was the old cemetery, with old, sunken graves and caved in tombstones with rubbed out names. It was almost impossible to read the names of those who were buried there, and it was because of all that that people seldom visited the old cemetery.

In the new cemetery, that was closer to the Kutno highway, there were visitors almost all the time. People came to the graves of their parents, to visit the graves of relatives of relatives. It was also a tradition in town that when one was marrying off a son or a daughter, the parents would go to the cemetery to inform their close ones about the upcoming wedding. They used to say that people would do this to invite these relatives to the wedding.

For the entire month of Elul, before the High Holidays, almost everyone in town would go to the cemetery. Who can even talk about when the 21st day of the month of Shevat arrived! That was the *yahrzeit* of the great *Tzadik* of Gostynin, Reb Yechiel Meyer, of blessed memory. The Gostynin cemetery was really crowded then, not only with the residents of Gostynin, but even with Jews from the surrounding towns. People kept on coming to the Rav's gravesite the entire day.

That's how the cemetery was never empty, because there were always warm, living people, among the cold tombstones.

[Page 321]

But suddenly, a black cloud stretched over Poland. Hitler's horrific devastation approached. The murderers herded out the entire Jewish community from Gostynin right into the gas chambers, and murdered them in the ovens. That's how the Jewish cities were destroyed. Even the cemeteries were wasted and destroyed.

Days, weeks, and months passed, and the emptiness and silence of the cemeteries remained, simply because there were no more Jews left in the town who could visit. The silence disturbed the rest of those deceased. It was difficult for them to understand why they were left so bereft and alone. They missed the cries of the orphans who would come to their parents' gravesites. They missed those pervasive sad melodies that carried the "*El moleh rachamim*" (prayers for the dead) across the cemetery. So, the deceased called a meeting in the old cemetery to discuss the situation and to find out the reason for the terrible silence.

It was still in the middle of the night, the fields in the surrounding mountains were yet wrapped in darkness, and all was still silent. But from the old cemetery, a white strip was seen, a whiteness that cut through the darkness. It was the dead wearing their *kittels* (white robes) and *taleisim* (prayer shawls), and also the white, caved in tombstones that partially covered the graves - it was there, among the graves, that the deceased gathered for the meeting.

Right in the center of the cemetery, there was a table covered with a white tablecloth. Around the table, were the faces of the holy people of the Gostynin community.

At the head was Reb Leybish Lipszycz, son of the Gostynin *Tzadik*, Reb Yechiel Meyer, of blessed memory. Reb Leybish was wearing a white *kittel* with a silver stole around his shoulders. He looked like he was standing before his congregation on the eve of Yom Kippur, just about to begin the prayers of *Kol Nidrei*. To the right of Reb Leybish was the hoary white Reb Shmuel Volf Pinczewski, the *dayan* (religious judge) of Gostynin, with his earnest face that recalled his *selichos* prayers as he recited this with his last energies and strained voice, "My soul is Yours, and my body is Yours..."

[Page 322]

On the other side of the table, there was Reb Yekel Alberstajn, the son-in-law of the Gostynin *Tzadik*, of blessed memory. He was a scholar, a masterful teacher, but he had his earnings from trade. He was wearing a white, satin *yarmulke*, and his long, curly, *peyos* (side locks) were tucked behind his ears. The seriousness of his face was the best testimony that there was now a serious matter at hand.

At the table were also seated the elderly sage Reb Shmuel Yosef Bagno who was always occupied with his learning Torah; there was the dark Fishel

(Tzivia), with his sharp mind that was a little involved in general knowledge too; and also the elderly Avrohom Yitzchok Lomzer, with his wide beard that covered a large part of his face and his bushy eyebrows that grew right over his eyes. Avrohom Yitzchok Lomzer was the man who blew the *shofar* in *shul* in Gostynin on *Rosh Hashana*, a man who blew the *shofar* without even one sound ever flawed.

There were more Jews sitting around the table with serious faces, but the majority of the people were standing around that table waiting.

Standing at a slight distance from the table were the women. They were all seated on the caved-in grave sites. This unique scene was reminiscent of the city's women's court ("*ezras noshim*" in the synagogue). So removed and unique were they, and swaying as if in prayer; they moaned and sighed. Others emitted sad, choking cries, and yet others cried aloud, and these cries echoed far into the mountains.

In the beginning, it was all so beautiful that the entire group was so still - but with the trained eye looking towards the new cemetery, of all those present in the old cemetery, it seemed that everyone was waiting for something important to happen and come forward from the new cemetery.

Then Reb Yekel Alberstajn informed everyone that the messengers were returning from their mission.

From afar, they saw Reb Itche Keller, may he rest in peace the primary manager of the *Chevra Kadisha* (community organization that takes care of funerals), a great scholar with a healthy aptitude for worldly matters. Everyone listened closely to Yisroel Itche's words, and therefore he was often elected to openly discuss complicated matters. He was also a constant attendee of the Gostynin *Tzadik*, of blessed memory.

[Page 323]

Reb Yisroel Itche, along with another three men of the *Chevra Kadisha*, were selected from this gathering to approach the Rebbe's <u>ohel</u> (tent-like covering over the gravesite) in the cemetery, and to find out from the *Tzadik* - if he would reveal the secret - the reason that no one was coming to visit the graves in the old cemetery, and why suddenly there were no more weddings or funerals. Was it that the Angel of Death was finally successful, meaning no one was left on this earth?

To deal with this mission, there were Yisroel Itche with the other three men of the *Chevra Kadisha*, Shmuel Klajnbard, Yakov Mendel Keller, Yisroel Itche's son, and Mendel Ichel Gostinski.

Shmuel Klajnbard was a difficult Jew, always leaning on his walking stick that accompanied him at every step. He never rushed. "Why?" he asked. "What should I rush for? Will the dead body run away?"

Yakov Mendel, who followed his father's ways, but one step ahead and more modern, was known in town for his immaculate clothing. Just as his father, Yakov Mendel was also highly regarded by the community, and later he took over the management of the *Chevra Kadisha*. Often he too was the advocate for the community in front of the city's governor who respected him greatly.

Mindel Ichel was a pious (*Chassidish*), religious Jew. His ancestry for generations was from Rabbis and scholars. In town he was renowned for his exactitude in issues of *kashrut*. He used to be called the "vinegar manufacturer" because making vinegar was part of his livelihood. He also made wine that the entire town used on *Shabbos* and on the holidays, and he was also involved in the general needs of the community.

[Page 324]

These four messengers returned from their mission to see the holy Gostynin *Tzadik*.

The mood was strained and serious. Everyone waited to hear what the messengers would tell. But the head of the messengers, Reb Yisroel Itche, for whom speaking was never a problem, came to the table with a furrowed brow, biting his lips that wouldn't open to speak.

After a short time, the crowd became restless. Finally, the messengers revealed the gruesome, tragic story that they searched for the Rebbe's tent throughout the length and width of the entire cemetery but could not find it.

The terrible news of the disappearance of the Rebbe's tent struck the crowd like thunder and everyone felt that something awful had happened, because if the Rebbe's tent could have disappeared from its eternal resting place, then who could imagine what had happened to the orphans and to the entire Gostynin community?

Everyone's face showed anguish and sadness. It was obvious that the community suddenly felt that Gostynin had gone through a terrible destruction. Everyone was rock still. Only from the women's side could one hear moaning and sighing.

But soon the white-haired Reb Shmuel Volf stood up wrapped in his *talis* (prayer shawl). Only his thin hands were visible. He stretched them out to the heavens, and with a trembling voice and his last energies he called out: "Raise your eyes to the mountains! From where will come our help?" From where, oh, will come our salvation?" Soon he collapsed in tears and soon the entire crowd joined him.

Suddenly, a mighty wind with fearful howling arrived, the surrounding trees and bushes bowed noisily. And from the mountain came a thick cloud of dust. There was a sort of moaning heard in the wind. It seemed that everything around - the mountains, the trees, the graces, and the tombstones along with the entire assemblage merged into one big mass, and were carried by the wind. And over the terrible howling of the wind, an echo was heard from the other side of the mountain. The voice became stronger and clearer, and through the noise was heard: "Pure souls, why do you storm and grumble there? Why are you so angry at your orphans? What complaints do you have of the Gostynin community? Do you not know that your children, your brothers and sisters, the entire Gostynin community were killed by the German murderers in gas chambers and crematoria in all the unsettled Polish cities and they didn't even make it to Jewish graves?."

[Page 325]

"Look west over the mountains and you will see the dense, powerful stench that is carried from the ash on the mountains. Those ashes are the remains of the millions of holy Jews, and there, among the millions, you will find the holy ones from Gostynin. ."

"That black cloud of wind will always face upwards toward the Heavens, as an eternal memory, that an entire Jewish world was destroyed."

The wind still howled, the trees and bushes still bowed. But the voice from Heaven was heard no more. The darkness suddenly thickened. The white strip of the old cemetery disappeared, even the tombstones became black from the darkness. There was not even any sign left of the dead.

The meeting ended, and the cemetery lies still between the Bug and the Kutno highway. Again the cemetery will be forlorn and bereft because there is no one left in Gostynin who would come to the grave of their families...

[Page 326]

These Candles Are Holy...

by H. Sztern (Israel)

Translated by Pamela Russ

Hershel Sztern

Reb Yeshaya opened the glasses [china] cabinet to take out the Chanuka candelabrum. He stood for a while, respectfully, as if in front of a great nobleman.

The Chanuka candelabrum that stared proudly out of the china cabinet all year, was the pride of Reb Yeshaya. This was his ancestry scroll [ancestral documents, because the Chanuka candelabrum came into his hands through the inheritance of his grandfather, the esteemed *Tzaddik* [righteous man], Reb Yechiel, of blessed memory. One of his *chassidim* [followers], with pure thoughts and pure hands, shaped the candelabrum from pure silver.

His followers recounted that when the Rebbe lit the Chanuka candles with a melody and in deep concentration, then God's Presence rested on him, and his holy face radiated such that one could not look at him just as one could not look at the sun. And in the small flames of the pure olive oil [that was used for burning] he saw, actually saw in reality, the holy Hasmoneans, the Jewish heroes, burning with rage and hatred towards the Greeks who invaded the Holy Land and desecrated God's Palace.

He saw how, dressed in the strength of self-sacrifice, the Jewish fighters threw themselves into the fire of the fight for the holiness and purity of the Jewish Land and for Jewish honor; he saw the humble cup of pure oil that the Hasmoneans discovered with trembling hands in a corner of the Holy Temple.

[Page 327]

On his face, one could see that he was experiencing, along with an ecstatic shiver, the Hasmoneans' discovery of the holy small cup of oil with the seal of the High Priest.

The *Tzadik* would knit together his long eyebrows, close his fiery eyes, and tell the large group that had assembled around him:

"This small cup of oil, this is the last reserve of strength and holiness that God Himself, as it were, hid for his People of Israel in difficult times, may He have mercy on us, when Israel's candelabrum was already flickering down; close, Heaven forbid, to being extinguished. When the soul of the nation falls, sinking into an abyss of impurity, and is threatened to go under, God forbid, then Blessed God takes His last reserve of holiness and purifies his nation, and the People of Israel once again return to their source.

"When enemies sharpen their wild teeth on the gentle lamb of Israel, when the entire measurement of cruelty from the whole world, that which finds itself among the nations, pours itself into the head of Israel, when the People of Israel is confused and is standing, God forbid, at the brink of going under – then the Creator has mercy on His children who are struggling in pain. He takes out the small hidden cup of oil, the final reserve of strength, and Israel infuses with exceptional energy and power.

"But," a deep sigh escapes from the Rebbe, "woe is to the nation when God has to use His last reserve. Only certain individuals are worthy of this......."

***

Reb Yeshaya was standing in front of the Chanuka candelabrum, and before his eyes stood his grandfather Reb Yechiel, lighting the Chanuka candles.

He remembered every word of his teachings. But his final words rang strongly in his ears...

It was the eve of Chanuka, year 5702 [1941]. The Nazi murderers were blowing like raging winds across the Jewish cities in Poland. Terrible laws and tragic news rained down like hail over the Jewish heads. The noose that they tied around the Jewish throats became tighter and tighter. They already heard the footsteps of the devil and the waving of his sword.

[Page 328]

Reb Yeshaya smelled the odor of death, and therefore the frightening words of his grandfather rang:

"Woe to this generation, when God must use His final reserves... Only certain individuals deserve this..."

When night fell, Reb Yeshaya locked the doors and gates, and lit Chanuka candles in a discreet, small corner.

His eyes cried rivers of tears. He felt that this was his final Chanuka and maybe even his final night. He saw before his eyes the entire world as one hell, one dark graveyard, and he was actually standing at the edge of a precipice...

When Reb Yeshaya's eyes became weary of crying, he called out:

"Master of the Universe, when You decided that my generation should drink the bitter cup until the bottom; when You poured onto us the whole world's murder and cruelty, that we should die a terrible death through wild brutality, I accepted all this with love. But don't forget, Master of the Universe, about the hidden cup of pure oil, about the individuals whom You will protect under Your wings and who will take from Your well of strength, and only they, as the Hasmoneans, will fight in the enemy's impure face, and destroy him and his temples, the stronghold of nests of murder and evil."

The next day, the first day of Chanuka, was a dark day in the city. Military trucks stopped in the middle of the market place, and fat, well-fed Germans with whips in their hands wildly chased after the elderly and the children to take them to the slaughter.

That day, the devil needed hundreds of victims to satisfy his wild blood thirst. The SS men led hundreds of Jews through the streets of the city. Old people and children to the slaughter.

The Germans led Reb Yeshaya, with his patriarchal beardat the head of the death march. His face was white as chalk, and he asked the profound question: "For what? For when?"

[Page 329]

He went on his final way with his eyes downcast, buried deep in his beard, sunk in his thoughts of glorifying the Name of God. He suddenly lifted his eyes to the heavens and whispered: "Master of the Universe, see how dark it is for your nation of Israel. Help, open the small cup of oil and give to those whom You will save, strength and courage that they should avenge the blood of Your servants whose blood has been spilled, and redeem the nation of Israel from their bitter exile!"

* * *

It was the first Chanuka in the new pioneering colony of the Negev. Groups, young pioneers, who not long ago arrived here from the valley of tears, have decided to celebrate the holiday of the Hasmoneans with great festivity. In their holiday clothes and with their glowing faces, they gathered in the reading room.

Around the large silver Chanuka candelabrum everything was decorated beautifully with colored decorations. The head of the *kibbutz* [collective community], Yechiel, the only surviving son of Reb Yeshaya, stood for a while, deep in thought. His grandfather's Chanuka candelabrum carried him back to the world of his father and grandfather. Like that, in a dream, he lit the Chanuka candles, and together with his father and grandfather, he recited the blessings with the ancient melody.

"Amen!"

The strong voice of the young hearts that beat with freedom and joy, stirred Yechiel from his dream. On his face, joy and sadness struggled.

Yechiel began to tell his friends the history and life cycles of the Chanuka candelabrum; the silent witness of the times of his esteemed grandfather in exiled Poland; the witness of the tragic deaths of millions of Jews and now of the rebirth of a new Jewish nation in Israel – a nation that was forged in fire by the hatred for the murderers of our parents sisters and brothers, and the fire of love, boundless love, for the Jewish People and the Jewish Land.

[Page 330]

"We are the remaining individuals who have been saved after the horrible murders of our nation," the head of the *kibbutz* thundered with his powerful voice. "On our shoulders, rest enormous historical obligations. Let us hope that God Almighty will give us strength and courage from that cup of oil, strengthen the hands of our fighters so that they will destroy all our enemies who place themselves like the devil in our way, and relight the darkened *menorah* [candelabrum], which will stream her rays from the mountains of Zion and spread the light across the dark world."

The memories from the dark past and hope for a beautiful and bright tomorrow melted the souls of the young sons of Israel and carved out unbendable, strong heroes, who, after hearing the speech of the head of the *kibbutz*, broke out in a long *Hora* dance.

And in spite of everything ----- The Nation of Israel lives! The Nation of Israel lives! Longed for Chanukah songs, with all kinds of melodies of the different tragic times of the exile, found their revival in the proud singing that rang in the air of the blooming Negev.

The Nation of Israel lives!
The Nation of Israel lives!
Stockholm, 1948

[Page 331]

A Letter to My Friend Hans

by Ezri Zajf-Etsmun

Translated by Pamela Russ

Ezri Etsmun

Do you remember me, Hans, your longtime friend
From childhood and youth's times?
In my thoughts I am writing a letter to you today
From Tel Aviv, from afar.

I fled from the storm at the right time,
When life was still flowing calmly.
I don't know if you are still alive or not,
It's not important, but let us talk...

I still see before me your gold blond hair
Your face so burned from the sun.
I hear your footsteps ... Is the dog still alive?
I would still recognize it today.

I speak and forget ... It's probably dead by now,
And you, Herr Schmidt, do not be angry,
Go try to understand, that in my heart there is still rings a clang,
A sentimental one, how to understand that!

[Page 332]

I'm curious, for example, if near the window still hangs
The small knife that gleamed on your belt.
With this toy, you drew blood from my sister,
From my brother, his life.

You remember my brother, you probably remember,
You greeted him warmly every morning.
Often he would accompany us to the train,
Under his coat he had hidden a toy.

And tell me, was your shirt, the brown one,
Ironed flat every day,
By the hands of Frau Schmidt, your mother, the refined one,
When you led Edy to his death.

Small Edy, so sweet, your friend,
You often pressed him against your heart,
Tell me, I beg you, did the little boy cry
When you suffocated him with gas?

And tell me one more thing, Hans, my good brother,
Forgive me for the angry remembrance,
How would you kill your friend, ME,
With whom you used to read together?

I am simply asking ... and what is the difference to you
To throw off a burden of memories?
And you, I am sure, would just like to know
What I feel towards you in my heart.

And odd, I don't wish that you encounter death.
On the contrary, that would make me sad.

[Page 333]

I want you to live, Hans, without escaping
The smell of blood that you spilled.

And from my look ... stiff and silent,

That should follow you all the days,
When a son or a daughter you will take into your arms,
Or a wife, when you will need some peace.

If you pick up a book – my stare will be in it,
In every single line and word.
Wherever you will turn, you will find
The memory of hideous murder.

(Translated from the Hebrew by Ludwig Zajf)

[Page 337]

Gostyniner Across the World
The Gostyniner Society in New York

by Y.K.

Translated by Pamela Russ

The Gostyniner Society in New York was founded in the year 1908.

The founders were Lipe Bresler, Yona Segal, Moishe–Dovid Rozental, Shloime Motilinski, Shloime Dobzhinski, Chaim Wand, Yakov Aryeh Herskowycz, and Y. Gliksohn.

The Society was set up according to the means and foundations of the then–existing Societies of the various *landsmanschaften* [immigrant benevolent societies formed and named after the members' birthplace in Eastern Europe], such as: to pay members' sick benefits; in the event of illness, to ensure their medical care and provide a doctor who would receive an annual fee from the Society. The Society also acquired its own burial ground for their members and families and organized itself based on the principle of shared support in a member's time of need.

When new members registered and there were elections, the first president to be elected was Yosef Wolman.

During the first period, a constitution was set up regarding how the Society should conduct its work, what the responsibilities should be of each member, and so on. According to the regulations, meetings were to be held twice a month.

The Society became the information center for Gostynin. When a member received a letter from Gostynin, with any kind of news, this was reported at the meetings. And when a Gostyniner arrived in New York, the *landsleit* [compatriots, Society members of the same town in Eastern Europe] already made sure that this newcomer would attend the Society's meetings, where he was warmly welcomed. This type of guest aroused the members' great interest, because usually he was able to give over personal regards. Because when someone left Gostynin to come to America, the entire town knew about this. That's how the Society maintained a constant contact with Gostynin.

[Page 338]

When the Society's membership grew, and the opportunities for social activities were no longer so limited, the Society made contributions to various charitable institutions and establishments. Meanwhile, financial assistance was also sent to the needy in Gostynin, especially for the holidays.

With the outbreak of World War One, contact with Gostynin was broken. So much so that there was no information about what was going on there. But as soon as the war ended, a special general meeting was called and a relief committee was elected that would help with the aide work to Gostynin, because there was no doubt that Gostynin would desperately need help.

The activists on the help committee were Moshe Flaum, Sholom Motlinski, Lipe Bresler, Philip Lefkowycz, Moshe Kalish, Harry Solomon, Meyer Dovid Tremski, Yosef Keller, Binyomin Kalmus, Dovid Kalmus, Zigmund Silverstajn, Itche Lewi, and Moshe Faiereizen. It should also be mentioned here that Esther Flaum, the daughter of Moshe Flaum, even though she wasn't a committee member, helped tremendously with this financial collection of money.

As soon as contact was reinstated, help was actually sent to Gostynin. The contact with Gostynin after that was maintained consistently, and in the post-war years, the Society also sent timely help for the Gostyniner, especially for those who needed assistance for the holidays.

There was a plan to celebrate a small holiday for the ten–years of the Society's existence. But the air was still filled with the war's gunpowder. So the celebration was delayed.

On Sunday, November 18, 1923, the 15th jubilee celebration was marked with a banquet. A journal was published in honor of this occasion. At that time, the president was Sholom Motilinski, vice president – Herman Lewi, treasurer – Yona Segal, protocol secretary – S. Bakh, finance secretary – Meyer Dovid Tremski, hospitality –

[Page 339]

Y.M. Motilinski, doctors – S.R. Peili and Y. Blum.

The other officials were: S. Silverstajn, Moshe Faiereizen, S. Klein, Binyomin Kolmus, Sam Solomon, Sam Gerst.

It's probably of interest to mention that in this jubilee journal there was a financial report of the fifteen years of the Society's existence:

Income	$22,208.60
Expenses	$16,423.91
Balance	$5,785.69

Among the expenses was the total of the sick benefits that was paid out to members $3,848.00

Contributions to charitable establishments and to other Jewish institutions $1,225.52.

The author of these lines stops here at the celebration of the 15th year's jubilee, disregarding the fact that the Society celebrated other jubilees in later years with more breadth and splendour, according to the progress in the life of the times – because for the 15th jubilee celebration almost all of the founders of the Society participated. The Gostyniner cantor, Reb Yankel Miller, of blessed memory, came from Detroit. It really felt like a Gostyniner celebration. The atmosphere and brotherliness was exceptional with the homey feelings Gostyniner warmth and intimacy.

In the later years, before the outbreak of World War II, the Society continued with its general activities: maintaining contact with Gostynin. But no more Gostyniner came to this land [the US] because of the anti-immigration laws. Many members did not demonstrate too much interest in this work, and so the meetings became more sparsely attended.

In the 1930s, when Hitler, may his name be erased, appeared on the German stage, a great unrest was felt in the societies of all the Jewish *landsmanschaften* of Poland, and naturally, the Gostyniner felt this as well. Many members received letters filled with ominous fear for the fate of the Jews of Poland. Others asked for an opportunity to come to America, but the gates to America were already shut by that time, and sadly, nothing could be done.

[Page 340]

It did not take long, when the horrifying World War II broke out, and once again, contact with Poland was severed.

Needless to say, during the war years nothing could be done for Gostynin. And when the end of the war was already in sight, and an assistance committee was created with money collections for the Gostyniner Jews, suddenly they found out about the terrible destruction that Gostynin, Jewish Gostynin, just like all the other towns in Poland, was wiped off the face of the earth.

After lengthy searches, if one discovered that there were several surviving Gostyniner living in Israel, immediately the Society sent them food packages, shoes, and clothing.

At the end of the 40s, when the Combined Jewish Appeal, along with the full cooperation of the entire Jewish press, undertook an intensive money campaign among the *landsmanschaften*, that was hugely successful, the Gostyniner Society also contributed a significant amount to the appeal. It is worth noting that Dovid Kolmus served as an example for others in the Society with his very generous contributions for the good of the Jewish Homeland.

When Dr. Chaim Weitzman, of blessed memory, was honored with a banquet in New York, Yosef Keller was the Society's delegate to the event, where he gave a check of $500 from the Society for the benefit of Israel, in honor of the esteemed guest.

The Society also gave $2,400 the price for building a house in Israel for new emigres. The Society also bought Israel bonds.

[Page 341]

It should also be mentioned that the Society sent a significant contribution to the non–profit loan fund [*Gemilas Chesed* fund] that was created by the Gostyniner Social Club in New York for the Gostyniner in Israel. The fund bears the names of the martyrs and is managed by the "*Irgun Yotzei Gostynin be'Yisrael*" ["The Organization of Emigrés from Gostynin in Israel"].

In November 1958, the Society celebrated its 50–year anniversary.

In the latter years, the Gostynin–born members remained a minority in the Society. The reasons for this phenomenon are the following: Many of the founders and original members have died. Many left New York, but at the same time many sons–in law, daughters–in–law, distant family members, friends, and acquaintances joined up, who had never in their lives seen Gostynin before their eyes, and more important, they have no feeling for the former homeland. In fact, now they are in the majority and in the management of the Society. The indifference to the Society went so far that the idea of publishing a Yizkor Book in memory of the Gostynin community received no support in the *landsmanschaft*. The Society declined participation in and even support for this publication.

The fate of *landsmanschaften* –societies in America is deplorable and the Gostynin Society is living through the same crisis that many other organizations of the same makeup are experiencing.

For this history, we should mention the names of important friends who held responsible positions in the Gostyniner Society's half–a–century's existence:

The office of president during this time was held by: Yosef Wolman, Lipe Bresler, Sholom Motolinski, who were exceptional with their devotion to the Society and were active in the organization until the final days of their lives. Moshe Flaum, whose house was always open for all our *landsman*; Herman Lewi, Itche Lewi, Max Winograd, Moshe Kalish, Harry Solomon, Mikhel (Michael) Mekler, M. Weinstajn, Moshe Faiereizen, Meyer Strauss, Y.S. Wajnerman, and Emanuel Shefer.

[Page 342]

The office of finance secretary was held by the following:

S. Bakh, L. Bresler, Sam Wand, Yosef Keller, Meyer Dovid Tremski (who glorified this position of office for eighteen years), Jackie Flaum, Emanuel Shefer, Y.S. Wajnerman, and Lewis Goldfarb.

Protocol secretaries were: S. Bakh, Lewin, Shmuel Keller, and Moshe Kalish, who held this office until this day, for the last 40 years.

For years, various offices were held by: Mordekhai Tabacznik and M. Hofman. Dr. Irving Mekler, even though he did not hold an office position, was exceptional in his active contribution in all areas.

[Page 343]

The Gostyniner Social Club in New York

by Y. K–R

Translated by Pamela Russ

In the years after World War II, the plan of publishing a Yizkor Book arose among the groups of Gostyniner *landsleit* [compatriots] in New York. The news that came from Poland bore witness that there was no trace left of Jewish Gostynin. Therefore, a group of Gostynin *landsleit* got together, with the initiative of Yissakhar Motil, to discuss the possibility of compiling a memorial book for Gostynin. This group consisted of Shmuel Keller, of blessed memory, Herman Krauz, Yosef Keller, Julius Bagno, Philip Lefkowycz, Shlomo Gostynski, of blessed memory, and Binyomin Tremski.

Even though all the participants were enthusiastic about this idea, a series of difficulties came up, and during the discussions it seemed that there was a pressing issue – the need to amass aide for the Gostynin refugees. At the meeting, it was decided to give priority to the aide activities of the *landsleit* and they sent out a message to all the Gostyniner in New York for them to collaborate in these activities.

After lengthy preparations, a general meeting of Gostyniner *landsleit* was held in spring 1949 in the Diplomat Hotel in New York, to which the Gostynin Society and its administration was also invited.

Meyer–Dovid Tremski was the chairman, and he underscored the urgency of helping the miraculously saved *landsleit*, and the responsibility to hold annual memorial gatherings in memory of the Gostynin holy martyrs. He summoned everyone to consolidate their activity in the organization that was created under the name of "the Gostynin Social Club." The goal of the club would be to maintain stable friendly relationships among the *landsleit* and to do constructive work for the new Gostynin *Olim* [emigres] in Israel.

[Page 344]

During the discussions, it became clear that there was a need for such a club: 1) because not all of the *landsleit* belonged to the Society; 2) the Society, lately administered by non–Gostyniner, did not demonstrate adequate understanding of the problems and needs of the Gostyniner: 3) the Society had remained frozen in its organizational format, and therefore had stopped its social activities.

The following officials were elected: Yosef Keller – president; Charlie Miller – vice president; Herman Krauz – treasurer; Shmuel Keller, of blessed memory – protocol secretary, and Binyomin Tremski – finance secretary.

Until now, the social club marked the *yahrzeit* [memorial date] of the liquidation of Jewish Gostynin and every year they held memorial gatherings. The idea came up to collect the means for the founding of a *kibbutz* [settlement] in Israel that would perpetuate the name of Gostynin. The appeal that was held brought in a significant amount. The activists of the club calculated that for this type of project there would have to be a collective effort made by all Gostyniner across the United States. The club reached an understanding with the Gostyniner Society in New York, to hold a collaborative money campaign. The officials of both committees created one collective administration with Betty Tremski as secretary. The Society withdrew from the partnership and the plan of the kibbutz fell through.

Socially, the club was very active. Contact with the Gostyniner in New York was strengthened. The club organized a series of musical evenings, in which, other than Shmuel Keller, of blessed memory, who sang folk songs, were Pauline and Clarisse Gostynski, the daughters of Shloime, of blessed memory, and Golde Gostynski, Iris Krauz, the daughter–in–law of Herman Krauz, and a series of professional performers and singers. Needless to say, the organization used the income for aide purposes.

[Page 345]

During that time, the club sent out help to the Gostyniner in Israel – food packages, clothing, and also money. A larger sum of money was sent over with Meyer–Dovid Tremski in 1952. This money served as the founding funds for the *Gemilas Khesed* [non–profit charity] fund in the name of the Gostyniner holy martyrs, administered by the *Irgun Yotzei Gostynin* [Organization of Emigrés of Gostynin in Israel]. Several years later Shmuel and Chana Keller went to Israel. They donated a significant amount from the club to the *Gemilas Khesed* fund.

The club did not give up the idea of a Yizkor Book. Shmuel Keller's visit to Israel caused the idea to be raised again.

The club decided to collect material, articles, and photographs, and to publish the book. It was understood that the *Irgun Yotzei Gostynin* in Israel would also commit to partnering in this plan. A special committee for the Yizkor Book was elected. The committee vigorously managed the work for a few years, and as a result, the *Pinkus* [record book] of Gostynin was developed.

[Page 346]

The Gostyniner Yizkor Book Committee in New York

<u>**Seated from right to left:**</u> Yisakhar Motil, chairman; Yosef Keller, secretary; Esther Stupej (Gombiner), Chana Keller (Bagno), Golda Gostynski (Frankel), Laya Keller (Miller); Moshe Kriger, finance secretary; Hersh Krauz, treasurer; –

<u>**Standing from right to left:**</u> Meyer Gostynski, Meyer Dovid Tremski, Dovid Bresler, Dovid Kunczman, Yehuda Bagno, Shlomo Gostynski, Shmuel Keller, Rakhtche Gosman (Gostynski), Yakov Gostinski, Yosef Gostynski

[Page 347]

The Gostyniner Society in Chicago

Translated by Pamela Russ

The Gostyniner Society in Chicago consisted of a small group of Gostyniner because there was never a large number of Gostyniner in Chicago.

The activists were: Yitzkhok Bruks, Eleizer Motil, his brother Yisroel Itche Motil, Polye Bagno, Sam Zajacs, and Mendel Holender.

The small number of Gostyniner who lived in the towns of the Midwest also belonged to the Society in Chicago.

From Kenosha, Wisconsin, those who belonged were Pesse (Miller) Kest and her husband Harry, Rivka (Zajacs) Kest and her husband Irving.

From Hammond, Indiana, those who belonged were Sam Zajacs and his wife Paula, Avrohom Neiman and his wife.

We also know some of the names of the individual Chicago members, such as the Millers, Chaim Itche Glantz and his family, Zelig Motil and his wife, Soroh Rabinowycz and her husband, Yoske Zajdeman and Zalman Zajdeman and their families.

Even though the Society comprised a small group, nonetheless, after World War I, they sent out a sum of money to the Gostyniner Jews to set up a *Gemilas Khesed* [non–profit charitable] fund. They also sent aide to those Gostyniner who needed help.

The Society in Chicago also contributed to the *Gemilas Khesed* fund that the Gostyniner Social Club in New York founded in Israel in the name of the Gostyniner holy martyrs and which is administered under the supervision of the *Irgun Yotzei Gostynin Be'Yisroel* [Organization of Emigrés from Gostynin in Israel].

The Society also helped in a big way, so that the Gostyniner in Chicago should socially remain together.

Regarding other places of activity where the Society was involved, we do not know any information.

[Page 348]

Some time ago, the Society lost two of its most active members with the death of Paula Bagno and Mendel Holender, of blessed memory. They were very missed in the Society.

Also, some members left Chicago, and several years ago, Yitzkhok Bruks, one of the most active members, former president for many terms, also left Chicago with his family. This left little vitality for the ongoing existence of the Society.

The result was that two years ago, the Society gave up its work. The funds that the Society had were sent to Israel and that strengthened the volume of capital in the *Gemilas Khesed* fund.

Truthfully, it is a great loss that other members did not take over the management, and the Gostyniner Society in Chicago had to dissolve.

[Page 349]

Organization of Emigrés of Gostynin in Israel
(The Organization of Gostyniner
in the State of Israel)

by R.M.

Translated by Pamela Russ

Until the end of World War II, the number of Gostyniner olim [emigrés to Israel] in Israel was small. During the wartime, some Gostyniner came to this Land with the Polish Anders' Army [Polish Armed Forces in the East in the period of 1941–42, named for its commander W. Anders] who came from Russia then stayed there [in Israel]. The main wave of *olim* from Gostynin began after the war in the year 1945. The Gostyniner used to meet privately from time to time and on the occasions of *simkhos* [festive events]. At these meetings they used to reminisce about their *shtetl* [small town life] that once was and is no longer. At the end of 1950, with the increase in Gostyniner *Aliyah* [immigration to Israel] the "hometown family" grew and they decided to organize a *landsmanschaft* [a society of compatriots] of Gostyniner in Israel, whose objective would be to strengthen the ties between the newcomer Gostyniner and those who came to the country before and to support them with everything possible as well as those who would come later on.

Irgun Yotzei Gostynin [Organization of Emigrés of Gostynin] in Tel Aviv with visitors from New York and Chicago.

Seated from right to left: Zushe Mikholski, Shloime Zweighaft, Julius and Berta Miller (Chicago), Meyer-Dovid Tremski (New York), Hersh-Leyb Leizerowycz. Standing from right: Manjak Mikholski, Mrs. And Sholom Rok, Regina Zweighaft, Moishe and Shoshana Motil, Dovid Kunczman, Regina Motil/Margalit, Mrs. Leizerowycz-Zweitfarb.

[Page 350]

The first meeting, when the organization was founded under the name of *Irgun Yotzei Gostynin Be'Yisrael*, took place on December 11, 1950. At that time, a committee comprised of the following was elected: chairman–Shloime Zweighaft, secretary–Sholom Rok, treasurer–Shmuel Gotfarb, Yehuda–Leyb Leizerowycz, Shmaya Kunczman, Danczinger, Shmuel Kruszniewski, and Ezriel Zajdman. At that meeting, a decision was passed: to publish a book compiled by the Gostyniner Jewish community that would reflect, as much as possible, the life of the Jews in our town, the outbreak of the war, the period of the catastrophe that would tell the horrors of the German concentration camps and deportation camps, and the fate of the experiences in Russia that our Gostyniner *landsleit* [compatriots] lived through. Also, about the life of the Gostyniner in Israel and in foreign countries.

The work of this book was taken up with intensive energy but because of different opinions that came up in this context, not all the material reached the committee. When it was discovered that the American *landsleit* decided to publish a Yizkor Book and had set up a special Yizkor Book committee from among themselves, it was decided to collaborate with the New York publication. Only a part of the material from Israel was successfully given over.

The main concerns of the committee concentrated around the aide work for the new Gostyniner *Olim* [newly arrived to Israel]. Understandably, at the beginning our aide was minimal because of a very lean budget that was at our disposal. Over a matter of time financial contributions arrived and clothing and food packages from the Gostyniner *landsleit* in the United States, helped those who were in need, with a generous hand and sympathetic heart. From time to time, gatherings were arranged as well as all kinds of social associations, with the objective to increase and strengthen the ties between the newly–arrived Gostyniner and the older established ones in the land, and also to create special funds for those who needed.

[Page 351]

On October 21, 1951, it was decided – upon the suggestion of *Khaver* [friend, comrade] Moishe–Leyb Pinczewski – to create a *Gemilas Khesed* [non-profit fund] whose objective it would be to provide material help to all those who needed it. At that meeting, *Khaver* Moishe Ben–Dovid, who not long before had returned from a visit to the United States, told of the pulsing life of the Gostyniner *landsmanschaft* in New York, and about the lively contact among these *landsleit* and about their activities.

For this committee, the following four *khaverim* [friends] were elected: *Harav* [the Rav] Y. B. Katz, Moishe Ben–Dovid, Moishe Mikholski, and Rivka Margalit.

The Gostyniner Yizkor Book Committee in Tel–Aviv

Seated from right: Shloime Zweighaft, chairman, *Harav* Yona Borukh Katz, Hersh–Leyb Leizerowycz

Standing from right: Moishe Mikholski, Rivka Motil Margalit, secretary, Moishe Ben–Dovid (Motil)

[Page 352]

✳✳✳

A tighter tie was established with the Gostyniner *landsleit* of New York, thanks to our American *landsleit* in Israel: M. D. Tremski, Bruks, Miller, Sh. Keller, Harav Y. B. Katz, and Yisokhor Motil, and their wives. These guests brought with them larger amounts of financial support for the Israeli *Gemilas Khesed* fund for the Gostyniner. That's how the fund filled up its capital, and in that way it enabled the yoke to be eased in a constructive way and provided more effective help for all those who needed it. The fund helped all the Gostyniner needy by providing loans and financial support.

At that time, *Harav* Yona Borukh Katz settled in the Land of Israel. He brought forth a spirit of vitality to all the general meetings at all kinds of gatherings.

A Yizkor gathering in Tel–Aviv with the participation of Shmuel and Chana Keller of New York

From right to left: Chana Keller, Shloime Zweighaft, Gutfarb, Hersh–Leyb Leizerowycz, *Harav* Yona Borukh Katz, Sholom Rok, Shmuel Keller
[Page 353]

The activities of the committee were expressed in the organizing of the gatherings, general meetings, and memorial meetings each year on the *yahrzeit* of the destruction of the Jewish settlement in Gostynin by the Nazi murderers, may their names and memories be erased. The appointed annual date of the *yahrzeit* was the first day of the Hebrew month of Iyar [corresponding to the month of May].

***

With this opportunity, in the name of all Gostyniner in Israel, we would like to express our regret for the untimely death of our beloved and esteemed *landsman* Shmuel Keller, who accomplished a lot for the close ties between our *landsleit* on both continents, and put in a lot of energy so that the plan of the Yizkor Book would be realized. His letters to Israel were filled with spirit and devotion and his deeds to alleviate the situation of the Gostyniner *landsleit* in Israel were a well of inspiration for all.

May his memory be blessed!

***

The current committee of the Gostyniner *landsleit* in Israel consists of the following *khaverim*: honored chairman – *Harav* Yona Borukh Katz, chairman – Shloime Zweighaft, secretary – Rivka Margalit, treasurer – Yehuda–Leyb Leizerowycz, members: Moishe Ben–Dovid and Moishe Mikholski.

[Page 354]

A Letter from the Other Side of the Ocean

by Adela Epstajn–Leszinski

Translated by Pamela Russ

Adela Epstajn–Leszinski

Adela Epstajn–Leszinski (Poland)

The letter from the other side of the ocean and the reports about the trial of the Germans murdering the Gostyniner Jews bear witness to the great tragedy. – There are no more Jews living in Gostynin now. When the trial against the German murderers took place in Plock, there were no more Gostyniner Jews left in Poland who could come forth as witness to this horrific murder.

Dear Friend,

When I returned to Gostynin, I found only very few signs of the fact that there was once Jewish life there. More clearly: The only signs remaining from that life – is the opposite of life – the destroyed cemetery of Jewish Gostynin; that is all that remains of the once blossoming community.

For me, this was a tragic and horrific picture. I searched for the graves of my dear ones and close ones. I found them empty and desecrated. Even the "tent" [over the gravesite] of the holy Gostyniner Rebbe was no longer there. Even more: The entire cemetery lay in chaos, with grass growing wildly and neglected. The fence, that once surrounded the holy place, was torn away. The cemetery had been totally destroyed by the dark powers of the German thugs. The graves and tombstones were completely broken up and destroyed. A great, wild desert and emptiness could be seen for miles long.

[Page 355]

A Non–Jewish Tombstone in the Place Where the *Shul* [synagogue] once stood

The Polish union of former political arrestees in Gostynin, after the war, buried and murdered Gostynin residents (there was not one Jew among them) and in their memory they set up a tombstone in the place where the Gostyniner *shul* and *Beis Medrash* [Study Hall] were once located.

On the ground, you could see goats roaming around aimlessly, calmly eating
the tall grass and vegetation that grew there exceptionally thick. These
creatures did not know of and certainly were not moved by the bitter
tragedy that had befallen our dearest ones who were torn apart. Quietly and
undisturbed, they chewed the grass. It was all forgotten by these around
about the catastrophe that the Nazi tyrants brought upon the Gostyniner
Jews.

[Page 356]

I looked for my father's gravesite. I couldn't find it. I tried to remember the
location of the grave, but, sadly, that too was impossible. I did remember
that in the center of the cemetery stood the "tent" and near the "tent" was
my father's grave, but for naught – I couldn't figure it out.

Along with a few other Gostynin Jews I decided to restore the cemetery. In
the centre of the cemetery, we set up a collective monument.

Walking through the Gostynin streets I stopped near the street that was our
home. I remembered many things from my youth, but this did not last long.
With curiosity, I searched for a few familiar faces, even though I knew that
you could no longer find anyone there. I did find a few friends – Polaks, who
greeted me warmly and expressed their sympathy for our national
misfortune that we had experienced. "Too bad for the Jews," they said. "Why
can those who remained alive not come back and start all over?" ...

But for me, Gostynin no longer exists. The memories remain; of a wonderful
Jewish inheritance that each of us carries in our soul, an inheritance that
many generations labored hard to amass and that so mercilessly was
destroyed.

I know that Gostyniner all across the world live with these memories.
Jewish Gostynin lives in our hearts and will live for as long as we live.

[Page 357]

One of the Gostyniner Murderers
Is Sentenced to Death[24]

by Avrohom Papjerczyk

Translated by Pamela Russ

Recently, the trial of the Hitlerist murderer Yakub Pohl took place in Plock. The accused Pohl, a German from birth, was born in the year 1904 in the town of Gostynin, in the district of Plock. He lived there until Hitler's soldiers marched into Poland. During the occupation, the accused was an active Hitlerist and head of an SS unit.

The accused Yakub Pohl is the executioner of the Gostyniner Jews and the Polaks. As the head of an SS unit, he arrested more than 300 Polaks and Jews in the town during the days before November 11, 1939, under the so–called guilt of preparing an uprising against the occupying powers. During the trial period, Pohl tortured the arrestees in a sadistic manner. During the first days of November 1939, 24 of the arrestees were led to a neighboring forest and were murdered there. Among those who were shot, there were: three priests from the town and from the surrounding area, a list of teachers from the school, a few doctors, the mayor of Gostynin, and the four Jewish councilmen: Leyb Pinczewski, Zajacs, Burak, and Yekhiel–Meyer Keller. Pohl actively participated in the murder of these 24 sacrifices.

In 1941, there were once again arrests made of Polaks and Jews in the town. Forty–two of those arrested were murdered by the SS in the Krasznicer Forest. Pohl forced the Jews to bury the dead and then they themselves were murdered. Pohl was also accused of tens of other crimes, such as sending hundreds of Jewish and Polish residents to death camps. The majority of these people did not return. In April 1941, following the orders of the accused, 105 city residents were arrested. They were shot in the yard of the Jewish

---

24. The above mentioned report was written by Avrohom Papjerczyk and was reprinted from the Warsaw "People's Voice" ["Volksstimme"]

municipality. Other than that, Pohl also was involved in robbing the dead bodies, forcing monies from the families of the arrestees, and so on.

[Page 358]

In the year 1943, the murderer was sent over to France to impose his bloody deeds against the local resistance movement. After the fall of Hitlerism, Pohl settled in West Germany. In the year 1952, the Fascist murderer came with a special "mission" to the German Democratic Republic[25], where he was discovered by the security powers who later extradited him with the permission of the Polish Department of Justice.

Thirty–nine witnesses were heard over the period of two days. All as one attested before the judge that the accused was the spectre from Gostynin.

The witness Nowakowski tells: He and his father were among the 300 arrestees. During their trial period, Pohl murderously beat the witness with a gun. The father of the witness was among the first 24 sacrifices.

The witness Bielinski tells the judge that Pohl decided about life and death of all the residents of Gostynin. The witness Lewandowski stated that Pohl took revenge on him because before the year 1939, he made the "*Sanatzia*" ["Healthy Politics Party"] Police aware of the open Hitlerist activities that were being conducted by Pohl and other Germans who lived in Gostynin. The chief of the *Sanatzia* Police told the witness at that time that he should "not stick his nose where you don't have to" and immediately proceeded to share this information with Pohl. For this, Lewandowski was immediately sent to Auschwitz and two of his brothers were murdered.

After the statement from the witness, the prosecutor spoke, demanding the death sentence for the Hitlerist. After the presentations from the defendant and from the accused, the judge sentenced the Hitlerist murderer Pohl to death.

---

25. In that part of Germany that was governed by Soviet Russia.

[Page 359]

A Yizkor [memorial] Gathering in New York for the Gostyniner Holy Martyrs [those who perished in the war], conducted by Cantor Yakov Breitman and Shmuel Keller with His Choir

From right: Helen Bal, under her, half hidden, a choir member, Shmuel Keller, a choir member, Yisokhor Motil, Chana Tremski, Cantor Breitman, Yosef Keller, Moishe Kriger, Hersh Kruczyk, Dovid Kunczman. –

Bottom row: Meyer Gostynski, Yakov Gostyinski

[Page 360]

A Yizkor [memorial] Gathering in New York for the Gostyniner Holy Martyrs [those who perished in the war]

Gostyniner Jews who lived in Gostynin at the time of the outbreak of World War II and who died sanctifying G-d's name and the nation of Israel,

This list was compiled by the book committee in Israel.

Transliterated by Haim Sidor

Explanation of Fields

Family name and *first name* are self explanatory.

Spouse: is wife or husband when named

Family code:
    wife = wife as well as husband is memorialized
    husband = wife is listed by name and husband is simply mentioned with no name given.
    s = son
    d = daughter
    cc = children
    family = no specifics given; just the family sometimes with one member named

Order #: the order in which the names appear on the original Yizkor List.

Family name	First name	Spouse	Family Code	Order #
Aichvitzki	Mendel			19
Aichvitzki	Moshe			22
Aichvitzki	Pesa			23
Aichvitzki	Tcharna			20
Aichvitzki	Wolf			21
Akavietz	Miriam			10
Akavietz	Sabina			12
Akavietz	Sala			11

Akavietz	Shmuel			13
Akavietz	Yosef			14
Alberstein	Avraham Aaron			3
Alberstein	Haim Simcha			6
Alberstein	Hannah			2
Alberstein	Naftali			7
Alberstein	Shalom			4
Alberstein	Wolf			5
Alberstein	Yisrael David			1
Alberstein	Yocheved			8
Alberstein	Yosef			9
Ashiel			family	18
Auerbach	Yosef		family	27
Baibok	Esther			91
Baibok	Marisha			92
Baibok	Tzvi			90
Bangna	Akiva			74
Bangna	Gedalia			69
Bangna	Genendal			75
Bangna	Hannah			70
Bangna	Leibish		family	77
Bangna	Miriam			71
Bangna	Shlomo		family	76
Bangna	Yehezkel		family	72
Bangna	Yitzhak		family	73

Batshan	Bertcha			89
Batshan	Esther			88
Batshan	Faiga			86
Batshan	Leah			87
Bechaza	Faiga			80
Bechaza	Hinda			78
Bechaza	Yitzhak			79
Belfer	Avraham			93
Belfer	Efraim			95
Belfer	Golda			94
Bender	Fishel			98
Bender	Fraidel			103
Bender	Laibish			96
Bender	Simcha			102
Bender	Yaakov			101
Bender	Yehudit			99
Bender	Yocheved			97
Bender	Yosef			100
Blum	Yaakov Eliyahu		family	85
Borak	Henach		family	81
Borak	Hershel			83
Borak	Raphael			82
Borak	Sara			84
Borenstein	Gedalyahu			36
Borenstein	Hannah		family	34

Borenstein	Moshe			35
Borenstein	Yitzhak Meir (HaRav)		w	33
Bresler	Adash			62
Bresler	Avraham		family	68
Bresler	Bluma			58
Bresler	Freida			52
Bresler	Haim		family	64
Bresler	Hertzka		family	59
Bresler	Leah			51
Bresler	Necha			56
Bresler	Sonia			54
Bresler	Tila			67
Bresler	Tuska			61
Bresler	Tzadok			50
Bresler	Yaakov			53
Bresler	Yaakov			57
Bresler	Yissachar			66
Bresler	Yitzhak		& w	63
Bresler	Yosef			65
Bresler	Yurka			55
Bresler	Zalman			60
Brodziak	Yehiel		family	104
Brostovski	Bluma			42
Brostovski	Esther			39
Brostovski	Esther			47

Brostovski	Hannah			48
Brostovski	Hudis			49
Brostovski	Ita			41
Brostovski	Ita			46
Brostovski	Leibish			45
Brostovski	Rachel			40
Brostovski	Sara Dina			38
Brostovski	Shmuel Meir			37
Brostovski	Yaakov		family	43
Brostovski	Yehiel Moshe		family	44
Chazan	Chaya			217
Chazan	Hannah			218
Chazan	Mena			219
Cohn	Avraham Mordecai		family	267
Cohn	Issachar		family	268
Danziger	Benyamin		family	134
Danziger	Binem			136
Danziger	Bunim			141
Danziger	David		family	144
Danziger	Eliezar			137
Danziger	Faiga			132
Danziger	Hershel			139
Danziger	Liba			140
Danziger	Mordecai Mendel			130
Danziger	Moshe		family	142

Danziger	Paula Sheva		cc	138
Danziger	Pola		family	143
Danziger	Shabtai Arie		wife	135
Danziger	Simcha Bunim			133
Danziger	Yehiel Meir		family	131
Domb	Aram	Sonia	wife	155
Domb	Shalom			156
Dzshenshol	Avraham		wife	148
Dzshenshol	Chaya Sara			151
Dzshenshol	Masha		family	149
Dzshenshol	Mindel			152
Dzshenshol	Shimon Reuven		family	150
Dzshenshol	Wolf			153
Dzshigainski	Eliyahu		family	145
Dzshigainski	Meir		wife	147
Dzshigainski	Yosef		family	146
Dzshorkovski	Sheindel		cc	154
Erdberg	Andzsha			440
Erdberg	Trantel		family	439
Ettinger	Dan		family	26
Ettinger	Dan		family	438
Ezriel	Shlomo			436
Ezriel	Yocheved			437
Feldman	Feivish			469
Finezilber	Leah	(Hoichgelernter)		478

Finezilber	Shmuel Hirsh			474
Finezilber	Tzirel			475
Finezilber	Yisrael Yitzhak			476
Finezilber	Yosef			477
Fleiderbaum			family	458
Fleischman	Avraham Meir		family	453
Fleischman	Eliezar		family	454
Fleischman	Liba			455
Floimbaum			family	487
Frenkel	Baltsha		cc	452
Frenkel	Chumtsha		cc	448
Frenkel	Feivel			447
Frenkel	Hersh		family	445
Frenkel	Mendel			451
Frenkel	Moshe		family	446
Gaizler	Avraham		family	121
Gaizler	Moshe		family	122
Gelbard	Avraham		family	116
Gelbard	Moshe			117
Gelbard	Sara			118
Gelbart			family	127
Gersht	Moshe Yosef		family	119
Gersht	Sender		family	120
Glantz	Basha		family	110
Glantz	Braina			108

Glantz	Esther			112
Glantz	Menna			106
Glantz	Moniek			109
Glantz	Nisan			113
Glantz	Roiza		family	111
Glantz	Saleh			107
Glantz	Yaakov			105
Glicksberg	David		family	126
Goldberg	Haim		family	114
Goldberg	Nachum		family	115
Goldreich	Moshe			123
Goldreich	Yehiel		cc	124
Goldstein	Golda			129
Goldstein	Yona			128
Gumbiner	Dalek		family	125
Haiman	Zusia			166
Hobergritz	Miriam		cc	165
Hobergritz	Mottel			164
Hodem	Yehiel		family	162
Hodem	Zelig	Saleh	wife	163
Holtzman	Binem			157
Holtzman	Daleh			161
Holtzman	Feivel			160
Holtzman	Mendel			159
Holtzman	Shulmit			158

Itzkovitch	Aikela		family	28
Itzkovitch	Mendel			30
Itzkovitch	Sender			29
Itzkovitch	Tzadok			31
Kahalani	Mattis			527
Kahalani	Yehudit		cc	528
Kahana	Ben Tzion			272
Kahana	Esther			271
Kahana	Feivish			269
Kahana	Shmuel			273
Kahana	Tscharna			270
Kahana	Yitzhak			274
Kaplan	Hinda			529
Kaplan	Leoush			532
Kaplan	Rachel			530
Kaplan	Yarka			531
Kara	Avraham		family	558
Kara	Feivel		family	557
Kara	Yossel		family	559
Karzel	Ita		cc	545
Karzel	Zalman			544
Kavadzsha	Rivka		& mother	526
Kavent	Chaya		cc	551
Kavent	Fraida			556
Kavent	Gershon		family	547

Kavent	Golda			548
Kavent	Masha			549
Kavent	Mendel			552
Kavent	Mordecai			550
Kavent	Moshe		family	562
Kavent	Peril		cc	553
Kavent	Pesach			555
Kavent	Shaul		family	554
Kavent	Yitzhak		family	563
Kazshan	Shaul		family	266
Keller	Aaron		family	523
Keller	Adela		family	514
Keller	Baila Faiga			512
Keller	Ben Tzion			518
Keller	Moshe		wife	513
Keller	Moshe Ber			517
Keller	Peretz			515
Keller	Rivka			516
Keller	Sarah			519
Keller	Shalom		family	522
Keller	Tabtsha			520
Keller	Yehiel Meir		family	521
Kenig			& daughter	525
Kirsch	Hersh		family	511
Kleinbard	Eliyahu			507

Kleinbard	Moshe			509
Kleinbard	Priva			505
Kleinbard	Tscharna			510
Kleinbard	Tzesha			506
Kleinbard	Yaakov			508
Kleinot	Getzel			546
Kontzman	Faiga			543
Kontzman	Fraida	(Tadelis)	cc	541
Kontzman	Haim			538
Kontzman	Laibel			540
Kontzman	Rivcha Braina			539
Kontzman	Shmuel Aaron			542
Kraitzer	Dovrish			535
Kraitzer	Laizer		family	534
Kraitzer	Moshe			536
Kraitzer	Yitzhak			537
Krantz	Shlomo	Sela	family	533
Krashnievski	Moshe		family	524
Krel	Mendel		w & daughter	560
Kriegerman			w & s & d	561
Lamski	Avraham Noah			287
Lamski	Fraida			286
Lamski	Hinda Leiba			289
Lamski	Meir			288
Lamski	Sara Dina		husband	290

Landwasser			family	291
Laska	Adash			294
Laska	Alexander			292
Laska	Marek			293
Laska	Vladic			295
Lasman	Baruch		family	277
Lasman	Simcha Bunim		family	278
Lazarovitch	Bracha			284
Lazarovitch	Ita			283
Lazarovitch	Moshe Pincus			282
Lepkovitch	Yaakov		family	285
Levi	Baila			281
Levi	Beril			279
Levi	Glicka			280
Levin	Yosef		family	297
Liberak			husband & wife	296
Linderman	Henoch		family	276
Linderman	Yaakov		family	275
Makovski	Henech			372
Makovski	Shulamit			374
Makovski	Zlata			373
Maritz	Hershel			389
Maritz	Libtsha			388
Maritz	Moshe			387
Maritz	Rikla			390

Markovitch	Avrahamala			382
Markovitch	Hannah			385
Markovitch	Hella			383
Markovitch	Leitsha			381
Markovitch	Malka			379
Markovitch	Meir			380
Markovitch	Shalom			386
Markovitch	Shmuel			384
Matil	Adela			319
Matil	Avraham			317
Matil	Avraham		family	338
Matil	Avraham		wife	355
Matil	Avramek			363
Matil	Baila			340
Matil	Baila			346
Matil	Baruch			349
Matil	Berek			308
Matil	Binem			351
Matil	Blima Miriam			327
Matil	Blooma			304
Matil	Braina			329
Matil	Bruchtsha			325
Matil	Chava			352
Matil	Chaya			310
Matil	David			322

Matil	David			343
Matil	Devorah			348
Matil	Edzia			312
Matil	Efraim	Tscharna	wife	306
Matil	Efraim		family	311
Matil	Elka			354
Matil	Esther Toiva	Moritz	husband	333
Matil	Faiga			299
Matil	Faiga			344
Matil	Franya		h & cc	341
Matil	Henia			364
Matil	Henia			314
Matil	Hershel			350
Matil	Hershel			357
Matil	Hinda			358
Matil	Isser Meir			313
Matil	Laibel		family	336
Matil	Laibish			305
Matil	Laibish			318
Matil	Lutka			335
Matil	Manusha			301
Matil	Mordecai			298
Matil	Mordecai			345
Matil	Moshe			339
Matil	Necha			334

Matil	Nuta ben Yaakov Leib			321
Matil	Pesha Roiza			332
Matil	Rachel			342
Matil	Raizel			316
Matil	Rifka			300
Matil	Rifka			323
Matil	Rikel			360
Matil	Rivtsha			362
Matil	Roiza			356
Matil	Sara Mindel			303
Matil	Shimon Yosef			309
Matil	Shlomo			315
Matil	Shlomo ben Tzvi			324
Matil	Shmuel Baruch		w & cc	361
Matil	Shmuelik			347
Matil	Tzela			326
Matil	Tzivia			302
Matil	Yaakov	Raizka	wife	307
Matil	Yaakov			330
Matil	Yaakov Leib			331
Matil	Yankel		family	337
Matil	Yehiel Moshe			328
Matil	Yehoshua		wife	353
Matil	Yitzhak			320
Matil	Yona Meir			359

Mazer	Yaakov		family	377
Mazer	Yona			378
Merlender			Dr. & W	391
Michalski	Avraham		family	367
Michalski	Esther			371
Michalski	Hershik		w & mother	369
Michalski	Maniek			370
Michalski	Yasha			368
Moshkovitch	Fraidel			375
Moshkovitch	Mordecai			376
Most	Necha			366
Most	Yosef			365
Naiman	Beril		family	406
Naiman	Laizer			400
Naiman	Moshe		family	403
Naiman	Moshe		family	407
Naiman	Pinchas			404
Naiman	Sheindel			401
Naiman	Shlomo		family	402
Naiman	Shmuel		wife	405
Narveh	Avraham Hersh			396
Narveh	Baila			398
Narveh	Hannah			395
Narveh	Levi			399
Narveh	Pesa			397

Nasenavitch	Avraham		family	394
Nasenavitch	Yaakov		family	393
Nasenavitch	Yochanan		family	392
Odit	Bracha			17
Odit	Shmuel Aaron			16
Odit			family	15
Ospeh	Eta			25
Ospeh	Zalman			24
Peltzman	Fraidel			471
Peltzman	Necha Dina			470
Peltzman	Yankel			473
Peltzman	Yitzhak			472
Perlgritz	Rozshka			450
Pintshevski	Akum			461
Pintshevski	Baruch			468
Pintshevski	Issachar			465
Pintshevski	Itka			460
Pintshevski	Kiva			462
Pintshevski	Liba Yiska			464
Pintshevski	Malka		cc	466
Pintshevski	Moshe			459
Pintshevski	Shmuel Wolf		family	467
Pintshevski	Yaakov Leib			463
Plotzer	Esther			480
Plotzer	Lipa			481

Plotzer	Michal Ber			479
Plotzer	Pesa			484
Plotzer	Shlomo			482
Plotzer	Yisrael			483
Potash	Mendel			485
Potash	Rachel		& son	486
Pozner	Hannah Liba			457
Pozner	Issachar			456
Prince	Avigdor		family	444
Prince	Menashe		family	443
Prince	Yaakov		family	442
Prince	Yeshiyahu		wife	441
Pshigada			family	449
Rabinovitch	Adela			575
Rabinovitch	Hershel			573
Rabinovitch	Mattis		family	574
Rabinovitch	Yaakov			576
Radzanover	Avraham			579
Radzanover	Braina		cc	580
Rafka	Merish			587
Rak	Mordecai		family	578
Rak	Shmerl		family	577
Ring	Benyamin			571
Ring	Haim Sender			568
Ring	Moshe		family	572

Ring	Shaiga			569
Ring	Shlomo			570
Romer	Avraham			586
Romer	Haim		family	584
Romer	Laibel			585
Romer	Shmuel Aaron		family	583
Romer	Yeheil Hersh		family	582
Romer	Yitzhak Yaakov		wife	581
Rosak	Faiga Sara		cc	565
Rosak	Nachum			567
Rosak	Yaakov		cc	564
Rosak	Yisrael Meir			566
Salmonovitch	Aaron		wife	421
Salmonovitch	Fraida			419
Salmonovitch	Moshe			422
Salmonovitch	Regina			420
Salmonovitch	Yitzhak		wife	417
Salmonovitch	Yossel			418
Sarna	Faiga			427
Sarna	Hannah			426
Sarna	Hertzka			428
Sarna	Sarah			425
Segalman	Meir		mother&brother	502
Shafran	Laizer		wife	588
Shafran	Rozshka			589

Shafran	Tzivia			590
Shaier	Nachum Yisrael			602
Shaier	Pesa		cc	606
Shaier	Sarah Leah			603
Shaier	Yeheil Leib			605
Shaier	Zanvill			604
Shatan	Akiva		family	595
Shatan	Ever		family	592
Shatan	Yaakov		family	591
Shatan	Yehuda		family	593
Shatan	Yitzhak		family	594
Shekerka			family	611
Shiavitch	Avraham		wife	599
Shiavitch	Hershel			601
Shiavitch	Hinda			597
Shiavitch	Pinchas			598
Shiavitch	Ruth			600
Shiavitch	Shaul			596
Spector	Avraham			410
Spector	Dartsha			415
Spector	Franya			411
Spector	Hannah			413
Spector	Meir			412
Spector	Rachel			409
Spector	Rachel			414

Spector	Yocheved			416
Spector	Yosef			408
Srebnagora	Fraidel			434
Srebnagora	Gittel			430
Srebnagora	Mordecai			433
Srebnagora	Moshe Yitzhak			429
Srebnagora	Noah			431
Srebnagora	Rachel			432
Steinman	Basha		cc	617
Steinman	Haim		wife	612
Steinman	Nachum			616
Steinman	Pinchas			615
Steinman	Yaakov Moshe			613
Steinman	Yoshka			614
Stern	Hannah			610
Stern	Shmuel Zalman			609
Stern	Yenta			608
Stern	Yitzhak			607
Strikovski	Avraham		family	424
Strikovski	Hersh		family	423
Strikovski	Yitzhak			435
Tauba	Lola			229
Tauba	Yehiel Meir		family	230
Tauba	Yehoshua		family	231
Tauba	Yitzhak		wife	228

Tenenbaum	Meir			224
Tenenbaum	Shaindel			225
Tenenbaum	Yaakov			226
Tiger	Avraham		family	232
Tiger	Avraham		family	235
Tiger	Yehiel Meir		family	233
Travinski	Hershel		family	227
Tremski	Chaya			221
Tremski	Hershel			222
Tremski	Reuven			220
Tremski	Yocheved			223
Troianovski	Haim Baruch		family	234
Troianovski	Michael		family	236
Tsharka			3 sisters	237
Unger	Yehoshua		w & cc	32
Vilner	David		family	171
Vilner	Pinchas		family	170
Vilner	Sarah			173
Vilner	Yosef		family	172
Vilner	Zurach		wife	169
Visipka			family	168
Volkovitch			family	179
Vorkovitch	Haim		family	167
Wasserman	Chava		cc	176
Wasserman			family	175

Weingard	Mendel		family	178
Weisman	Hersh Leib		family	177
Wolf			family	174
Yabloinski	Bina			239
Yabloinski	Moshe			238
Yabloinski	Pelka			240
Yabloinski	Sarah			242
Yabloinski	Yaakov		family	244
Yabloinski	Yisrael		family	245
Yabloinski	Yitzhak			241
Yabloinski	Yoska		family	243
Yakobovitch	Chavacha			252
Yakobovitch	Gutsha Chaya			246
Yakobovitch	Heniak			250
Yakobovitch	Moniek			251
Yakobovitch	Moshe			247
Yakobovitch	Sarah			248
Yakobovitch	Tuvia		wife	249
Yazsher	Shlomo Mendel		wife	253
Yeshan	Aaron		family	265
Yeshan	Chaya			262
Yeshan	Hannah		family	257
Yeshan	Hannah			261
Yeshan	Leah			263
Yeshan	Leiber		family	264

Yeshan	Yosef		family	256
Yizraelavitch	Berish		family	259
Yizraelavitch	Tzipa			260
Yizraelavitch	Yosef		wife	258
Yutkovski	Zarach			255
Yutkovski			husband & wife	254
Zaidman	Avraham Haim		family	207
Zaidman	Moshe		family	208
Zaif	Avraham			203
Zaif	Mirel		cc	204
Zaklikovski	Fraida		cc	213
Zaklikovski	Frimet			216
Zaklikovski	Laibish			215
Zaklikovski	Noah			212
Zaklikovski	Zelig		w & cc	214
Zandman	Machtcha			209
Zandman	Roiza		cc	210
Zarchin	Solomon		family	181
Zarchin	Yaakov		family	180
Zimmerman	Mordecai		family	504
Zimmerman	Pesa			503
Zinger	Gella			202
Zinger	Laibish			201
Zinger	Mordecai		wife	200
Zinger	Moshe			198

Zinger	Tscharna Leah		cc	199
Ziontz	Aaron		wife	185
Ziontz	Avraham		family	187
Ziontz	Esther		family	188
Ziontz	Hanan		family	186
Ziontz	Marek		family	189
Zonenshine				211
Zshalandzsh	Dela			195
Zshalandzsh	Hanan		family	197
Zshalandzsh	Sertsha			194
Zshalandzsh	Yaakov			193
Zshalandzsh	Yaakov Lipa		family	196
Zshalandzsh	Yehuda Hersh			190
Zshalandzsh	Yenta			191
Zshalandzsh	Yitzhak			192
Zshichlin	Lilly			206
Zshichlin	Berish		wife	205
Zshichlinski	Gedaliyahu		family	184
Zshichlinski	Rushka			183
Zshichlinski	Yaakov		wife	182
Zveibaum	Asher		family	501
Zveibaum	Benyamin			498
Zveibaum	Shmuel Meir		family	500
Zveibaum	Sortsha			499
Zveighapt	Anka			492

Zveighapt	Feivel			495
Zveighapt	Franya			496
Zveighapt	Machla			489
Zveighapt	Marek			493
Zveighapt	Mordecai			491
Zveighapt	Yona			488
Zveighapt	Yoska			490
Zveighapt	Zlata			494
Zvier	Mottel		family	497

[Page 361]

Yizkor

Translated by Pamela Russ

[Page 364]

Book of Lamentations, Chapter 2, verse 2:
God destroyed without pity
All the dwellings of Jacob,
In His anger, He razed
The fortresses of the daughter of Judah,
Bringing them down to the ground.

(Translation from Yehoash)

[Page 364]

For an eternal memory

Of our dear husband and beloved father and grandfather

Shmuel Keller,
may he rest in peace.

(Died on October 2, 1959, Rosh Hashana eve, 5720)

May his memory be honored!

Chana, Morris, Florence, Barbara, June, and family (New York)

Shmuel Keller,

May He Rest in Peace

Shmuel Keller, of blessed memory, was one of the first who gave thought to, and later began working on the realization of the idea of the Gostyniner Yizkor Book. Shmuel could not come to terms with the thought that his hometown, its Jewish community, the activities that went on there, the accomplishments and struggles of its beautiful youth, the fights for the existence of its Jews – that all of that would be lost and forgotten. Yes, he gave himself a clear accounting that along with the destruction that came upon the Polish Jewry, the Jewish settlement of Gostynin was also wiped away – but he sought to eternalize the memory of Gostynin.

And it is no wonder then that he was the initiator of the Yizkor Book project. Shmuel was a Gostyniner through and through, even after tens of years of living in New York, thousands of kilometers away from his beloved hometown. Here, on this American soil, he did not forget the smallest detail of what went on there. With every fibre of his being, he was tightly bound to that place of the past. His grandfather Reb Yisroel Itche and his father Reb Yakov Mendel did not cease to affect his character – they always stood in front of his eyes. From his youth onwards, his gentle soul was open to the influence of both of these men, for whom he carried within him the greatest honor and respect. At the smallest opportunity, he mentioned both of them and all his days he reaped benefits from their deeds, which he remembered well, in spirit and inspiration.

Characteristically, when he was on his deathbed and was lightheaded by the large dose of sleeping pills that they gave him in the hospital, without stopping, he mentioned the names of his grandfather and father. He likely believed that they were standing at his head and he was conversing with them.

In his early youth, Shmuel was already joined the choir of his beloved cantor, chazzan Yakov Miller, may he rest in peace. As a choirboy, he knew all the chazzan's compositions. He took very seriously the music of the Gostyniner chazzan, and loved to sing the sweet melodies of the Shabbat hand holiday prayers. In his later life in America, Shmuel sang and preformed with choirs and well-known cantors. Everywhere he went, he brought along the personal songs of his beloved cantor and his choir glowed with authentic Jewish homey flavor that penetrated everyone who heard him and his choir. It was not only the music that he inherited from the Gostyniner chazzan, but he also, just as his teacher, behaved with respect and seriousness toward his position, to the prayers, and to the congregation, since he felt like the chazzan's ambassador.

At home [in the town], Shmuel Keller was one of the most gifted amateur actors that participated in the performances of many plays. He was able to bring a role to life. He understood how to identify himself with the personality that he was portraying. His presentation was authentic and convincing. He was also active in the work of the library. For him, a book, a sefer [religious book], a Jewish book with Jewish content – was a treasure. He wanted Jews to read and to know how to appreciate their own culture. He himself did not stop acquiring Jewish books and his book shelves continued to expand. In particular, his thirst for Jewish knowledge grew after the destruction [Holocaust]. He swallowed every letter, every word, with curiosity. He wanted to immerse himself in the wisdom of the generations.

As a Gostyniner coming to America, he soon became active in the Gostyniner Society of New York. He was ready to participate in every issue. He was active in the Gostyniner Social Club that was formed, and in the creation of the Yizkor Book. When he found out about the horrific termination of his family, he could not rest, and he searched and found every Gostyniner survivor that remained alive, stayed in contact with him, found means to help the needy, and sent packages of food and clothing, and often even cash. With this work, he hoped to forget his own tragedy. But his health was now compromised. His task was to mark the yahrzeit [anniversary of the death] of the Gostyniner martyrs. When he recited the prayers at the memorial gatherings you could feel the deep anguish and endless pain that he carried inside himself.

With the establishment of the State of Israel, Shmuel became like a different person. He became involved with the activities of the established Jewish independence. In 1953, he went to Israel to see with his own eyes what Jewish strength can demonstrate. Of course, he met with his Gostyniner compatriots, particularly with the victims of the evil Hitlerism, who found their home in Israel after their horrifying experiences. He knew about everyone's ancestry, what happened with someone's grandfather, uncle and aunt…

With his growing interest in Israel, he joined the Bialik branch of the Jewish Nationalist Labor Movement. His contributions to the funds were done with an open hand. He thought of going once again, but it was not fated for him to do so.

It was also not fated for him to see the Yizkor Book. He worked very hard for this book, lived and breathed with it. He was torn away from the living too early, unjustly for him, for his family, and for his compatriots and acquaintances.

Never, never will we forget this humble, fine man and good brother.

Yosef Keller

[Page 368]

For the holy memory of our beloved husband and father

Shlomo Gostinski,
may he rest in peace

Died on December 5, 1957

Honor his memory!

**Golde and daughters: Pauline and Clarisse
and family**

[Page 369]

Shloime Gostinski,
May He Rest in Peace

When Shloime left Gostynin, he left behind a city with all sorts of activities and many different schools of thought. He himself was active in many areas, in political life as well as in the cultural life of Gostynin.

His life in Gostynin was an interesting one, because he was very interested in all of the city's activities. But since all his brothers were already established in America, and his dear ones had already left Gostynin, he too left for America.

Here, in this new country, he did not give up his interests in social life. He now became an active member of the bakers' union, involved in the Poalei Zion [Zionist Labor Party] movement, and also an active member in one of the Workman's Circle branches.

When a group of Gostyniner established the Gostyniner Club, with the goal of helping the Gostyniner refugees, Shloime was one of the founders and was very active in the aide work. And when the plan developed to publish a Gostyniner Yizkor Book, Shloime quickly became one of those who devoted himself to the creation of the book.

He devoted a lot of energy and work to this book. He attended all the meetings of the book committee and also wrote about Gostynin himself. Of course, his article is published in this book. He hoped to see the final product of this book, but sadly death suddenly tore him away and he did not merit to see the published final piece.

Honor his memory!

Y. K –R

[Page 370]

In holy memory of our dear brother

Meyer Gostinski,
of blessed memory

Died in the year 1955

Honor his memory!

**Brothers: Yosef and Yakov
Sisters: Tzivia and Ruchtshe
and family**

[Page 371]

**The Gostyniner Yizkor Book Committee
in New York**

**expresses its anguish and sorrow on the untimely
passing of our dear friend**

Meyer Gostinski,
may he rest in peace,

**who did not live to see the fruition of this book, about
which he dreamed, and in which he was active.**

Honor his memory!

**Gostyniner Yizkor Book Committee
in New York.**

[Page 372]

Meyer Gostinski,

may he rest in peace

Golde Frenkel-Gostinski

Golde Frenkel-Gostinski

I have known Meyer Gostinski from the time that I came to the United States. Actually, I knew him before that because when his brother Shloime – my husband – came to Poland to be married to me, he introduced me to his brothers in New York, describing each one of them. But mostly, we spoke about Meyer. When I mentioned to my future husband about the places and things of the greatly developed technology of America, I received this answer: that Meyer will show me everything.

When my husband and I came to New York twenty-eight years ago to the house of Meyer and his brothers, I really connected more to Meyer than to any other family member. He won over my care and love from the very first day that I stepped onto American soil. For every tear shed, whether it came for yearning for my family or friends, or whether I was caught up with the thousands of threads from which I was uprooted – Meyer comforted me and found a good word to say. He was more than a brother-in-law. He showed himself to be a sensitive person, understanding the other person's situation.

He descended from generations of chassidic-rabbinic roots, and this ancestry influenced his education and the future path of his life. The awareness of his lineage shaped his character and even though he was not a religious man, he never forgot this. He possessed extraordinary capacities, a good head for everything, but sadly, sometimes a will that was too weak to push large things through [to the end]. For that, there were several contributing factors. One was his frail state of health. Whatever he undertook, he always had to fight against a difficult obstacle – illness.

While still a boy, he was pulled into the Zionist movement. He ran to the Beis Medrash and to shul [synagogue] and did not keep his convictions secret. This gave his chassidic parents much heartache. He always remembered that Simchas Torah [last day of Sukkos holiday, celebrating with the Torah scrolls], when the Zionists dared to sing the Hatikva [Israel national anthem] during the Hakafos [dancing with the Torah scrolls]. With an open pride, he described the smacks he received from the gabbai [sexton] for this Zionist affront ...

During his lifetime, he had rises and downfalls. But failure never discouraged him. On the contrary, through each cloud he could see the sun's rays. This strength gave him energy to get through both the physical and spiritual experiences, when even deep in his heart there remained yawning open wounds, may no one know of this.

One of his great attributes was that he could fit into society and take part in the discussions that took place. He showed particular zeal in discussions about Zionism. Here he used every argument to convince his opponents of the correctness of his views.

He was very aware of words: a smart and good person. Truthfully, he was easy to anger, and in the heat of his anger you could see a characteristic expression on his face: He raised his lower lip over the top one. Those who knew him and noticed this, that now, now, now, he was becoming angry, because he was already biting his lips...

Because of his sincerity and other qualities of his personality, people were attracted to him with love and respect.

In his heart, he carried warmth and love. He tried to express his feelings in the lyrical poetry that he wrote and would then sometimes read to select people. More than once I asked him to send in one of his poems to an editor to have it published. But he declined. He writes – he used to say – for himself and in the best case, for his close ones...

He was completely broken up by the horrifying devastation that the last World War brought to European Jewry. He mourned to himself for the terrible loss of millions of Jews. Pained, he raged against the German beast that tore apart his nation, his tragic nation.

Is it a wonder, then, that at one of the assemblies of his Gostyniner compatriots, Meyer requested that the memory of the devastated home town be eternalized? He was of the first ones to support the idea of a Yizkor Book.

It was not fated for him to see the book published, dear Meyer Gostinski. His shining face will remain forever deep in our hearts.

[Page 375]   **For an Eternal Memory**

Forty-five Jews who died or who were killed in the Konin camp were taken by Rav Aronson right after liberation to a separate part of a Christian cemetery and given a burial.

Among these 45 were Jewish from Gostynin. These are the names:

Weitzner Avrohom
Born in the year 1890 – died or was killed on the 5th of April, 1942

Shurin Yosef
Born in the year 1891 - died or was killed on the 5th of June, 1942

Isaak Shloime
Born in the year 1897 - died or was killed on the 12th of May, 1942

Goldberg Nachum
Born in the year 1884 - died or was killed on the 12th of May, 1942

Kowend Yitzchok
Born in the year 1911 - died or was killed on the 19th of May, 1942

Lefkovitch Yosef
Born in the year 1911 - died or was killed on the 29th of May, 1942

Fajnzilber Yosef
Born in the year 1914 - died or was killed on the 2nd of June, 1942

Brustowski Lipe
Born in the year 1928 - died or was killed on the 16th of June, 1942

Losman Eliezer
Born in the year 1913 - died or was killed on the 2nd of July, 1942

Rak Moshe Yakov
Born in the year 1909 - died or was killed on the 4th of July, 1942

Nasinowycz Avrohom
Born in the year 1897 - died or was killed on the 7th of July, 1942

Tzimerman Chaim Mordechai
Born in the year 1906 - died or was killed on the 20th of July, 1942

Motil Yakov Leyb
Born in the year 1893 - died or was killed on the 31st of January, 1943

May G-d avenge their blood!

[Page 376]

For an memory of our comrade and friend

Fishel Lefkovitch,

may he rest in peace

Who was untimely torn away from us.

Gostyniner Yizkor Book Committee in New York

[Page 377]

Fishel (Philip) Lefkovitch,
may he rest in peace

Philip Lefkovitch was one of the founders of the Gostyniner Social Club. Even though he was one of the most active members of the Gostyniner Society in New York, when he found out that a group of Gostyniner were getting together to establish a group to help the Gostyniner in Israel and all the Gostyniner who managed to save themselves from the great destruction in Poland, he immediately joined the group and helped found this club.

Fishel Lefkovitch was born in Gostynin into a poor family what worked hard and honestly to earn a living and did not have the means to give their children an elementary education.

As a young boy, they already made a worker out of him, and when he came to America, he was already a practiced tailor.

Here he joined up with the Cloakmaker's Union, where he was active. He read the daily newspapers and began to take interest in issues outside of the confines of the sewing machine. The union, as well as the workers of the shop where he worked, recognized and praised his activities. He was elected as chairman in his shop, which was one of the bigger shops.

His work in the Gostyniner Social Club was also active and multi-faceted. He was particularly active in the aide work for the good of the Gostyniner.

Unfortunately, Fishel became ill with a heavy, incurable illness. He went through several difficult operations, but whenever he had the opportunity, even when he was sick, he did not cease and was active with his last energies.

After a long and difficult illness our comrade and friend, Fishel, died.

On the day of his funeral, the shop – where he worked and was chairman – was locked so that all the workers would be able to give him his final respect.

He will always be missed in our group. Honor his memory!

Y. K-R

[Page 378]

For the holy memory of our dear and beloved father

Dovid Bresler,
may he rest in peace

Who was so suddenly torn away from us

**Wife Rochel and daughters: Ruth and Gloria
Bresler (New York)**

[Page 379]

Dovid Bresler, may he rest in peace

Dovid Bresler was one of the few survivors of the entire Jewish community. His rescue did not come easily. He went through all seven gates of hell. He suffered for years in the German labor camp "Ginskirchen," and agonized with terrible troubles and pains. His number was 144573 and he remained there until Hitler's downfall.

From Ginskirchen, he was taken to the well-known "Fernwald Camp" [DP camp]. When he left Fernwald, he went to America, and arrived in New York in May 1949.

He arrived in America sick, a broken person. He suffered terrible, constant headaches, and spent 17 months in the hospital. And when he finally left the hospital he was still dangerously sick, but he was recovering.

Just as he was active in the Bundist organization in Gostynin, he immediately joined the Bundist Club in New York. He also joined the Gostyniner Social Club, and was one of the founders of the Shloime Mendelson Branch of the Workers' Circle.

As soon as he learned that the Gostyniner were preparing a Yizkor Book, he immediately joined the book committee, and also contributed to the book fund and attended the sessions of the book committee.

His sudden death tore him away from us on the 11th of June, in the year 1950. Honor his memory!

May his valuable social work be a comfort for his wife Rochel and his two daughters, Ruth and Gloria.

Y. K-R

[Page 380]

For the holy memory of our father

Yakov Miller, may his memory be blessed

Cantor for many years and *shochet*[1] in Gostynin

Died in Detroit in 1942

Our mother Sarah,
of blessed memory
Died in Gostynin in 1910

Yoel Miller (Chicago)

Moshe Ber Miller (Chicago)

Leah (Miller) Keller (New York)

Mashe (Miller) Litov (Detroit)

Pesse (Miller) Kest (Kenosha)

1. Ritual slaughterer

[Page 381]

For the holy memory
of our devoted wife and beloved mother

Tille,
of blessed memory

the daughter of the Gostyniner *chazzan*[2] and *shochet* and *bodek*[3], Reb Yakov and Sarah Miller

She left us in the middle of her life.

May she rest among all the other holy ones.

Her husband: Meyer Dovid Tremski and the children

2. Cantor

3. Ritual slaughterer and examiner of meats for purposes of kashrut

[Page 382]

For the holy memory of our dear father

Feivel Kruczyk,
may he rest in peace

Honor his memory!

Herman and Sonia Krauz
(New York)

[Page 383]

For the holy memory of our dear mother

Fradel Kruczyk,
may she rest in peace

Died in New York in 1940

Honor her memory!

Herman and Sonia Krauz
(New York)

[Page 384]

For the holy memory of my father and mother

My mother,
Baila Faiga Keller,
may she rest in peace
Murdered by the Hitler devils in the destruction of Poland

My father,
Yakov Mendel Keller,
may his memory be blessed
A community leader in the Gostyniner community
(died in Gostynin 27, Shevat, 5697 [Feb. 8, 1937]

Honor their holy memories!

Yosef Keller

[Page 385]

For the holy memory of my entire family

Gathered around the gravesite of my father Yakov Mendel Keller, of blessed memory

All those gathered around the gravesite were killed along with their children by the German murderers in Poland.

Left Side: Women from right to left:
Chantche Keller (Zerochyn) – Yechiel Meyer's wife; Manya (Zerochyn) Keller – Aaron's wife; Charna (Motil) – my sister, Efraim's wife; sitting – my brother Yechiel Meyer

Right Side:Top right:
My brother Sholem; next to him – my brother Moishe; near the gravestone – Sholem's wife; sitting – my brother Aaron
Top left:
My father's brother Ben-Tzion and my brother-in-law Efraim-Motil (Charna's husband)

Yosef Keller

[Page 386]

The Gostyniner cemetery became shamed because of the bestial
Hitler murderers who tore up the gravestones of the graves and used them
to pave the streets.
For that reason, we are placing a gravestone here for our grandfather

Reb Yisroel-Itche Keller,

of blessed memory,

one of the pillars of the Gostyniner Jewish community.

Also for our grandmother

Chaya Sarah Keller,

may she rest in peace

a truly modest woman.

Here also, may these names be perpetuated of our uncles and aunts
who lost their lives together with their families in the terrible Hitler murders:

Peretz Keller, Benzion Keller, Fraida Hadas and her husband
Zalman Czarnabrode and their three daughters, and Shayna Brocho.

Honor their memories!

Yissachar Motil   Josef Keller
(New York)   (New York)

For the holy memory of my sisters

Pesse Keller,
may she rest in peace
Died in Gostynin in the years
before World War I

Chava Keller,
may she rest in peace
Died in Gostynin before
the outbreak of World War II

Honor their memories!

Josef Keller

[Page 387]

**For the holy memory of our sister and brother-in-law
may they rest in peace**

Yitzchok Izayev and wife,
may they rest in peace

Died in Grodno after the First World War

Our sister
Miriam (Miller) Izayev
was killed by the Hitler bandits along with the 6,000,000 martyrs.

Honor their memory!

**Julius Miller, Morris Miller, Leah (Miller) Keller
Masha (Miller) Litov, Pesse (Miller) Kest**

Rochel (Motil) and Naphtali Korn,

may they rest in peace

Rochel Motil left Gostynin in the early years of this century, when, across the entire Poland the revolutionary freedom movements began to ignite everywhere. Even though in those years few girls joined the movement, Rochel was found at many party meetings because she belonged to the intellectual class of girls in the city.

Here in America, Rochel met Naphtali Korn, a boy from Warsaw, a warm idealist who was active back home in the Poalei Tzion [Zionist Workers' Movement] movement. Later on, they married and moved to Detroit.

Rochel never forgot her hometown of Gostynin. After the destruction of Poland, when she found out that the Gostynin Social Club in New York was running aid activities for the rescued Gostyniner Jews, she participated warmly and extensively.

Naphatali Korn was very active in Detroit in the Zionist Workers' Movement, and was dynamic until his last days of life. He managed to visit the State of Israel, which for him was the holy realization of a lifelong dream.

Rochel died very early, on November 7, 1950. Naphtali died suddenly on April 26, 1958. They left behind two wonderful daughters: Selma and Phyllis, who received, other than a general education, a fine Jewish education.

The Gostyniner will always remember Rochel and Naphtali.

Y. K-R

[Page 388]

Mendel Ichel Gostinski,
may he rest in peace

My father, Mendel Ichel Gostinski, may he rest in peace, the vinegar maker, was a religious Jew, a Gerer *chassid*. He was the founder and activist of the Talmud Torah, and a member of the *Chevra Kadisha* [Burial Society].

Rachtshe Gostinski, at her father's gravesite in Lodz, in the year 1933

My father always took care that the needy children should have warm clothes for the winter.

With an exceptional warmth and joy he welcomed the children of the Talmud Torah when they came for testing [of their learning] on Shabbath afternoon. He gave each child a Shabbath fruit.

[Page 389]

Each Friday night, my father also studied with a number of workers of the town, who wanted to study Torah.

When my father found out that there was a needy widow in town, he took care that there should be some money for her, and he himself went to the market, bought some bundles of wood, and took them to those who needed.

They heavy yoke of earning a livelihood that rested on my father's shoulders forced us to help him. Even so, he required that we study Torah. We got up every day at five in the morning. My father had already prepared the lantern to light up the road so that we should go study Torah before going to work.

In general, my father took care of the people and kept the *mitzvos* [religious commandments]. If someone died in town, my father put aside his constant social ventures until after the funeral.

Every Friday night, he made sure that the guests in town were taken care of for *Shabbath*, and he too brought home a guest.

My brother Meyer, may he rest in peace, tells the following of the final moments before my father's death:

> "It was on the final day before his death. My sister Zisse and I did not leave his bedside. Silently, my sister and I were looking at his yellow-brown face that had almost no sign of life left. With our glances, we filled ourselves with his almost dead face, to remember his appearance forever, because we knew that his hours were few.
>
> "As two devoted guards, we did not leave him. And at this moment, my father opens his mouth and says: 'Children, it is time to *daven Mincha* [recite the afternoon prayers]!' And he makes a gesture as if to get off his bed. Both of us went over to him trying to stop him from doing this. I told him that I would *daven Mincha* and he could participate through me. Suddenly he sits up, puts his feet off the bed, and says: 'I am getting down and will *daven Mincha*.' And with those words, he fell down."

Today, 44 years after his death, I remember my father who was always ready to help the poor people in town. I will always hold dear this memory and the beautiful Jewish character traits of my father.

Yosef Gosman-Gostinski

[Page 390]

This is a memory of life long ago…

Shlomo and Tzivia Gostinski
at my mother's gravesite in 1927

[Page 391]

Pesse Gostinski,
may she rest in peace

It is the eve of Yom Kippur, candle lighting time. The house is prepared for the holiday. The table is covered with a snow-white tablecloth. The silver candelabra glisten and shine; prepared with the candles inside them. A holy, awesome atmosphere reigns in the house. The entire household, all the children, the parents, are together in the house. My father, as is his custom for Yom Kippur eve, does not leave to Kol Nidrei [Yom Kippur prayers] until my mother has lit the candles. Dressed in his satin gabardine and in his only socks, my father is pacing back and forth through the house and is lightly humming a tune which they used in the shteibel [small, informal synagogue] for zochreinu le'chaim [special prayer for Days of Awe, "remember us with life"]. With that, he deepens the holiday spirit in the house. The children are gathered around the table and wait with a religious tremble for the mother's candle lighting.

My mother, tall, pale, and delicate, is dressed up in her satin dress that she only wears to shul [synagogue] for the Days of Awe. She moves majestically and approaches the table. She places her white, delicate hands onto the table. Her beautiful black eyes are shining with unshed tears. She remains like that, motionless, for some time. Soon, she stretches out her hands and gestures as if to embrace the candles. This, several times. Silent prayers flow through her fingers. Her fine hands are bright over the candles, just as the tablets are bright over the Holy Ark.

I overhear as my mother, with her blessings, mentions one name, then another. She mentions my father, the children, and other names that are lit along with the fire of the candles.

"May the Al-mighty bless them." My mother finally lets her hands drop and she recites a religious blessing.

That is how our mother remains in our memory.

Meyer Gostinski

[Page 392]

For the eternal memory

My beloved sister   My dear mother

Rivka'le Heiman   Zisse Heiman

Killed by the Nazi murderers, may their names be erased

I will always carry their memory

The only remaining daughter and sister
Pessy Weingott-Handelsman

[Page 393]

For the eternal memory of
Zisse Heiman-Gostinski,
may she rest in peace

Killed by the Nazi murderers in April, 1942

For the eternal memory of

Yehudis Epstein,
may she rest in peace
Died in Warsaw

Family Gostinski

[Page 394]

In holy memory of
Reb Avrohom Yudel Gostinski,
of blessed memory

(Died in 1916, in Lodz, Poland)

He was a *Talmid Chochom* [learned scholar], a student of Torah, a respected scholar, and the author of many religious books.

The grandchildren of the great grandfather:
Yosef, Yakov, Tzivia and Rachtshe Gostinski
(Zisse, Meyer, and Shloime, may they rest in peace)

[Page 395]

In memory of

Binyomin Levi,

may he rest in peace

(*Shochet* [ritual slaughterer] of Gostynin for the last 35 years)

Photographed with his wife Leah in honor of their 50thwedding anniversary

Family Gostinski (New York)

[Page 396]

As a holy memory of my beloved and dear parents, brothers, sisters, and sisters-in-law
who were killed by the Nazi murderers.

Honor their memories!

אָנשטאָט

אַ

מצבה

פאָטער

צבי בן יעקב לייב ז"ל

(געשטאָרבן אין 1936 אין גאָסטינין)

מוטער

בלומע מרים בת ישראל

איטשע קעללער ז"ל

Center of photo (box):

Instead [of]
a gravestone [for]

Father
Tzvi ben [son of] Yakov Leyb,
of blessed memory
(Died in 1936 in Gostynin)

Mother
Bluma Miriam
bas [daughter of] Yisroel Itche Keller,
of blessed memory

Seated from right to left: **Father Hershel, Esther Tauba, Mother Bluma Miriam : -- :**

Standing from right to left: **Niche, Moishe, his wife Breine Burak, Shloime, his wife Bruch'tche, Yakov Leyb; near them: his wife Pesse Roize and Lutke**

[Page 397]

**In holy memory
Of my brother-in-law and my brother's children
who were killed at such a young age by the Nazi murderers**

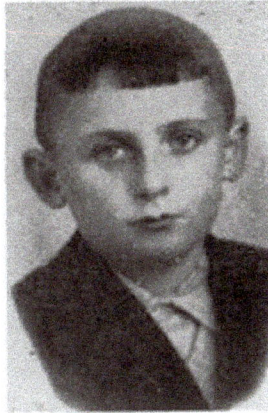

Tzilia Motil   Yakov Motil   Moritz Aleksander

Daughter of Shloime and Broch'tche   Son of Moishe and Breine   (Esther Tauba's husband)........

Born 1938, killed in 1942   Born in 1928, died in 1942   Lived in Koval

Honor their memories!

**Yissachar and Zisse Motil
(New York)**

For a holy memory

Of my dear and beloved parents and my entire family
that was killed by the hands of the Nazi murderers.

Honor their memory!

**Father Isser-Meyer, Mother Henne, brothers Shloime, Leybish and Yitzchok,
sister Broche'tche, grandchildren Tzilia, Avrohom, and Noson**

Regina, Sholem, and Amir Margalit
(Tel Aviv)

[Page 398]

In holy memory of our father and mother
Mendel and Genendel Bagno

My Mother,
Killed at the hands of the Nazi murderers

My father,
Died in Gostynin in the year 1929

Honor their memory!

Chana Keller (New York)
Julius and Bess Bagno (New York)
Leybish Bagno and wife (Tel Aviv)
Shmuel Beiruch Bagno and wife (Brussels)
Yente and Felix Miller (Brussels)
Yakov Bagno and wife (Brussels)
Baile Roize (Brussels)

[Page 399]

For the holy memory of our brothers and sisters
of our family Bagno

who were killed in Belgium by the hands of the Nazi murderers

Yosef   **Hinde**

Sholem   **Gutman,**
                              died in New York in 1950

Honor their memory!

Chana Keller (New York)
Julius and Bess Bagno (New York)
Shmuel Beiruch Bagno and wife (Brussels)
Yente and Felix Miller (Brussels)
Yakov Bagno and wife (Brussels)
Baile Roize (Brussels)
Leybish Bagno and wife (Tel Aviv)

[Page 400]

In holy memory of our dear and beloved parents

Their tombstones were destroyed by the German murderers. May these few words serve as a memorial for our father and mother.

Honor their memory!

Sarah Dvoire (Bresler) Gonshor
(Died in 1904 in Gostynin)

Elazar Gonshor.......
(Died in the year 1915 in Gostynin)

Daughters Chava'tche Krieger and Zisse Motil
(New York)

[Page 401]

In holy memory of our dear brother

Yosef and his family
who died at the hands of the German Nazi murderers in the Warsaw ghetto

Honor their memory!

Daughter Faigele, son Elazar   Yosef Gonshor and his wife Chan'tche

Chave'tche and Moishe Krieger
Zisse and Yissachar Motil
Max Rozental
(New York)

[Page 402]

In memory
of our brother and sister-in-law who
left us so very young

Charna (Melamed) Gonshor   **Yitzchok Ber Gonshor......**
Died in 1954 in New York   Died in 1944 in New York

In his young years, Yitzchok Ber was very active in *Poalei Tzion*[Labor Zionist Movement] in Gostynin; also a member of the administration in the Peretz library; an active member in the drama circle; one of the founders of the movement for professionals in Gostynin. He left Gostynin and came to New York in the year 1921. Throughout all these years, Ber maintained a close contact with Gostynin.

Sister Rochel Melamed
Brother-in-law Max Rozental
Chave'tche and Moishe Krieger
(New York)

[Page 403]

In eternal memory

You left us, dear and beloved

Blanche

And we, your close ones, remember you.
We mourn for you and will not
Forget you until our final breath

Your Max

Your sisters
Chava and Zisse

Your brothers-in-law
Moishe and Yissachar

Let this serve as a tombstone
for our
dear father

Avrohom Rozental

whose gravesite the
German cannibals
destroyed.

Also a tombstone for
our mother

Chaya Soroh

Our sisters: **Pesse, Hinde** and her husband **Elazar Rozental**, and
their child; **Yitte** and her husband **Shapiro**
and **Esther**, who were killed by the sadistic murderers in the
burning ovens.

In pain and sorrow, we remain the son and brother

Yisroel-Moishe and Itzik Rozental
(New York)

[Page 404]

A picture of my father, my teacher
Reb Yehuda Leybush
son of Yakov, of blessed memory, Tremski
(born in Gostynin)

Learned, a merchant and an activist for the needs of the community – "Others praised him, not his own mouth" [comment on his humility].

Died in Gostynin on the 7th of Iyar, 5683 [April 23, 1923].

May his soul be bound up in the bond of life
Meyer Dovid Tremski

[Page 405]

**For the holy memory of our dear family
that was killed by the Nazi murderers.
Honor their memory!**

The family Gombiner

From right to left: **Dolusz, Chana (Zhichlin)**, mother and **Romek.
Dolusz** and **Chana** were killed by the Nazis; father **Itche**(died in
Gostynin); **Romek** (died in Gostynin in 1936); mother (died in New York
in 1945).

Itche Gombiner, may he rest in peace

Yakov Gombiner, wife, and daughter
(lived in Wloclowek)

Itche Gombiner, may he rest in peace

Among the few businessmen in Gostynin who did not fear the currents of the freedom movement, which also pulled in the Gostynin youth, there was also Itche Gombiner.

Itche was considered one of the progressive persons in town. He possessed a healthy spirit and logic.

In general, he was a loving person and respected by the community. He was one of the prestigious members of the Burial Society, which at that time was one of the most important institutions.

He tried to give his children, other than a Jewish education, a general education, and in fact his son Yakov, was one of the first Jewish young boys who studied in the city's new public school. Later, when it became apparent that Yakov had an aptitude for music, he was sent to the Warsaw conservatory.

Itche partnered with several forest [land] merchants in the city, but he was the most active and managerial force of the company. He was tall, healthy, and relatively young when he became ill and had to undergo an operation. At that time, there were no surgeons in Gostynin, so he was taken to the hospital in the nearby town of Plock. But it was already too late, and he did not leave the hospital alive.

May these lines serve as a tombstone for his children.

Gutche Lowy and husband
Salle Kupersmith
(New York)
Esther Stupei
Regina Frushein and husband
(New York)
Shloime Gombiner (Sam Gomberg)

[Page 406]

In holy memory of my parents, sister, and brother-in-law

My mother
Soshe Krieger

died in Warsaw
1933

My father
Shlomo Krieger

died in Warsaw
1930

My sister Rochel'e and her husband H. Korfinkel
Died in the Warsaw ghetto

Honor their memory!

Moshe and Chava Gonshor-Krieger

[Page 407]

In holy memory

Of my sister and brother-in-law and their family died in the Warsaw ghetto

Sister Nechele Breintuch-Krieger; her husband Shimon Breintuch; their son Pesach

Their children: Lola, Manya, and Rivka'le

Eliezer Breintuch

My sister **Rivka** and her husband **Leibel Grinfeder**
murdered by the Nazis in Paris.

Their son died in Paris after the liberation

Sholom Breintuch

Dovid Grinfeder

Honor their memory!
Moshe and Chava Gonshor-Krieger

[Page 408]

In memory
Of my beloved parents

Chaim and Rivka Kuntzman

When I look at pictures of my father and mother, may they rest in peace, I remember the horrible days when the German murderers mercilessly completely wiped out so many Jewish communities in Poland. One scene in particular remains before my eyes, when I came to take leave from my parents, because I had decided to run away from the terrible hell. With tears in their eyes, my mother and father pleaded that I should not run away, because they did not believe I would come out alive while trying to get through the Polish border that was fenced in by the German killers who did not allow any Jew in their clutches to remain alive. They couldn't imagine that their son would even try to tear himself out of the murderous claws.

It was not easy to tear myself away from certain death. The sufferings were very great. Hiding and endless wandering were very difficult to experience. But after all the difficulties and pains, I miraculously made it to Israel and remained alive. My brother Shammai, who lives in Israel today, made it along with me.

But sadly, my parents, who vehemently opposed my leaving, were killed in the devastation of Poland.

Dovid Kuntzman, wife, and children
(New York)

[Page 409]

In memory of my dear family

May this serve as a tombstone for their unknown graves

Sister: Tzirel and husband Hershel Sonicki

Parents: Shloimeand Tzivia Frenkel

Their son Nanek

Brother: Mendel Frenkel

and his wife Baltche (Moritz)

**Sister: Dr. Laitche Bursten (Frenkel) and her husband Dr. Yosek
Bursten.**

**Killed as underground leader of the intellectuals in "Drancy Prison" in
France.**

Honor their memory!

Golde (Frenkel) Gostinski and family
(New York)

[Page 410]

In holy memory
of my family that was killed in the terrible destruction of Poland

Left: Lay'tche Makowsky and her husband Meyer Markowycz
Right: My dear parents Henoch and Zlate Makowsky

My brother Avrohom, a widower, and four children; my oldest sister Rivka
and two children; my sister Laya (Lay'tche), her husband Meyer Markowycz,
and two children; my sister Shulamis, her husband Binem Holtzman, and their
three children; my brother and his son who were in Chelmno from the year
1941 and were killed there along with my mother Zlate, may she rest in peace,
who was transferred from the Gostynin ghetto to Chelmno when the ghetto in
Gostynin was liquidated.

May these lines in the Yizkor Book serve as a tombstone in their memory

Shmerl and Elke Makowsky
(Belgium)

[Page 411]

In holy memory

Of the family of

Moshe Yitzchok Srebnagura

And the family of

Ch. Y. Peltzman

Two *chassidic* families of Gostynin

**Of the entire family, those remaining alive are Etke (Peltzman) Makowsky
in Belgium and a grandchild who lives in Israel**

Honor their memory!

Sam and Elke Makowsky

In brilliant memory of
Our destroyed families

**In the years of the great destruction
we participated in this Yizkor Book.**

S.M. Pierson	**Tzivia Marks**
A. Dobryn	**G. Mitchel**
A. Segal	**H. Salomon**
Saul Zajacs	**M.B. Miller**
N. Goldberg	**Chana Kusman**
Family	**Regina Kest**
Rosenberg	**Family**
Dr. K. Bach	**Tabatchnik**
Jay Jakobs	**Yona Segal**
Bluma Motil	**S. Wolfson**

[Page 412]

In memory of
Hershel, Hinde, and Eliyahu Motil

Our father, who was known for his perpetual smile and goodness, and our mother, who was always busy and harried, gave us a Jewish, Zionist upbringing.

Their devotion to the children was limitless. When our brother Eliyahu became ill and was in the hospital, our father did not leave his side, and our mother came to see him several times a day. With Eliyashe's death, a deep sorrow enveloped the family.

Our father Hershel, who all his life dreamed of a Jewish national home, did not live to see the establishment of a Jewish state. He did merit to die in his own bed. He died on the 25th of Adar Bais, 1941.

Our dear mother Hinde was sent to the camp in Konin. A day before her death she sent us a request. She knew that these would be her final days and she told us to stay together and take care of one another.

In fact, we honor this request in a holy manner, and we believe that our parents are watching over us. We went through indescribable anguish in the camps. Our brother Shmulik was already sentenced to being shot in the Death March, and I, Gershon, was registered in the liquidation. But we always had faith, we believed that we would remain alive, and this belief saved us from all dangers.

Soon after the war, Shmulik was in Gostynin, and he went to the cemetery to the gravesites of our parents. But there was no sign of this entire cemetery. The earth was ploughed and seeded, and the past – erased.

May these lines serve as a tombstone in eternal memory of our loved ones. May this also be a memory of our father's two brothers: Simon Yosef, his wife Chaya-Soroh, and their children Efraim-Pinchas and Charne; and our uncle Efraim and his wife Charne. And also for our mother's brothers: Moishe Erdberg from Kutno, his wife Golde and son Mendel; our uncle Yehoshua and Aunt Mindel. I also want to mention my bride Gute Motil, the daughter of Leybel.

Gershon and Shmulik Motil

In memory

Of my grandfather and grandmother

Yakov Leyb Motil and Niche (Holtricht)

Honor their memory!

Yissachar Motil

In memory

Of our dear grandfather and grandmother

Simcha and Tzivia Bresler

Honor their memory!

Chava Krieger and Zisse Motil
(New York)

[Page 414]

In loving memory of

Our father, our teacher,
Rabbi Eliezer son of Betzalel Shmuel,
may he rest in peace
Luzer Okolica
Died on June 12, 1941;
Hebrew date 17th day of Sivan, 5701

Our beloved mother

Mrs. Ryfka daughter of Rebbe Moishe,
may she rest in peace
Ryfka Okolica

Died on January 14, 1956;
Hebrew date Shabbath, 1ˢᵗ of Shevat, 5716

Our beloved sister,
The child **Ita Roiza daughter of Reb Eliezer,**
may he rest in peace
Ita Rojsa

Died on January 11, 1913;
Hebrew date Shabbath, 3ʳᵈ of Shevat, 5673

Our grandfather
Moishe son of Izak
Our grandmother
Ita Roiza daughter of Leybush Zaklikowsky

HaRav Henry (Chaim-Henoch) Okolica
Samuel (Betzalel Shmuel) Okolica

For the blessed memory of my father and mother

Chaim-Meyer and Chaya-Faige Salomon

Died in Gombyn before the war years

And my three brothers

Matis, Avrohom-Moishe, and Mendel Salomon

Sacrifices in the terrible devastation of Poland

Honor their memory!

Harry Salomon
(New York)

[Page 415]

**In holy memory of my brothers and sisters
and their families who were killed by Nazi murderers**

Moishe, Yitzchok, Beryl, Yosel, Esther Kruczyk,
of blessed memory

Honor their memory!

Herman and Sonia Krauz
(New York)

**In memory of our parents and families
Who were killed by the Nazi murderers**

Sister Golde Belfer	**Yonah Tzweighaft**
(Tzweighaft)	**Tzvi and Esther**
Brother-in-law Yosef	**Beibuk**
Spector	**Brothers: Yoske amd**
Children Franya and	**Mordechai Tzweighaft**
Meyer	**Sister: Rochel Spector**
Brother-in-law	**(Tzweighaft)**
Avrohom Belfer	

Shlomo, Rifka, Aliza, and Dvoire Tzweighaft (Tel Aviv)
Wolf and Gedaliahu Belfer (Israel)

[Page 416]

In holy memory
Of our dear parents and family

Moshe Wolf, Simele, Shloime, Sender, Leybel, Yankele Gelbard Volya Neiman and family Boruch Lasman and family

**Who were tragically murdered by the Nazi killers.
Honor their memory!!**

Sam and Faige Borenstein and family
(New York)

As an eternal memory of our dear father
Leyzer Lefkovitch,
may he rest in peace

Died in March 1935, in New York

Honor his memory!

Jack and family Lefkovitch
(New York)

[Page 417]

In memory of my beloved parents

Yakov-Sholom and Tzipora Bagno

My sister Tola and brother-in-law Bernard Hershkovitch

Sister Manya and Angie

Brother Shia, sister-in-law Manya, and daughter Tzelinka.

May these lines serve as a tombstone for their unknown graves.

Ruzhke and Yakov Stein

In holy memory of my beloved wife

Esther Kalmus,
may she rest in peace

Daughter of Reb Yakov Yechiel Gold

Her husband Dovid Kalmus

As an eternal memory of

My dear parents

Lipe and Bashe Bresla (Bresler)

Lipe died on March 12, 1943, in New York
Bashe died on March 28, 1947, in New York

Honor their memory!

Noach Bresla
(New York)

[Page 418]

In holy memory of

Professor Yakov Zerachin and wife

And their two daughters

Chantche and Manya

Who were killed along with their families in the Terrible devastation of Poland.

Honor their memory!

The Zerachin family settled in Gostynin, and Professor Zerachin took on the position of teacher of religion in the public gymnasium. He also organized courses in Hebrew. As a fiery Zionist, he planted the kernels of Zionism deeply into his students.

Professor Zerachin was an overall loving and social person, and quickly became settled in town, where the people welcomed him warmly and established him as director of the Jewish people's schools.

Zerachin's two daughters, Chantche and Manya, also quickly became citizens of Gostynin, and married the two brothers Yechiel-Meyer and Aaron Keller.

All of them died in the years of the horrors.

Y. K-R

[Page 419]

In holy memory
of my close family and friends (male and female) who were killed by the
German Nazi murderers

The families:

Pinczewski   Motil
Feinzilber   Keller
Brown   Printz

Male friends:	**Chaim Bresler, Itche Katz, Refoel Burak, Yakov Leyb Pinczewski, Betzalel Gombyner, Avrohom Zajacs, Zalman Ospe, Lipe Plutzer, Otke Moritz, Shmuel Markovitch, Ben-Tzion Moritz**
Female friends:	**Chav'tche Kaufman, Rochele Zweighaft, Irena Lefkovitch, Tila Kleinbord, Baltche Moritz, Blima Goldman, Blima Dzhiganski**

Honor their memory!

Yissachar Motil
(New York)

[Page 420]

In memory of Family Tabatchnik

Chana-Rochel Tabatchnik

I am joining in the cries of all our compatriots to honor the memory of our holy martyrs who were killed by the Nazi murderers in the gas chambers of Auschwitz and Treblinka.

My language is too poor to allow me to express my deep pain and anguish.

At the moment, scene after scene, event after event, swim by in my memory, of terrible pain that I and all of us experienced and suffered through, and of the horrible pains and agony.

Each one of us who miraculously remained alive could write complete volumes of the evil and cruelty of the Germans.

But at this moment, I only want to remember and honor the holy memory of the near and dear ones of my family.

My father was Hershel Tabatchnik. He merited dying before the Jewish tragedy began.

But my mother, with all her sons and daughters, were killed in the German death camps.

And I, only I, remained alive from my entire family. I survived to bear witness and carry deep sorrow my inside me my entire life.

I don't know where, and in which death camps, my brothers and sisters were killed. They died leaving absolutely no memories behind them.

But I want to relate how my brother Avrohom-Aaron and my eldest sister Chana-Rochel were killed. I want to tell about their tragic martyr's death.

The German murderers assembled ten Jewish young people in a barn in the camp Konin in order to take them to the gas chambers to their death. Among these young people was my brother Avrohom-Aaron. But these ten young people decided that it would be better to kill themselves rather than to fall into the hands of the German murderers. And they decided to hang themselves and to burn down the barn.

They threw lots as to who would be the first to hang himself and who would be the last, and then [that last one would] burn the barn. The lot fell to my brother to be the last one, and the one to burn down the barn. And that is how it went.

One after the other, each young man hanged himself on their self-constructed gallows. And when it was my brother's turn, he ignited the barn and then proceeded to hang himself.

This is how these ten Jewish holy martyrs met their death, and with these multiple deaths, my brother Avrohom-Aaron died as well. How can I forget that?

I will also never forget how the German killers and slaughterers viciously tore my oldest sister Chana Rochel from me, and took her to Auschwitz to murder her.

I fell at the feet of the murderers, sobbed, and pleaded with them not to leave me alone; begged that they take me along with my sister, who was like a devoted mother to me, so that I could be burned to death alongside her in the ovens of the crematoria.

But the killers tore her away from me forcefully and cruelly pushed me aside and cynically remarked: "Soon, soon it will be your turn."

My dear sister then turned to me and said her final words: "Remember, Helen, you are the youngest and the last sister of our large family. Don't give in to the enemy. Strengthen yourself and see that you remain alive. At least let one limb of our family survive. Let there remain a memory of us all.

"You will outlive the murderers and devils and will bear witness to tell what all of us have experienced and suffered. You will have the merit to see your brothers in America."

And I experienced it and lived through it all. And now I am in America.

I married and have a good husband and two dear children. I could say that I have a wonderful family life.

But I will always carry in my heart the deep sorrow and agony of my closest and dearest ones, who died so young and so horribly by the hands of the Nazi executioners in the gas chambers of Auschwitz and Treblinka.

I will never forget this!

Helen (Tabatchnik) Boll

[Page 422]

Martyrs

Ezriel Zajdeman

We will never forget our dearest ones, our parents, brothers and sisters who were killed so cruelly by the hands of the German murderers. We will tell our children, and our children's children, so that they will never forget our devastated families.

With the publication of this memorial book for the martyrs of Gostynin, I would like to mention here the names of my parents, brothers and sisters, as well as the names of my relatives of my father's family, which was considered one of the largest families of Gostynin.

My father, Avrohom Chaim Zajdeman, of blessed memory, my mother Elke Zajdeman, of blessed memory. My older brother, Moishe Zajdeman, was on the Russian side during the time of the war. Sadly, no one knew what happened to his body.

My sister, Gutche Zajdeman, married while in the ghetto. A picture of the ghetto, and a picture of the yellow Jewish star, which everyone in the ghetto had to wear – we received when we were sent to Siberia.

My brothers Dovid and Nisen Zajdeman, of blessed memory; our sisters: Sonia, Yente, and Esther Zajdeman, of blessed memory.

I want to mention those who died from my father's side. Our grandfather, Volf Zajdeman, of blessed memory; my father's sister: Kashe, of blessed memory, married to Nachum Steinman, and two children; Soroh, of blessed memory, married to Yisroel Meyer Rusak, and two children; Baile, of blessed memory, married to Artche Lichtenstein, they had four children.

My father's brother, Yitzchok Zajdeman, lived in Rodzhiwe, near Plock.

A sister of my father, Rochel, lived in Kutno, died along with her three children.

May this memory book of the martyrs be a holy tombstone for their destroyed lives.

[Page 423]

Life in the Gostynin Ghetto goes on
A Wedding in the Gostyniner Ghetto in March 1940

The bride is Gutche Zajdeman
In this group are also the parents of the bride,
Avrohom-Chaim and Elke Zajdeman, may they rest in peace

[Page 424]

A picture of the Gostyniner ghetto

Jewish youth wearing the symbol of the Jewish star

[Page 425]

In holy memory of my family

My father **Chaim Goldberg** and my mother**Chava,** may they rest in peace

My brothers: **Yisroel Moishe, Yissachar Mendel, Aryeh Leyb,** and **Yosele**

My sisters: **Malka, Soroh Rifka,** and **Mene**

All who died in the destruction of Poland by the hands of the Hitler executioners

Honor their memory!

Yechiel Goldberg
(Paris)

Reb Chaim Goldberg was known as Chaim "blue-maker," because he was a dyer. He prayed in the chassidim shteibel [informal, small synagogue], but on Rosh Hashanah and Yom Kippur he would pray in the synagogue. And no wonder: Reb Chaim was a first class Baal Tokeia [the person who blows the shofar on the holidays]. In his hands, the shofar was like a musical instrument. And who of those congregants who used to pray in the Bais Hamedrash and experienced the dramatic blowing of the shofar there, did not enjoy the skilled shofar blowing of Reb Chaim Goldberg? Because of that, the synagogue Jews were determined that only Reb Chaim should be the Baal Tokeia for them.

Reb Chaim was a warm Jew. He was never a very wealthy man, even though G-d blessed him with a good livelihood. With all of this, he never had any conflicts with anyone, and was a man of great faith all his days.

Reb Chaim was one of the most respected businessmen in the city.

Y. K-R

[Page 426]

In eternal memory

Soroh Goldman (Szcuwnik), who is now in Israel, writes that her parents, Yakov and Fraide Goldman, settled in Gostynin in the year 1911, where they lived until the year 1926, when they left Gostynin for economic reasons, and went to Lubraniec. "But Gostynin," she writes, "was always their home."

She perpetuates the names of her family. Her mother Fraide, who died in the Lodz ghetto in 1942; her father Yakov Goldman, who left this world at a young age in 1943; her sister Baile, who was tortured in the Lodzher ghetto at the age of 28; and her brother Shloime, who died in one of Hitler's camps.

May their names never be forgotten!

Moishe Yehuda Pinczewski in Israel, writes:

My father, Yissachar-Dov, son of Avrohom and grandson of the Gostyniner *dayan* [judge in religious Jewish court] Reb Shmuel Volf Pinczewski, in his young years, was already considered one of the best students. And as was the case with a student of such prestigious lineage, he was taken as a son-in-law for a prominent family, for the daughter of the honored Moishe –Leyb Dobriner, actually from the town of Dobrin.

As the father-in-law Reb Moishe Leyb, so the son-in-law Yissachar-Dov was also a Gerer *chossid* [follower of the Gerer Rebbe].

It is interesting to note that when Malke, Yissachar-Dov's wife, became ill, and the illness, despite her doctors, dragged on, both father and husband lost their trust in the doctors and both went to see the Gerer Rebbe, whom they trusted very deeply. Naturally, they asked the Rebbe to pray for the daughter and wife. And when G-d helped, and Malke became well again, both Gerer *chassidim* knew that this was a result of the Rebbe's prayers.

In the great destruction of Poland, both my father Yissachar-Dov and mother Malke lost their lives.

May their names be remembered eternally.

Yonah Klingbeil (Tobtche Boczan), who is now in Israel, writes with great yearning and heartache about the destruction of Gostynin. She warmly describes the town of her youth; the natural geographic beauty and the cultural institutions and activities that were described many times in many ways on the pages of this book.

With particular warmth and love, she remembers her beloved brother Avrohom, who was a scholar, a serious student of Torah studies; the melody of his studying still rings in her ears. And even if they separated in their ways and beliefs, nonetheless, the love between brother and sister was truly a warm one.

In agony, she relates that her brother, the fine student, was sickly, and in the year 1928, left this world as a young man. His death had a terrible impact on his father, so much so, that he too left this world as a young man.

"The rest of the family," – she writes – "died in the destruction of Poland with the other Gostyniner holy martyrs."

Fraidel Pinczewski (Sheier), in Israel, writes in memory of her father Nachum-Yisroel Sheier, and her mother Soroh-Laya Sheier (Danciger):

My father, Nochum-Yisroel, of blessed memory, born in Wiszegrad, where he was one of the best Wiszegrader young men, was the husband of my dear mother Soroh-Laya, the daughter of Mordechai-Mendel and Toibe [Toba]-Chaya Danciger. As was done in those years, the young man, the student Nochum-Yisroel, was taken as a son-in-law and given board.

So, my father actually studied Torah day and night, without any concerns for having to earn a livelihood.

But when business for Mordechai-Mendel and Toibe-Chaya Danciger worsened daily, my father declined continued boarding and undertook, with the help of my mother, to do a little bit of trade. And even though earning a livelihood was difficult, my father nonetheless did not forego any of his studies, just as it is said: "It is good to have Torah with the lay of the land" [*Tov Torah Im Derech Eretz*"]. And even though my parents did not earn fortunes of money with their business, there was always a guest at the table and no one ever declined to give charity.

My mother died in Gostynin two years before the outbreak of World War Two, and my father died during the second year of the war.

The rest of my family died during the war devastation. I am the only one remaining.

May these lines be an eternal memory for them.

INDEX

L

M

T